Mabogo P. More

Creolizing the Canon

Series Editors: Jane Anna Gordon, Professor of Political Science, with affiliations in El Instituto, Philosophy, and Women's, Gender, and Sexuality Studies, University of Connecticut, and Neil Roberts, Professor of Africana Studies and Faculty Affiliate in Political Science, Williams College

This series, published in partnership with the Caribbean Philosophical Association, revisits canonical theorists in the humanities and social sciences through the lens of creolization. It offers fresh readings of familiar figures and presents the case for the study of formerly excluded ones.

Creolizing Rousseau
Edited by Jane Anna Gordon and Drucilla Cornell
Hegel, Freud and Fanon
Stefan Bird-Pollan
Theorizing Glissant
Edited by John E. Drabinski and Marisa Parham
Journeys in Caribbean Thought: The Paget Henry Reader
Edited by Jane Anna Gordon, Lewis R. Gordon, Aaron Kamugisha, and Neil Roberts, with Paget Henry
The Philosophical Treatise of William H. Ferris: Selected Readings from The African Abroad or, His Evolution in Western Civilization
Tommy J. Curry
Creolizing Hegel
Edited by Michael Monahan
Frantz Fanon, Psychiatry and Politics
Nigel C. Gibson and Roberto Beneduce
Melancholia Africana: The Indispensable Overcoming of the Black Condition
Nathalie Etoke
Translated by Bill Hamlett
Afrocubanas: History, Thought, and Cultural Practices
Edited by Devyn Spence Benson, Daisy Rubiero Castillo and Inés María Martiatu Terry
Translated by Karina Alma
Creolizing Rosa Luxemburg
Edited by Jane Anna Gordon and Drucilla Cornell
Mabogo P. More: Philosophical Anthropology in Azania
Tendayi Sithole

Mabogo P. More

Philosophical Anthropology in Azania

Tendayi Sithole

ROWMAN & LITTLEFIELD
Lanham • Boulder • New York • London

Published by Rowman & Littlefield
An imprint of The Rowman & Littlefield Publishing Group, Inc.
4501 Forbes Boulevard, Suite 200, Lanham, Maryland 20706
www.rowman.com

6 Tinworth Street, London SE11 5AL, United Kingdom

British Library Cataloguing in Publication Information Available

Library of Congress Cataloging-in-Publication Data

Names: Sithole, Tendayi, author.
Title: Mabogo P. More : philosophical anthropology in Azania / Tendayi Sithole.
Other titles: Global critical Caribbean thought.
Description: Lanham : Rowman & Littlefield, 2022. | Series: Global critical Caribbean thought | Includes bibliographical references and index. | Summary: "This is the first book-length work to focus on the philosophical and anthropological contribution of Mabogo More, a prominent and influential black South African existentialist thinker"—Provided by publisher.
Identifiers: LCCN 2022000049 (print) | LCCN 2022000050 (ebook) | ISBN 9781538166116 (cloth) | ISBN 9781538166130 (paperback) | ISBN 9781538166123 (epub)
Subjects: LCSH: More, Mabogo Percy, 1946- | Philosophy—South Africa. | Philosophical anthropology.
Classification: LCC B5644.M67 S58 2022 (print) | LCC B5644.M67 (ebook) | DDC 199/.68—dc23/eng/20220111
LC record available at https://lccn.loc.gov/2022000049
LC ebook record available at https://lccn.loc.gov/2022000050

For My Beloved Mama
Lebohang Thelma Sithole
August 1, 1956–August 9, 1999

Contents

Acknowledgments

This book could have been done much earlier, but due to anxieties, frustrations, deferrals, and the pen failing to pour ink, it kept on being between postponement and abandonment. But it has always been troubling me, yet there was no grammar to birth its scripting. Since this is the book that I have been dreaming to write, its realization has been nightmarish. With the endurance of sleepless nights, fits and starts of the day, it proved to be therapeutic. The book brewed, sedimented, and distilled into maturity. Also, executing it in the hostile intellectual environment that is grounded in epistemic violence that is masked by the liberal consensus, I have stayed with the weight of provocation, and this has been haunting me to act through the protocols of doing the otherwise of black thought.

The Africa Decolonial Research Network, which refused to die many deaths it has been institutionally subjected to, has been a refuge for fugitive practices, and I am thankful that its pulse—The ADERN Seminar Series—a laboratory where I experiment with my critical investigations by means of three lecture part series. This will always be a home and its founder, Sabelo Ndlovu-Gatsheni, left a living monument—a home in a true sense where the body, mind, and sound find refuge.

Lewis Gordon is the one who provoked this book, and I want to thank him for his generosity. Keeping me in check and ensuring that I get enough sleep, something which I miserably fail at, has been Boshadi Semenya, Lebohang Motsomotso, Zingisa Nkosinkulu, Thabang Monoa, Thulisile Shongwe, Mahlomola Nchabeng, Cyprian Mpungose, Mzwandile Buthelezi, and Nomalanga Tyamzashe. You deserve special mention as you took care of me in tough times of writing this book and I am eternally grateful.

To Mpumelelo Masumbuka, Steven Motlhamme, Moladi wa Sekeke, Clement Leshika, Lebohang Motsomotso, Musa Motha, Njabulo Zwane,

Nathan Brown, Ronald A. Judy, Tumi Mogorosi, Thabiso Lekgong, Sakhiwo Mbatha, Tshepo Madlingozi, Simphiwe Sibiya, Mzwandile Nkutha, Linda Tshabalala, Isaac Khambule, Lunga Mkila, Siyasanga Tyali, Lerato Mokoena, Siphamandla Zondi, Maurice Vambe, Mark Michael, Nokuthula Hlabangane, Bongani Madondo, Mojaki Makhuza, Dorcus Ndou, Julia Simango, Sibusiso Maseko, Athi Joja and many others I forgot to mention, thank you for being there as this unfolded.

My late aunt Dikeledi Lebele and brother, Tshepo Lebele, thank you for being my loving family. My niece, Katleho Motseki, thanks for being my friend and cheering me up with your crazy jokes and inciting our mad and loud laughter.

My wife, Lindiwe, it is not enough to say thank you for everything. Words cannot go there, just to draw from the words of the jazz saxophonist, Charles Lloyd, by way of Fred Moten, the latter whose amity I value fondly. Robin D. G. Kelley and Ronald A. Judy, I appreciate your support.

I am fortunate to have a mentor and friend like Mabogo P. More. I wrote this book without him knowing and surprising him with a completed manuscript, words escaped him and a scat exclamation—"yay" whose correlate "wow"—said it all. As always, my mad love for him.

I want to thank Jane Gordon and Neil Roberts, series editors for *Creolizing the Canon* book series who warmly received this manuscript. How can I forget the care and guidance of the editorial team Frankie Mace and Scarlet Furness? I want to say thank you for your continued support.

For the anonymous reviewers, thank you for reading the manuscript. Thank you for taking your time in shaping it. Where I did not take some your criticism and advice, I shall, in bearing responsibility, take all the errors as solely mine. Those whose names could not be lettered here, please forgive the fog in my memory. I, however, in this failed gesture, would like to note that you are here, albeit under erasure.

My bambinos, Tendayi Jr, Chanise, Sibusiso, and Dyani wa Matekwe, this is for you, as always. Your grandfather, Marapuse "Madala" Sithole, who is my number one fan, as you know, deserves special thanks for his prayers that kept me going in lonely times of writing this book. At least, as always, the sound of jazz, and specifically bebop and avant-garde, kept me writing.

Lastly, thanks Mama for your love of jazz and pursuing my ear to its sound at the age of 12. I know you keep on snapping your fingers and tapping your feet when I play this music every day and not on Sundays only. This book is for you!

Introduction

Of a Philosopher in Black

A philosopher who puts philosophy to work, rather than applying and practicing it as pure abstraction, names and invents it as a distinct project which, in its radical form, is called *philosophy in black.*

In having to meditate in the name of this philosophy and its philosopher, the concern is not of a biographical subject. Instead, it is about the philosophical conduct of a philosopher who engages in philosophical anthropology.

The name of a philosopher who names philosophy as philosophy in black is Mabogo Percy More. As a philosopher who is located in the territory called South Africa, and which he rightfully calls Azania, More is rooted in the black lived experience, and he undertakes a particular mode and generative way of philosophizing. It is in his name that this intervention is undertaken. His name, for obvious reasons, is of the one who is a philosopher who is known in some circles and also not known in some. Those who know More, in discursive terms, have not only encountered his work, but they were, and continue to be touched and provoked by it in different ways. This, of course, depends on the relational and interlocutory dynamics that prevail. Appositional or oppositional, More makes it clear where he stands and what he stands for, and also, against. This, consequently, is what philosophy in black is. The questions that animate More's philosophical project, his conduct thereof, makes philosophy in black to be a disposition, a locus even.

Who, principally, is Mabogo Percy More? The answer to this question cannot be a form of totality or any definitional closure. There is, in this encounter, the discursive rupture that is a philosophy of a different kind which clearly sets More apart. He is not allured by the claim of being universal, and thus making philosophy to be the objective affair and whose basis in dealing with philosophical matters being abstract and detached from reality and its materiality. From the perspective of being black, More gives a different account on matters that he is philosophizing on. So, philosophical anthropology, from Azania as a locus, gives More's philosophy in black not only a currency to be a relevant project, but what is necessary. This necessity is informed by philosophy as the quotidian practice. The question of the contemporary, which in no way disavows of its past, is what More grapples with.

Born under settler-colonialism, before the instituting of apartheid, in the year 1946, More's birthplace is Benoni Old Location, east of Johannesburg. This place does not, in the present, exist anymore because of the forced removal most blacks were subjected to during apartheid. Blacks were, arbitrarily as apartheid felt, designated to townships like Daveyton and Wattville. The name Benoni Old Location is not in the current map. Where More was born, the place is now Actonville (which was established for the habitation of the Indian population), and this was in line with the enforcement of Group Areas Act to make sure that blacks are not near the town of Benoni "proper" which was for whites only. The Old Benoni Location is what More can point out as what was whipped out.

Evidently, the life and times of More have been, for the most part, informed by apartheid. This draconian regime, and its racist machinations and legal excess, made More to philosophize differently by taking the black situation as seriously a site of study, reflection, and critique.

A professor of philosophy, More taught at University of Limpopo, University of Cape Town, University of Durban Westville, University of KwaZulu Natal just to name a few. His stature as a philosopher of Azania is uncontestable. That is why, for More, it has been of importance that his philosophy has been concerned with the particularities and actualities of the lived experiences of Azania.[1] This makes More to be concerned with the lived experience of being black and this, under apartheid and even its aftermath (the post-1994 era), is the terrain of the existential struggle whose nexus of reflection stems from the black lived experience.

Philosophical anthropology in Azania, according to More, is concerned with the "emergence of black selfhood, black suffering, embodied agency, freedom, racism and liberation, in short, it deals with *being-black-in-the-world*."[2] Philosophical anthropology is centrally a human activity. Its questions are rooted in the meaning of being human. But this meaning, in this instance, is investigated by those who have their humanity questioned. This is the basis of More's philosophical anthropology and in Azania, by way of black radical thinking, it becomes existentialist in form, content, and expression.

> More's work is a meticulous interrogation of what it means to be human, the importance of dignity and freedom, and the dynamics of philosophical and

> political reasoning. It is these elements of his work that earned him a place not only in African philosophy but also in Africana philosophy.[3]

More's standing, as a philosopher, earned him what Lewis Gordon articulates as a South African great living philosopher. In not being a world-known philosopher, or a local celebrity intellectual, More is known, commonly, in small circles of those who are fighting for liberation and those who, in making philosophy a quotidian practice, are in the effort to make it the radicality of black life. But it is worth underlining that his influence is immeasurable. It stands to reason that More's greatness also lies in him being a philosopher of life. This is the generative life, one which is not only concerned about the production of meaning, but on how to live a meaningful life—that is, a livable one. Even though More is a trained philosopher, a professor in academic ranking, he is not bound by its "disciplinary decadence" as Gordon states, and he does not valorize it and thus not reducing it as a disciplinary formation.[4] More is concerned with the situation of being-black-in-an-antiblack-world, and at the center of his philosophical conduct lies the radical practice of doing philosophy not only as a discipline but as what Julia Suarez-Krabbe calls the "life project."[5] It is in this mode of philosophizing that More will foreground his philosophical anthropology, and the name Azania, as the rightful name for the territory known as South Africa, being his field. The philosophical conduct that stands in the name of being black, and where philosophy is put to work, it as the work of freedom, demands liberatory orchestrations. It is in these liberatory orchestrations that philosophy in black finds its radical expression. For, it is a philosophy that is foregrounded in the black point of view, and its canonical articulation and interlocution do not shy away from the situation of being-black-in-an-antiblack-world. This world, in More's philosophical conduct, is subjected to the radical drive. These liberatory orchestrations are undertaken not only as diagnostics of the problem, nor professing solutions, but what radically orients the philosophical conduct not to concede to the absolutes, strictures, and edicts of philosophy but its rupture.

Philosophy, for More, is a living practice which is worked on and through by human beings. It is clear that philosophy is not a mother of all disciplines as it is banally propagated. Obviously, it is a discipline among many other disciplines. It is what is within the realm of everyday life and not some abstract private sphere of Western episteme.

In having to be born and living through the hellish life of settler-colonialism and apartheid, Gordon attests: "More was keenly aware of what it meant to fight, day by day, for life in a world that offered continued denigration and despair."[6] This is the world that More stood up against and one which, in his force and might, sought to fundamentally change. Even when things are not corresponding with the effort that he puts, to still remain committed to what has to be done is something which has been radically consistent.

> Professor More has given more to South Africa, the country of his birth, than he received. What he expected, however, is not what those whose values are governed by market forces would proffer. A man guided committed and love for a people and their struggle for dignity and freedom finds little value in conventional forms of recognition.[7]

The revitalization of thought means that the eruptive spirit will signifty the development and recalibration of concepts. If who More is becomes what is defined and elaborated as a philosopher in black, whose philosophical conduct is philosophy in black, that demands the exposition that accounts for who he is and what continues to be in the name of his philosophy in black. More is the one who, in his philosophical conduct, brings to the forth the social, cultural, political, and philosophical tonalities and expressions into one. All these are fused in the name of freedom and the phrasing of More's social, cultural, political, and philosophical inscription articulates what is radically charged. His philosophical conduct has always been robust because, with justification, the pursuit of freedom is always a robust affair. Refusing to be a fence-seater and confronting things directly, the phraseology and articulation of his philosophical anthropology has been grounded on the radical commitment and the love for his people.

The thematic content of More's philosophical anthropology, with Azania as the foci and loci, makes it telling that More goes against the liberal consensus which has been officiated by the post-1994 settlement which, in the name of the South African regime that is called "post-apartheid," claims that freedoms were gained and the "triumph" against apartheid birthed a "new" South Africa. Everything is turned on its head and the modulation that unfolds in the name of freedom makes it possible to locate the radical expression of More's philosophical anthropology. If Azania is a field, that as a stand and standard, à la the modulated forms of philosophy in black, that makes More to hold a unique position in the field of contemporary thought. That is why philosophy in black speaks in the name of More's philosophical conduct. If a philosopher of change is what remains true when it comes to More, it still means that he intentionally effects change and it is what should come into being as a matter of his philosophical conduct, in his own name. More writes: "So the meaning of an ascription of an identity, even though it may or may not be indicative of one's character, nevertheless constitutes one into a character within a sociality that gives meaning to it."[8] Freedom, which is a yearning for fundamental change, its radical pursuit even, is all in the name of what More calls "free intention." It is the intention of what he wants and it comes from him—freely. That is to say, More is the being who lives with free intention. This is only because he chooses to be free. Change comes with More's character and that he is a black philosopher, a radical one at that, who is in combat with apartheid and antiblackness, this would mean the continued reshaping of his character and that would mean, on the basis of free intention, choosing what he wants. This, in short, means More is what he wants *to be*. Since he makes freedom to be one of his principalities, and that being engraved in his modes of philosophizing, that is the constant reshaping of his identity. His philosophical questions, themes, and concerns will be determined by the situation of his blackness. This, also, has to do with the way that More chooses to do philosophy in that mold and that does not necessarily mean that when one is black one does philosophy in black. But, for More, to be specific, his free intention to do philosophy in black is what makes his blackness to be the fulcrum of his philosophical anthropology and by the way of valorizing Azania, this makes it apt. Again, it is key to keep on insisting that More is a black contrarian and it is from his blackness that he is articulating reality in a different way that does not parade the dictates of the liberal consensus. This facticity, which is More's blackness, makes philosophical anthropology to be in line with liberatory orchestrations that radically call for Azania.

This change is not only in terms of the outcomes, but the very intention and action of making it. Briefly put, this is putting philosophy to work. Change is what is in the making and that, for More, is largely grounded in blackness.

Philosophy in black is a radical expression that speaks in the name of various traditions which are liberatory and that stands for the name of Azania in this case. Chief among them is Black Consciousness which, for More, as his contrarian position, does not draw from political parties but from the thought of Steve Biko. More is not, at all, a member of any political party. This does not mean that he is apolitical. He is, just to punctuate, one of the most politically engaged philosophers. That is why he refuses to disentangle philosophy from politics. More is radically committed and he is, consistently so, committed to the cause. That is why Black Consciousness is his fold and it is through it that philosophy and politics are enjoined. Just to emphasize, Black Consciousness is not a formation of singularity's enclosure. Even though it is called Black Consciousness philosophy, it is a meta-political formation that is not enclosed by political parties. There are, currently, political parties that espouse Black Consciousness, namely: Azanian People's Organization which broke into factions of two parties (Socialist Party of Azania and Black People's Convention) that do not have any impact in the political landscape dominated by the African National Congress. Black Consciousness philosophy, in its ante-party politics, is what More adheres to because this is not what is in a party-line. For More, then, there is no such thing as toeing the party-line.

Richly so, Black Consciousness has intellectual (re)sources that are religious, social, cultural, political, and for More, in particular, philosophical. The philosophical conduct of More centralizes and deepens Black Consciousness as a philosophy without reducing it to what is philosophical in a disciplinary sense. Black Consciousness philosophy is a form of rupture. In focusing on its origins and development, More argues that it is a philosophy thus: "Black consciousness has always, with justification but sometimes without justification any attempt at justification, been the only liberation movement whose ideas were generally referred to as a philosophy."[9] The centrality of blackness and that being the intentional and definitional basis of Black Consciousness philosophy, and this being the philosophic force that advocates for Azania, makes its roots and canonical formations to be "an intertextually embedded philosophy that draws from multiplicity of sources of black intellectual productions."[10] More even goes further to even state that Black Consciousness philosophy is rooted in Africana philosophy which, indeed, is its mode of philosophical expression. Also, more fittingly, More states that Biko is its foremost philosopher—say, Africana existentialist philosopher.[11]

Besides, More, just like his black radical forbearers and contemporaries, refuses to be complicit with apartheid and any other form of dehumanization. He advocates for what is in his own name. This is not reducible to the act of individuation, but the collective struggle for a just and free world.

More makes it clear that he refuses to be confined and defined by the articulation of his situation, and as a philosopher in black, his philosophical anthropology is premised on the very idea of fundamental change.[12] To say philosophy in black is to be attuned to the ways that a black philosopher authorizes the modes of philosophizing and thus in the grounds of Azania and in Black Consciousness philosophy as one of the intellectual frames that More engages, what comes out clarifies the radical demands of this philosophy.

> A student of existential philosophy, which he saw manifested in the revolutionary thought of Steve Bantu Biko and which he respected in the courageous philosophy of Frantz Fanon and Jean-Paul Sartre, More instantly recognized a kindred spirit. He held in his hands a text of Black existential philosophy, which was also part of Africana existential philosophy.[13]

In this rich philosophical tradition that Gordon paints, the radical demand to be free means that More advances fundamental change. In the regime that is considered to be post-apartheid—or, more acutely, post-1994 dispensation—or, what More terms "neo-apartheid," the scandal remains that this is a regime that is invested in the refusal to confront the reality that has to fundamentally change.[14] As a philosopher of fundamental change, More is located within the annals of philosophical anthropology because the study of the human situation is all about change. The effort, in More's philosophical conduct, is effecting that change. What has to fundamentally change is the ending of racism. Being born in a racist polity and still continuing to live in one (even though South Africa is claimed to be non-racial), there is an effort to make sure that this reality changes absolutely. In the name of this change, More inaugurates the conditions of possibility which comes in the name of what Gordon names as "critical reflection."[15] The eruptive nature of More's philosophical anthropology and by way of centralizing Azania, at all times, is what has been in the name of the lived experience, and the self is not an individuated subject but the being that is in relation with others. This is what demands and also necessitates critical reflection. To add, disciplinary decadence and enclosure will not have the last word as the study of change is advocated.

More attaches blackness not only as the racial marker but his own being, a being that has its own point of view, a being that is free and also in relation with other beings. For there to be freedom, there must be the imagination and the actualization of change. It will not be amiss to assert that a philosopher in black is the being of freedom. It is all that is in the name of freedom that makes More to take a clear stance of being a contrarian who is contra unfreedom. For, in order for him to act and pursue freedom, he must declare and assert himself as a free being who, in effecting change, will, and must, in the name of his philosophical conduct, generate the conditions of possibility. For this to be actualized, it is key to ask: What does it mean to be free and to live the life of freedom? More avers:

> Of course, by freedom I do not mean absolute freedom to be whatever I want; that would be absurd. As a human being, a free consciousness, there are things I choose and those I cannot choose. I did not, for example, choose to be born at a particular time in a particular place by particular parents of a particular racial stock.[16]

It is clear, in having the freedom to choose, despite More's naming being something that is imposed on him, and what he could not do anything about, coming to consciousness and being in pursuit of freedom is what More always chooses. Freedom is not license and for More, it is responsibility and it is in the name of this freedom that he made his name to be aligned with it as a matter of his philosophical conduct. In choosing freedom, in him being a conscious being and acting according to the desires of his freedom and self-definition (a philosopher in black), More is named as the basis of his identity construction and that, later, will be up to him as a philosopher of freedom on what he does with his name. In his own name, his principles and philosophical concerns, More takes philosophy in black as not only a discursive project but the exercise and actualization of freedom.

In terms of his own blackness, something interesting emerges and it is in what meaning he constructs a liberatory project. Here is More: "That I am black is a given, it is my facticity, but it is entirely the meaning I give to my blackness that gives it significance."[17] More's blackness is the one of freedom. It is the blackness of the one who acts in the agency of blackness and that is why his philosophical conduct is all about change. Starting from his own name, More has this to say: "Thanks to Black Consciousness philosophy, we became tired of pursuing a whiteness that was impossible to achieve, we reverted back to our African names, and we said: 'Anybody don't like calling me by my African name, go to hell.'"[18] This is one important fact that the name "Mabogo" is principal and it comes before "Percy" (which is not in his identity document) and the name "Samuel" (which is in his identity document) is the one that he does not use. Also, the way he names himself, and taking his name seriously, that is evident in the manner that he philosophizes.

In Azania, which is the name that More chooses as opposed to South Africa, the same principle of choosing to be free still applies. It is in More's effort of choosing freedom that leads him to take the act of naming very seriously. Since the settler-colonialist project has been the one of arbitrarily imposing names on blacks and also whitening their original names through systematic bastardization and erasure, the change that More effects is one of freedom. It is in the name of this change that More will not accept the stasis and decadence of settler-colonialism and apartheid—that is to say, dehumanization writ large.

More refused to be a usable thing or a misused person in a way of ingratiating himself to those who dishonor him. Instead, More stands for the recognition that is set out in his own terms. He stands out as a black philosopher and that is in the name of what can make him to be incorporated in the accommodationist discursive frames. Gordon correctly notes: "The demands placed on him, as they are for all black philosophers, were often seductive."[19] To be seduced is to be made impotent and that, in the name and guise of importance, is a misleading deed. Seduction, by means of being subjected to the dimming of consciousness, is to be misled, blinded even. The radical refusal to be seduced has made More to stand for the principle—a costly affair. What makes More to charge forth has been the very idea of thinking. "As all philosophers, Black philosophers must 'think,' but given the exigencies of life posed in antiblack societies, such philosophers cannot think in terms leisurely or luxurious."[20] What Gordon advances, in the annals of philosophy in black, or any other philosophical project carried by a black philosopher, is that thinking cannot be decoupled from urgency. Thinking is done in the now and it is in the name of what must be done—that is, it is necessary to think urgently.

During clutches of its dehumanization, the formation of a philosopher who will not submit to this world will lead to a radical commitment to institute a new reality altogether. This reality will mean not being defined in the name of being an object, but a living being who takes philosophy as a life project. And, its radical expression, grounded in Africana existentialist philosophy, will mean engaging philosophical anthropology as one that reflects and inflected by the social milieu More is in. Having grown up in racist South Africa, and living what is considered to be township life, which is the segregated milieu of the black, apartheid as radical separation, the cutting off of blacks from things fabricated white, the world of More and his philosophical concerns will be informed by urgency. Even more pertinently, More refused the world that the racists constructed for him. He is his own image, his own face, the "human face" which Biko called for.[21] He had to have the urgency to create a different world that, according to Gordon, will make racists irrelevant.[22]

In the contested terrain called South Africa, what emerges is the call for its rightful name—Azania. South Africa is the name of the country that carries a baggage of the racist history and this even haunts the present. Even in the post-1994 formation, that goes in the name of non-racialism or South Africa being a cliché and façade that goes by the tag of the "rainbow nation," a lot is at stake in terms of the reality that confronts the present. South Africa is confronted with a scandal of antiblack racism and this is what, even in the face of the liberal humanist impulse, cannot wipe off the reality that racism, in its antiblack form. It cannot be overemphasized that South Africa is racist. There is no amount of peppering this truth under the clutches of complexity, sophistication, fluidity, entanglement, change, or whatever that is used to sanitize. The modes of disavowing this truth, and clutching the straws that there is no problem of racism, it being structurally sedimented, the perversity of the everyday life as it is, the antiblack reality as it were, demands the ways of dealing with reality as it is and not denying blacks the language to articulate their demands, and to name the reality that they are in through their own terms.

South Africa, in its antiblack formation, is what is subjected to the radical change that aims to give it another form of a radical expression in the name of Azania. In his work, More does not name South Africa in a valorized sense, and what he does, instead, is to call for Azania. His philosophical anthropology, in its radical disposition, challenges the meta-narrative of the post-1994 South Africa. He is a philosopher who engages reality from a radical point of view.

Philosophical anthropology, in More's philosophical conduct, is what is embodied and also lived—say, living thought. This is not a matter of what

Gordon calls "floating abstractions" but, as it were, the reality as lived.[23] In other words, what is the lived experience of being black and that being the actionality of what must emerge, is what More's philosophical anthropology is. The lived experience is not something that is fixed or the experience of those who cannot alter their situation and the reality that surrounds it.

More privileges the question of being and this is what, in Azania, cannot be forgotten. "To be more precise, the preoccupation with 'being' is the fundamental concern of the philosophy known as ontology and, by extension, philosophical anthropology."[24] The manner in which Black Consciousness philosophy responds has been a clear attendance to the human question. This is by the way of "bringing to life that question of Black being."[25] This is the being that is questioned and what erupts is the spirit that combats this dehumanization. More writes: "The consequences of a questioned and denied humanness, of being treated as a sub-human, sub-person, or animal invariably leads to the profound experience of existential dread and anguish in the face of non-being."[26] What More takes seriously is the essence of accounting to the meaning of being whose humanity is questioned.

By being born in settler-colonialism and then its apartheid perfection, More is, as a black person, affected by dehumanization. It is from this concern of his being that he will radically insist on being free and not taking dehumanization as the definer of his existence. The denial of the humanity of the black being is confronted by way of having a different conception of being-black-in-the-world which, for Chabani Manganyi, sets the basis of the redefinition of the black self—say, Black Consciousness philosophy as the re-articulation of being *otherwise*.[27] This is the being of the black in its own terms that insists on the vocabulary of freedom which refutes the logics that justify dehumanization. In the post-1994 regime, there is no way that the question of being suspended remains dormant. More takes this up and asks: "This being the case, how then can Black people fail to engage in existential and ontological self-interrogation?"[28] There is a concern for More and it is framed in a question: "If a person's humanity is questioned or denied, what can that person do except assert his or her humanity?"[29] The redefinition of the self, by way of More, his philosophical conduct even, takes seriously the task of asserting the humanity of those who have their humanity questioned. There is no way that philosophical anthropology in Azania will not be concerned with the question of being, and thus extricating it from the conception of freedom. What is apparent in More's philosophical conduct, in his assertion of being, is the emergence of a radical conversion whose occurrence means the affirmation of the self. Self-definition is the assertion of being and for the black, it is clear that ontological questions are fundamentally distinct.

A black philosopher, that being More, is the one who is not concerned with matters that concerned other philosophers who, the question of race and their humanity not being questioned, featuring as matters of no concern at all. That would lead to the question that More asks: "What does it mean to be a philosopher of African descent in South Africa today?"[30] It is this question that defines who More is and that, even, explains his philosophical conduct.

> The black experience is not incorporated into the philosophical experience despite philosophy's putative universality and generality. In other words, the peculiar features of black experiences such as racism, apartheid, oppression, colonialism, slavery, and more are not part and parcel of the experiences represented in the abstractions of white philosophy. Philosophy stays away from messy issues such as racism, slavery, colonialism, phenomena that beget poverty, crime, pain, death, and more to African people.[31]

More's philosophical conduct, its justification thereof, makes a clear statement and takes a standing that More does not contradict his conscience. By being a contrarian, being a black philosopher qua philosophy in black, he does a subversive kind of a philosophy. It is a philosophy that is denied of being a philosophy, and More—without seeking any legitimation, qualification, approval, justification, and thus not ingratiating himself to injustice—does philosophy in his own accord. This is because he is the one who acts in the name of philosophy in black.

More rejects the internalization of the black being as non-being. He stands to wrestle with naturalization of dehumanization as a given and does, at all times, affirm "a being who has freedom as her/his foundation and goal."[32] The being of freedom and the being who is in pursuit of freedom is the one who radically refuses to submit to any form of ontological closure but always calls for rupture. The being of radical conversion is, for More, the one who necessitates and accelerates freedom.

So, this is who More is. He is the being of freedom even if such a freedom is frustrated, withdrawn, denied or whatever that will make it to fail. Always, there is something generative and the ways of willing this freedom come as a result of working from the limits. Radical conversion, for More, is having to authorize the self.

> Let us be clear what was at stake here. At the heart of the matter was an issue of authority—the authority of Blacks to describe reality as they perceived it and to define themselves as they saw fit within that reality. At stake here was the power and authority to define.[33]

It is the self-definition of those who are dehumanized to rehumanize themselves. It is their refusal to see themselves through the eyes of those who dehumanize them. The basis of self-definition is what always depends on them. It is through their honor and dignity (no matter how denigrated and denied) that they will uphold the way they define themselves. By radically refusing to be what others make of them, they make themselves in their own imagination and image of their freedom. That is why they are radical and do not compromise on what this freedom is. More, in this case, is a philosopher of freedom. That is why he is even free to instate philosophy in black.

That is why philosophy in black, as the life project, is the radical antithesis of what Suarez-Krabbe refers to as the death project.[34] In philosophy in black, there is the emergence whose radical potentiality, or its mark of conditions of possibility, will mean the re-making of the world that is radically different from the one that is antiblack. South Africa, in its antiblackness, is substituted by the institution of Azania not only of what is the name in the lettered spirit, but the whole refiguring of reality, and the modes of philosophizing that animates this radical force being everything that has to do with creating alternative forms of existence that refuse to concede to what is the name of no change.

Azania is instituted to even refashion alternative forms of being black, and this is the image of invention that comes from the philosophical conduct that stands from the field of those who claim freedom and act on its will as opposed to the enclosure of unfreedom. By his philosophical anthropology and Azania as the axis, More is doing the study of fundamental change. Here, in acting by the way of a liberating (im)pulse, the political dimension of things "also construct new forms of life."[35] The actional gesture, also to note, is generative, in that it brings things to life. Also, the creation of new meanings is what is there in More's philosophical conduct. By this, More always renews tensions and recalibrates the resolve. If Azania is change, it would mean that More's philosophical conduct will have to be understood in its generative force and it is what stands against what Gordon calls "disciplinary decadence" which, in its "epistemic closure," has nothing generative about it and as such, being resistant to any form of a philo-praxis.[36] Philosophy in black, what is in the name of constant change, stands rooted in the Azanian political field where More resides and philosophizes. In the eruptive sense of things being otherwise, refigured from what they were, that as the result of figuring stuff out, knowing, doing, and thinking differently as Walter Mignolo states, new questions and modes of inquiry are all about instituting different attitudes.[37]

In the name of More, in the name of his philosophical orchestration, Azania is not only centralized as the renaming of South Africa. Rather, attention is made to Azania as a field of thought qua thought—say, philosophy in black as More's philosophical orchestration. It means that things are put in motion and what is in the realm of "living thought," as Gordon coins it, is being able to be something generative even in the midst of any form of stasis.[38] There is a radical break from stasis because More refused to be named in the ways that have to do with his insignificance, but he registers his significance without seeking recognition or ingratiating himself into the disciplinary fold of philosophy. Philosophy in black, for More, is the rightful orchestration whose name means not only a liberatory project but a large scheme of re-making the world. Even in the face of failure, there is no end in having to rise up again and again and doing what has to be done in the name of responsibility. More is a responsible philosopher. He is responsible for what he is orchestrating—philosophy in black—that is, the philosophy that faces enclosure whenever it is advanced. But there is nothing that stops More in puncturing these enclosures and insisting on freedom. He is responsible for what comes in the name of responsibility. What bears the name of responsibility is what is in the name of freedom. Therefore, the philosophical project that More does, in the name of Azania, and that being the name that signifies freedom (as opposed to a mere geographic location), makes the ethical task of being responsible to come in the name of responsibility. That is to say, there is no responsibility if More is not responsive to the world he is in, the world he is responsible for—what, in fact, is in his own name. As a philosopher, More is not responsible for his name in the individuated sense, but in the relational form with his interlocutors whom his thought is what he is in conversation with (through texts, dialogues, critique, and otherwise). Since philosophy is the communication of ideas, and that not being reducible to the field of pure abstraction, More takes philosophy to work to respond to the life project as the antithesis of the death project. Taking from Suarez-Krabbe, it is clear that the world is being created in the ethical sense where response and responsibility are entwined, and that, in itself, generates something that is fundamentally different and what, as a result, can blur enclosure.[39]

In chapter 1, a submission is made that More is a revolutionary teacher. This is a teacher who is not a mere pedagogue but the interlocutor who engages in the relational dynamics with what is in class. It is here that this goes beyond the call of his profession and the case is made that More is a giver, a generous one for that matter. The class that More teaches, this chapter argues, is a different formation altogether because it becomes the experimental formation which abolishes the teacher–student hierarchy. This, then, as the enriched and proliferated way of teaching, which is the revolutionary operation, turns philosophy's monasticism in its head. The critique that is launched under the conception of undermonastic practices is what makes More as a revolutionary teacher to be bold.

In chapter 2, the reconfiguration of the concept of Azania in undertaken, and by way of More, this is distilled by critiquing the state formation and territory named South Africa. It is clear that More's philosophical conduct fosters a livable world, a world of freedom and Azania is the land of the free.

This chapter will deploy More's Africana existentialist phenomenology to make a case for Azania and that is the name that critiques the foundation of settler-colonialism, and what is advocated is not only a name-change, but the uprooting of the infrastructure of racism that informs South Africa even in its post-1994 formation.

In chapter 3, an interlocutory encounter is staged to illuminate the shifting of the geography of reason and this is done from Azania as an enunciation. The shifting of the geography reason is taken upon as the testament of More's philosophical practice, and he having a home in the Caribbean Philosophical Association has to do with him not having a philosophical home in the land of his birth. The chapter critiques the Philosophical Society of Southern Africa and, in particular, its complicity of disavowing racism and not to take the black lived experience as a point of departure. In a country that is plagued by the past and present of racism, there is no way that attention cannot be paid on it as a philosophical problem.

In chapter 4, a meditation is undertaken to locate More as the figure of rebel and the claim is that he fights for the cause. This goes against the myth that the rebel is the one who is without a cause. Instead, as More shows, the rebel is the one who fights to live, and in this sense, to rebel is to exist. That is why he is, all the time, radically committed to say yes to freedom and no to unfreedom. As an existentialist philosopher, and a philosopher of freedom, More argues for radical demands and fights for different conditions of possibility. As a rebel, More ensures that there is rupture, the claim is made and substantiated that he is all for freedom.

In chapter 5, an exploration on the conception of the death text is dealt with and that being tied to the forms of authorship. The chapter begins by thinking through More's obituary of Aimé Césaire, and this is only authored if the one who is being written about is deceased. Also, the chapter examines another death text which is known as the Will and it is shown how authorship becomes a way of exercising power from the tomb to the living. The chapter, then, examines the auto-obituary which is a death text where More, the living author, writes about his own death.

This book, in the concluding chapter, makes a case for the way in which More articulates liberation and that, in fact, is not reducible to a utopic register. Instead, the radical insistence on liberation will always mean waging the existential struggle to create a different set of conditions and mapping the radical sites of possibility even in the face of enclosure. What is always at work—that is, More doing philosophical anthropology in Azania—is a grammar of this liberation. This must be taken as a trait of who More is, a philosopher in black. And, this will come out clearly in the unfolding of this intervention because of the unique way he philosophizes from Azania.

NOTES

1. Mabogo P. More, "Biko: Africana Existentialist Philosopher," *Alternation* 11, no. 1 (2004): 79–108. This is the life-world of those who philosophize from the manner in which they see the world. This means, in a way, philosophy cannot be in abstractions, but the facticity of the black, and things being seen from the black point of view.

2. Ibid., 82. These are not the concerns that pre-occupy white philosophers. They are not coming from a dehumanized reality of being racially marked.

3. Lewis R. Gordon, "Foreword," in *Looking through Philosophy in Black: Memoirs*, edited by Mabogo P. More, xv–xx (Lanham: Rowman and Littlefield International, 2019), xx.

4. Lewis R. Gordon, *Disciplinary Decadence: Living Thought in Trying Times* (Boulder and London: Paradigm Publishers, 2006).

5. Julia Suárez-Krabbe, *Race, Rights and Rebels: Alternatives to Human Rights and Development from the Global South* (Lanham: Rowman and Littlefield International, 2016).

6. Gordon, "Foreword," xv.

7. Ibid. The idea of love and commitment for his country and people has made More to engage in philosophy as a project for change. That is why More refuses to be complicit with any form of the status quo. He is, as it is known, a non-conformist to boot. He is keenly aware how conformism breeds complicity and that would mean not being responsible for the project of freedom.

8. Mabogo P. More, *Looking through Philosophy in Black: Memoirs* (Lanham: Rowman and Littlefield International, 2019), 6.

9. Mabogo P. More, "The Intellectual Foundations of Black Consciousness Movement," in *Intellectual Traditions in South Africa: Ideas, Individuals and Institution*, edited by Peter Vale, Lawrence Hamilton, and Estelle H. Prinsloo, 173–195 (Scottsville: UKZN Press, 2014), 177.

10. Ibid., 179.

11. More, "Biko."

12. More, *Looking through Philosophy in Black.*

13. Gordon, "Foreword," xix.

14. Mabogo P. More, "Fanon and the Land Question in (Post)Apartheid South Africa," in *Living Fanon: Global Perspectives*, edited by Nigel C. Gibson, 173–185 (New York: Palgrave Macmillan, 2011).

15. Gordon, "Foreword."

16. More, *Looking through Philosophy in Black*, 4.

17. Ibid.

18. Ibid., 5.

19. Gordon, "Foreword," xvi.

20. Ibid.

21. Steve Biko, *I Write What I Like* (Oxford and Johannesburg: Heinemann, 1978).

22. Ibid.

23. Lewis R. Gordon, "A Phenomenology of Biko's Black Consciousness," in: *Biko Lives! Contesting the Legacies of Steve Biko*, edited by Andile Mngxitama, Amanda Alexander, and Nigel C. Gibson, 83–93 (New York: Palgrave, 2008).

24. Mabogo P. More, "Black Consciousness Movement's Ontology: The Politics of Being," *Philosophia Africana* 14, no. 1 (2012): 23–39, see 23.

25. Ibid., 24.

26. Ibid., 26.

27. N. Chabani Manganyi, *Being-Black-in-the-World* (Braamfontein: SPRO-CAS/Ravan Press, 1973).

28. More, "Black Consciousness Movement's Ontology," 30.

29. Ibid., 31.

30. More, *Looking through Philosophy in Black*, 17.

31. Ibid., 20.

32. Ibid., 34.

33. Ibid., 35.

34. Suárez-Krabbe, *Race, Rights and Rebels.*

35. Gordon, "Phenomenology of Black Consciousness," 87.

36. Gordon, *Disciplinary Decadence.*

37. Walter D. Mignolo, *The Darker Side of Western Modernity: Global Futures, Decolonial Options* (Durham and London: Duke University Press, 2011).

38. Gordon, *Disciplinary Decadence.*

39. Suárez-Krabbe, *Race, Rights and Rebels.*

Chapter 1

The Revolutionary Teacher

A teacher is a giver, a generous one at that. But what to make of the revolutionary teacher, the one who teaches in times of crisis, the one who is in crisis or declared a crisis by those who cannot stand his or her revolting thoughts, articulations, and expression that turn what is known upside down? The curriculum of a radical disposition, one which is deemed radical as it marks a clear line and speaks where it is coming, one which does not allow itself to be relevant (whatever what relevance means, to being popular and palatable)? What to make of that teacher who is deemed disorganized while reorganizing thought for learning to be side by side with unlearning?

The subject of concern here is the revolutionary teacher. Mabogo P. More teaches philosophy, for a long span of his life, more than four decades, and this has been done with the revolutionary intent. Teaching has been a lifelong practice. More is, as a professor too, continuing to learn. Besides, him being a revolutionary teacher means being a studious student too. Learning to unlearn has been his radical practice. Re-reading the world otherwise, from a point of view, which is denied—the black point of view—has been the disposition of his teaching that makes it to be the transformative force of his philosophy.

More will be framed in registers that give an innovative account of the revolutionary teacher. It is this account that will not only give a clear sense of who is More, but the important part will largely be based on his revolutionary teaching, his philosophical thought and practice—his philosophical anthropology in general. For this frame to be brought into meaning, its generative capacity being installed, More's revolutionary role as the teacher will be engaged with him as a giver. It is in giving that revolutionary teaching is understood because in giving human beings knowledge, he also learns from them. This giving is radical, in that it is based on the principle of expecting nothing in return while giving and giving oneself. The pedagogy of More is one of those material that are a canon and non-canonical; the ones which are deemed exterior due to the protocols of philosophy's radical exclusion of black thought. More teaches philosophy and exposes its racism by being concerned with the question of race that is regarded as nonphilosophical.

The philosophy class that More teaches is revolutionized by questioning the conventional notion of the class itself. In his revolutionary teaching, the class becomes a sort of an ensemble, a space where thought is experimented and it ceases to be business as usual but a radical project where experiment and experience go together to facilitate the fugitive protocols that animate different ways on thinking, knowing, and doing. From More's revolutionary teaching, the question of human existence is what is undertaken as philosophical anthropology's question of being-black-in-an-antiblack-world.

A GIVER

Why is More a revolutionary teacher anyway? He is engaged in the acts of giving. More is, according to Reiland Rabaka, in a "dark dungeon."[1] As Nahum Chandler attests: "It seems we are in a black hole."[2] It is in this black hole where light must be shed, and the result of that being is getting out of that hole. It is also known, that there is a world out there, outside this hole, near and far from it. The revolutionary teacher must be there to get his students outside the black hole. This is a demanding task and, according to Rabaka, it demands hard intellectual labor.[3] But this is what has to be done, and there is no any other way around it. The only way is to forge ahead. It is by getting out of this black hole that will make students to be free. But being free must be a value that must be instilled while they are in the black hole so that they will know how to get out and to also know what is out there and how to continue to fight for freedom out there. The revolutionary teacher, then, is the one who gives this gift of freedom. It is in this gift that minds will be in possession of this gift. This is a form of a disposition which, to Kwame Nkrumah, "can enhance, intensify, even develop the consciousness."[4] This means that students become revolutionary agents and not empty vessels that must be filled. They must engage in action, and that is the ideal of the revolutionary teacher. As Nkrumah notes: "Positive action is revolutionary and negative action is reactionary."[5] More's positive action is what makes him a revolutionary teacher. Something has to be done in engaging in positive action. This is the concrete materiality and not some abstractions. "Without positive action, a colonial territory cannot be truly liberated."[6] But positive action, as being driven by the revolutionary teacher, does not yield anticipated outcomes all the time. However, effort has to be put.

> Positive action must, furthermore, seek an alignment of all force of progress and, by marshaling them, confront the negative forces. It must at the same time anticipate and contain its own inner contradictions, for, though positive action unites those forces of a situation which are, in regard to a specific purpose, progressive, many of these forces will contain tendencies which are in other respects reactionary.[7]

The predicament of the revolutionary teacher is to live with this reality. It is to embrace disappointment, failure, and betrayal as they often outweigh success, fulfillment, and accomplishment. The risky undertaking that the revolutionary teacher is in has always proven to be far much costly than beneficial. The revolutionary teacher agitates for change in the condition that does not want change.

There is more that the revolutionary teacher must give. There is less that is received. With passion, dedication, and love, the revolutionary teacher does not invest in receiving. The weight is on giving. This giving is the radical disposition. As a revolutionary teacher, More should continue to give, and this is something that comes from his love and commitment for a different reality, the one that is against antiblackness.

As a teacher, one who is committed to what Rabaka calls "revolutionary decolonization," the ethical imperative of giving is principal.[8] This becomes the impassioned assertion for liberation. The purpose of giving is done by More knowing that, according to Nkrumah, "rudimentary minds are nothing but active matter."[9] Rabaka argues that revolutionary decolonization is placed in the service of the present and futures with the focus of "black being" and "black becoming." The present and future are urgent marks that propel the insurgent eruption and marks that propel the insurgent to erupt into what is necessary to be done, the radical unfolding of the doing itself without the preoccupation of the outcome. Revolutionary decolonization is the opening of possibility, and it is that opening that is essential.

There is no obsession with universality but what matters is the dissimulation that comes with this universality, as this is the particularity of the elsewhere. Revolutionary decolonization, from that root, is a serious matter, one that might be called, according to Rabaka, "a matter of intellectual, political, and racial life and death."[10] What is clear here is that revolutionary decolonization is defined and refined by Rabaka to call for modes of urgency and insurgency. This is the conceptualized and calibrated way of putting More's philosophical project into perspective, and thus locating him as the revolutionary teacher. By saying revolutionary decolonization, Rabaka intensifies more heat so that the revolutionary project can steam ahead. This will mean the articulation of the project that will not be palatable to liberal sensibilities which are there to stand against the project of blacks thinking for themselves and standing up for themselves. Blacks are those who see the world with, and from their own eyes, their inner eyes, their ways of seeing.

Teaching is change. Thus, it is revolutionary. The one who is teaching, and More in this case, is revolutionary. But not any other teacher is revolutionary. Teachers who demand change and do not become complicit in dehumanization are revolutionary teachers. More as the revolutionary teacher comes from a disposition that his project is about giving. To give, as the imperative of revolutionary teaching has everything to do with love. A gift is what is offered in the name of love. The love of teaching is what More embodies. He continues to give even what he offers to give is taken away. Nelson Maldonado-Torres explains this situation as the paradox of the gift where those who are giving from nothing are giving with their lives.[11] They know the worth of their gift, in that they continue to give even if they are subjected to precarious modes of being alive. This really attests to the fact that the revolutionary teacher is the one who is filled with a heightened capacity to love. It is here that passion and compassion are knotted, and there is nothing that will stop the heighted revolutionary spirit having to do what has to be done.

The spirit of critique is what animates the revolutionary teacher. The revolutionary teacher exists to create a different set of conditions. This, according to Chandler, "is the conception of the necessity."[12] The necessity is propelled by the fact that different set of conditions stands against the status quo that hides behind reason. The revolutionary teacher is the one who would be cast as being unreasonable. In the colonial conditions, the revolutionary teacher will make this necessity to combat the decadence of reason, and show that what is masked as reason is unreasonable. By teaching philosophy, More shows how philosophy, being weaponized for racist ends, presents itself as reason. More, for that matter, is opposed to philosophy that claims that reality can only be understood through reason.[13] This valorization of reason makes it to be the only way, while there are many ways. This has led Lewis Gordon to articulate reason "as a cat-and-mouse game."[14] When blacks make claim to reason, reason will disappear. It will only appear to be used against blacks. For More, in him being a revolutionary teacher, what Gordon calls "a revolutionary who demands systemic change"; this is the imperative that is insisted upon without end.[15]

Moten intimates: "There is more-than-critical criticism that's like seeing things—a gift of having been given to love things and how things look and how and what things see."[16] As the revolutionary teacher, More undertakes what Moten calls the intellectual project that is disruptive in the normative order of things, and this is the animating force of critique. Things are, then, according to Moten, radically altered in what was their free form, subjected to a constant alteration of a given in the spirit of generativity.[17] This is what revolutionary decolonization insists to see clearly, and thus altering things in the absolute. It is here where, in the context of the university, the distinction is collapsed between what is the inside and the outside.

> A self-critical practice will therefore not strive for a de-differentiation, a blurring of the differences between the inside and the outside of the institution, but rather for temporary overlaps, for precarious processes of exchange and differentiation. In both contexts, in the institution of the university and in self-organized initiatives of knowledge production, and all the more in their overlaps, a common problem inevitably arises: the complex relation between teaching and learning, between differently developed specific competencies, between different formal or informal hierarchy positions, between forms of empowerment and of fixing power.[18]

This inside and outside has led Gerald Rauning to argue for the concept of the absent teacher.[19] This means the need for those who teach and not interpellated into mechanical and mechanistic forms of the university, and thus performing robotic functions as opposed to critical thinking beings. The absent teacher is, according to Raunig, the one who deserts, and this means one who is inside and outside of the university.

> Desertion does not mean praise for fleeing from the world, but rather creating worlds. In the context of knowledge production, this power of invention is most likely to be found in self-organized contexts. Nevertheless, there is good reason not to lose sight of the institutional terrain, to use its resources and potentials to try out practices even in the belly of the institution, which are not easily digestible. For this reason, the starting point here is initially that of an institutional perspective of teaching.[20]

Stefano Harney and Fred Moten have this to say:

> In the face of these conditions one can only sneak into the university and steal what one can. To abuse its hospitality, to spite its mission, to join its refugee colony, its gypsy encampment, to be in but not of—this is the path of the subversive intellectual in the modern university.[21]

The revolutionary teaching that More undertakes is, while on the inside and outside, a way of not wanting to submit to the dictates of what is antithetical to revolutionary decolonization. This is what Moten calls "another way of living that exhaust imposed arrangements."[22] Where More stands has nothing to do with hanging in the balance, or mind dangling. Steadfast and resolute, he stands for something—principle. This is what distinguishes the revolutionary teacher, one who abhors opportunism, but one who creates opportunities.

Even if there are no opportunities, the indomitable will is the intensive drive that will yield opportunities. Moten has this to say: "I think I figured out what my job is: to support you in the development and refinement of your own intellectual practice."[23] But this is done in a radically different way than what might be expected from the university. Rather, this is the revolutionary teaching of life that the university has chosen to abandon. If More's emphasis is being rooted in the lived experience and fact of his blackness in an antiblack world, this means that he has to teach from the lens of that world. Those who are being taught become in touch with the reality that they are in. By giving the students their world as lived and experienced, and through engaged scholarship, is the task that More makes clear in his revolutionary teaching.

The revolutionary teacher is the one who yields opportunities of this nature, and this to Moten is creating the opportunity where the students will be made unsuitable to the demands of the world that is there to work them out, the overworking world. In this unsuitability, the whole point is the generation of life, a critical life. "Intellectuality is fugitivity, as a mode, and as a quality, of life."[24] Intellectuality is the combustion that must change into a thundering bolt to minds that must be of revolutionary decolonization.

More's gift is one that offers intellectuality. This is a serious gift. And, as such, More states: "I learned not to go to class unprepared."[25] What intellectuality demands is preparation and having to teach in the manner that is unconventional and not pandering to the sensibilities of the status quo, the task beforehand is not an easy one. Intellectuality, as the quality of life, as Moten attests, means that More, in teaching by way of freedom in the condition that it is resisted and denied, the effort of giving more has to be cemented. The gift of life, of quality, from intellectuality, is a different project altogether and that is what makes the being of the revolutionary teacher. In practice, the manner in which intellectuality is undertaken and executed is, by way of thorough preparation, of having to deal with the uncertain and the unknown. The search is not for solutions but diagnosis and critical investigation.

> This is the disavowal of the very idea of an endpoint; the task at hand, the activity in question, is aleatory. This is not about achievement; more specifically, and more generally, as we move in the weighted, weight air of enlightenment, this is not about the achievement of freedom.[26]

Intellectuality demands more work to be done to understand the existential condition that the black is in, and the ready-made answers that come to be definable and absolute are subjected to interrogation. There is no utopic arrival. The investigation still goes as new questions are (re)formulated. Intellectuality is, in the context of revolutionary decolonialization, a tool of diagnosis and re-elaboration of critique. This, in terms of the quality of life, demands modes of investigation that will even question the very nature of this life. Of course, it is not the life that is a given, but one denied. If, then, the radical pursuit of intellectuality is the mode of working through the ethos that animate the quality of life, this means that change, as Moten states, should be taken seriously as "change is better than development . . . change become a change bearing nothing, differentially, in particular."[27] That is, revolutionary teaching should be understood outside the logics of the university.

Revolutionary teaching is change. It is about learning to unlearn. Time is devoted when it comes to teaching. The creative energy is elevated, abstracted, and concretized in synthesized ways that should disseminate not only the structured pedagogic content but also the investigation of inquiry itself. More's commitment as the revolutionary teacher is a trait, one whose bar cannot be lowered because it is demanding. He teaches only to give the best. That is why the laziness of thought is not encouraged. By the fact that there is utopic suspension and the revolutionary decolonization should be engendered in rigorous and tireless ways, there is no instant gratification but more and more demands on the labor of thought. If development is what is subjected to suspension and change is what is principal as Moten says, the demand is having to work with something that is not easily noticed as change is gradual and often seen as minimal if non-existent. Since everything is about the quality of life, change is in the service of the life that has to be lived and the radical refusal of the current life that encourages laziness of thought so that there will be no change taking place.

This is the change that requires the opening of critique, and if there is closure, that critique must open, and if that critique is closed, it must engage in intellectuality that will withstand and stand against any form of discursive enclosure.

What is put forth, principal, is what Chandler articulates as the radical task that "disediment the dissimulation of a war."[28] It is the articulation that has to do with having to come face-to-face with a reality that needs to be disedimented and to reveal what has been masked and to bring all that is unseen to the realm of the seen. This is an effort that the revolutionary teacher should undertake.

What to make of a giver in what David Marriott calls the "ocular truth?"[29] This is the truth that should be seen. It is the one which is against any form of dissimulation. Ocular truth, according to Marriott, should not be mirrored in distortions. But, then, it is worthy to ask: What is the form and content of this ocular truth? What does it mean to give it if this truth is what is wholly unacceptable to the hegemonic sensibilities of dissimulation? It is clear, from the disposition of More as the revolutionary teacher, that things are radically different. The way he is going is a radically different route. More testifies: "I felt that the focus in analytic philosophy on analyzing English sentences and words was not something so much removed from my reality that I started drifting much more toward substantive ethical and political philosophical issues."[30] That clearly makes things to be the radical opposite. There will be no truth, and if there is the stubborn insistence that there is, here is a clear account of this as illuminated by Marriott who, then, writes: "The illusion of illusion is therefore that it can be communicated when it is false, but not when it is truth."[31] But these illusions, in the context of having been the revolutionary teacher, are always there since the racist infrastructure is created on mirrors and fantasies that fabricate reality, and they are armed with the spirit of dissimulation. There is more to hide than to reveal, and the task of revealing, by the revolutionary teacher becomes a demanding one because it is not a dialectical unfolding. As Marriott states, "the colonised should not be satisfied with a white or bourgeoisie truth, for such truth will never amount to more than the imaginary warrant of a mystified disenchantment or delusory re-enchantment."[32] What Marriott is hinting and hitting at is going underneath the surface and unearthing truth. The task of not accepting the given is such a task that the revolutionary teacher should undertake. The way of insisting on freedom has been what More has been contenting with and the route that he chose. More writes: "So I had some leeway and some freedom as to what I can teach."[33] Ocular truth is not the condition of the absolute, but the critical quest for truth, infinitude. Since dissimulation is not static, and it will invent its own truth through intensified conjuring, there should be no stopping in seeking truth—there must be the intensification of this task insofar as revolutionary teaching is concerned. In having to confront lies and deceit, the revolutionary teacher should be in constant battle with treachery. To be a revolutionary teacher is uncovering and uprooting "the political effects of that treachery."[34] Even this can be seen as the symptomatic exercise, it is not because having investigated the inner workings of that treachery, the combative nature of revolutionary teaching will trace the roots of those effects and uproot what makes them to be dissimulated.

More's revolutionary teaching, in service of the ocular truth is a way of seeing, and this is a way of seeing differently. Marriott attests: "Such seeing allows one to peer into the 'bones' beneath the constantly changing surface, via analyses that are themselves bound up with the movement of time; in such a vision one does not look down from on high on what happens, or endured, from a realm somehow beyond time."[35]

What More's teaching stems from is the spirit of revivification which allows the persistent ways of seeing, the revolutionary vision, that way of seeing. This, to Marriott, is "perspicacity"—that way of seeing, the one of seeing dissimulation, revolutionary teaching against treachery. Based on the long history of dehumanization, this seeing will not blind itself, but relive what has been unfolding to be to the black condition. It is this truth that attends to what Marriott calls "the truly social dimension of the real."[36] This truth should not be a distorted truth, and as Marriott points out, it should not be the one that leads to delusions. The best gift that the revolutionary teacher can give is one that will not mislead those who are being taught. Marriott writes: "A profound knowledge of the actual is not required to understand that marking something as actual is not required to understand that marking something as actual means primarily naming it as such and making a sign or gesture which evokes permanence and establishes a link between the visible world and its truthful presentation."[37] This has nothing to do with the sense of the objectivity and the verification of empiricism, but the ethical task where truth means thinking from the subjective condition. It is the thinking from one's existential conditions as opposed to teaching what is alienated from the lived experience. In amplification, More has this to say: "The socioeconomic and political matrix of my township black experience began to have a concreteness and social realism that tended to explode the value and relevance of traditional philosophical concerns."[38] The axis of the world is the one that revolves from where the revolutionary teacher is grounded. It is in that world that philosophy comes into being. More teaches philosophy as lived, as experience, as reality, as the ocular truth. It is the philosophy at the level of being seen from the perspective of being-black-in-an-antiblack-world. It is a living philosophy, the what of the quotidian testament.

Fidelity to truth means that the revolutionary teacher does not conjure up tricks. It means sharing knowledge as it is. By confuting lies that are embedded in canons stems not only from the position of opposition for its own sake, the revolutionary teacher, and More in particular, departs from the lived experience and the fact of blackness in the sense of Frantz Fanon who refuses for blacks to be acted upon in their quest for freedom.[39] Since More is teaching philosophy as the revolutionary praxis, it is the critical conjunction of various epistemes which are then engaged, foregrounded, and synthesized from the perspective of being black-in-an-antiblack-world. If knowledges are coming as universal, it is from the particularity of More that truth claims and totalities are subjected to critical examination. The confutation of lies comes after an engaged critical practice as opposed to *a priori* assumptions and *ad hominen* criticisms.

More's teaching is "a precondition for the understanding and edification of a revolutionary anticolonial culture."[40] This culture, one that More lives, and one that comprises the totality of his philosophical project, is not only out of choice. Everything stems from the matter of necessity as reality has to be that of a fundamental change, and this change should come through, as Marriott suggests, through a revolution. Nkrumah attests: "Any change of ethics constitutes a revolutionary change."[41] This revolution demands forms of writing which are different from the writing that propagate themselves as the absolute truth. The ethical imperative of the ocular truth is the foundational basis of teaching that is revolutionary. Here is More: "I felt tired of dealing with propositional truth-claims; I wanted a *lived* framework that made important links between philosophical truth-claims and *lived-experience*."[42] The continued practice of writing is what, in relation to More's philosophical project, the writing of what Marriott calls the "decolonial text" which insists on seeing clearly by way of a "sober view." By way of revealing the masquerade, Marriott insists on having the spirit of disenchantment. The decolonial text as the writing of form not only demands just a radical different but also the radical insistence that drives the revolutionary anticolonial culture. It is this continuity that makes the writing of the decolonial text to be, in itself, to come into being through what Marriott calls "revolutionary writing." More is a giver, and he presents his philosophical corpus through this revolutionary writing that Marriott attests to as the form of the ocular truth.

More's teaching is not wallowing in nostalgia. It is the radical critique of the present which is not only the residue of the past but its very embodiment. The lived experience of being-black-in-an-antiblack-world is the living presence that does not face the relic but the reality of colonialism's past. This is the mark of the present. To teach about colonialism, More does this to attest and contest the living presence.

> We want to get rid of nostalgia. But nostalgia is stubborn. If nostalgic longing is illusionary, this illusion is not necessarily an error, and we have to admit that we cannot make allowance for it by accepting that the things that come down to us from the past are never simply past, then denying that the same is true when we apprehend the present and the future.[43]

There is no need to wallow in nostalgia, as there will be no retrieving of what was, and the quest for purity is not the mission. Rather, in fidelity to truth, More is emphasizing the modes of teaching where being conscious of one's own being is the best gift that can be given. To be alien from oneself and wallowing in dissimulation, and being trapped in nostalgia, does not help matters when it comes to dealing with the reality of being dehumanized.

THE CLASS

Teaching is what More's philosophical project is all about. It happens in class. It is this space that teaching takes place. It is in class where those who More teaches come together to do study which, according to Harney and Moten, is a space where "collective labor" is undertaken.[44] It is, in point of fact, where experiments are conducted.

The revolutionary teacher in class does a different kind of teaching. It is in class that radical practices of thinking, knowing, and doing are incubated. The attitude that More instills in his teaching is not to produce students who are "ready for the world out there." This is the mantra of the modern university where students are treated as if they are products that must be ready to be cogs in a machine. Those who are ready out there are the ones who are seen as "the right ones" who are made ready. An antiblack world where More is teaching philosophy needs not only critical thinking students but radical ones who are yet to see the world for what it is—antiblackness. It is from this disposition that the preparation that goes into the making of the class is a different one.

The class ceases to be a place of command where rules are laid down. Since More is not a disciplinarian invested in didacticism, he creates a revolution in a class. Ways of thinking, knowing, and doing philosophy are not done in a canonized fashion, but there are dialogical practices that are set afoot. More attests: "Ignorance of the fact that philosophy did not actually begin in Greece renders me vulnerable to the racists arguments that African philosophy does not exist, that Africans not only are incapable of abstract thought but that they also lack rationality itself."[45] Not only a different form of philosophy is taught. The practice here in this class is to unmask philosophy. So, More teaches philosophy through decolonial practices. This demands the truth that philosophy prides itself with, to be subjected to ways of thinking, knowing, and doing that are far from being blinded by the lie that philosophy began in Greece and not investing in any effort to prove that African philosophy exists. As a black philosopher, More is questioned whether he is indeed a philosopher. It is from this doubt and denial that he does not make himself palatable and legible. In standing for the fact of being black, and having to teach philosophy from that disposition, he philosophizes against that grain that claims that he cannot philosophize. He does unmask this claim by unmasking the constitution of its making, and bringing this to class, this changes the way in which philosophy is taught right from the canon, epistemic statements, claims, facts, propositions, speculations, questions, and problems. Here, everything is question. By way of illumination, More writes: "Given all this information, once can immediately hear a remark: 'Africans are now claiming everything!"[46] What More is not invested in is not the nostalgic and purist arguments that claim the glorification of the African past, but he is decolonizing philosophy through Enrique Dussel's claim that "we shall be able to begin a philosophical discourse from another origin."[47] It is this decolonial departure that unmasks the claim that the origin is Greece. Human beings all over the world have been philosophizing, and it cannot be ignored that colonial projects were expanded by destroying other civilizations and ways of life. By way of freedom, More is teaching philosophy from another origin. It is the origin that is informed by the lived experience of being-black-in-an-antiblack-world.

Those who are in class are those who appear. They have been rendered absent. The class that More teaches comes into being as what, according to Dussel, is the revelation of the oppressed. This revelation is not life as it is lived. But it having to be lived differently. More as a revolutionary teacher gives a different conception and account of life. Dussel opposes "naïve everydayness" and calls for attention to be paid to critical ways of facing life.[48] This is what More emphasizes as a way of the quest of having to reclaim life that has been denied.[49] By privileging black experience, there is revelation that More brings into being and this, when engaged in class, reveals what has been concealed. Dussel writes: "A phenomenon is a being with a certain sense."[50] This is because what appears in the world appears as a phenomenon, and by way of philosophizing, Dussel makes it clear that what was known before will be discovered. "There is no phenomenon without the constitution of sense."[51] It is from the lived experience being a black philosopher that More comes to class and delivers radical ways of sensing the world, and this is what makes those who are absented in the realm of philosophy to appear. It is the revelatory protocol that makes the class to be a space where making sense of the lived experience and giving the account of oneself becomes a radical disposition of taking philosophy as a task of reflection and also going to the extent of taking philosophy to task.

The revelatory protocols that inform More's revolutionary teaching, according to Paulo Freire, "expresses the consciousness of students themselves."[52] It is in class that this gets articulated. More, as a revolutionary teacher, delivers philosophy as the pedagogy of struggle.

> A revolutionary leadership must accordingly practice *co-intentional* education. Teachers and students (leadership and people), content on reality, are both Subjects, not only in the task of unveiling that reality, and thereby coming to know it critically, but in the task of re-creating that knowledge. As they attain this knowledge of reality through common reflection and action, they discover themselves as its permanent re-creators. In this way, the presence of the oppressed in the struggle for their liberation will be what it should be: not pseudo-participation, but committed involvement.[53]

The revolutionary spirit of More is not only in his teaching practice. By being a radically committed philosopher, he takes matters very seriously. Below is a noteworthy account:

> I definitely was not going to far-off Cape Town to teach students analytical philosophy in a different form. I was certain that they could get someone better than

> me to do that. Remember, this was 1989, and the news of an imminent political change, the possible release of Mandela, and the unbanning of liberation organizations was already floating around. I couldn't resist the suspicion that I was going to be used as window dressing because they wanted to establish a new course titled "Philosophy in the South African Context," and therefore give it legitimacy by employing a black philosopher as its coordinator. In other words, I was not going to be included in mainstream philosophy as such but was going to be located at the periphery of a service course as a supernumerary (superfluous, extra, temporary) lecturer to boost the institution's image before Mandela came out of prison. So I declined the offer and accepted nearer home, Durban, which offered a lot of focus Social and Political Philosophy.[54]

More made a radical choice, and he revealed what was hidden. He made a choice that will enable him to teach a class that will be in line with his philosophical project. He refuses to be a tool and an artifact. It is from the spirit of this principality that More will want to be in that class which will not be in conflict with his philosophical orientation and to be in a place that he will be able to practice his revolutionary teaching. More's class is of those who, according to Freire, accept and take "their total responsibility for the struggle."[55] More, as a revolutionary teacher, engages in what Dussel calls "philo-praxis"—that is, philosophy put in service for the struggle for liberation.[56]

> The insistence that the oppressed engage in reflection on their concrete situation is not a call to armchair revolution. On the contrary, reflection—true reflection—leads to action. On the other hand, when the situation calls for action, that action will constitute an authentic praxis only if its consequences become the object of critical reflection. In this sense, the praxis is the new *raison d'être*, is not viable apart from their concomitant conscious involvement.[57]

It is clear from Freire that liberation has to be necessitated and in More's philo-praxis, teaching becomes not the instrument but the practice that takes students seriously. As Freire states, the student's capacity to reason should be taken seriously, and More as the revolutionary teacher is one who is informed by conviction. This has to fundamentally change in what philosophy is, and in his decolonial orientation, this is the task that he does not neglect but takes seriously so that fundamental change can be actualized. The principality of More's conviction means that he deploys liberation as the philosophical imperative. This conviction, argues Freire, is authentic. By More making it clear that he teaches philosophy from the lived experience of being-black-in-an-antiblack-world says a lot about the revelatory nature of his revolutionary teaching as opposed to hiding behind objectivity and neutrality. His conviction, an authentic one—one that he makes very clear in his corpus opus, his practice qua philo-praxis—makes the class to be thought as a radical space. It is in the class that his conviction is made manifest as it appears in his corpus opus and philo-praxis.

> The revolutionary leaders must realize that their own conviction of the necessity for struggle (an indispensable dimension of revolutionary wisdom) was not given to them by anyone else—if it is authentic. This conviction cannot be packaged and sold; it is reached, rather, by means of a totality of reflection and action. Only the leaders' own involvement in reality, within an historical situation, led them to criticize this situation and to wish it to change.[58]

It is in class that More is effecting change with students. He is not a didacticist pedagogue, but a philosopher of praxis. This, according to Dussel, is put thus: "The praxis of liberation, on the contrary, puts the system into question—not just as a possible or ideational question, but as a constitutive questioning, one that opens a world from itself, its own road from within itself."[59] Praxis in the class, where More is, and where, according to Dussel, person-to-person relationship are, becomes the operative function where the struggle for liberation is initiated. It in this person-to-person where George Ciccariello-Maher sets out to think of "a network of communes" which comes as a form the congregation of thought.[60] This, also, what can be said to be "the conceptual contours of radical planning from below"—that is to say, "grassroots planning from below"—the experimental sites of the struggle for liberation.[61] It is in the class where there is what Ciccariello-Maher articulates as "form" and "working-out" where in the class, the plan is there as since the class is the commune, it being inseparable from planning itself. The antagonistic struggle is waged in More's class where philosophy as the canon gets engaged from the position that will be ignored, neglected, ridiculed, and rejected. But the amount of planning that informs form and working-out engenders the spirit of conviction to effect change, and this does not happen by way of accommodationist gestures that get easily appropriated and corrupted by the liberal consensus. It is this liberal consensus that creates what Harney and Moten expose its politics as the repeated attack on those in the class.[62] This is the continued assault that More's class stands against by holding on the revelatory praxis. It is this revelatory praxis that serves as that mode of self-defense and also antagonism. "The self-defense of revolution is confronted not only by the brutalities but also by the false image of enclosure."[63] Those who are in the class and their revolutionary teacher do not concede. Instead, the revelatory praxis that Rabaka calls "revolutionary decolonization" which was discussed earlier becomes one of the principalities of the class.[64] It is from this disposition that paradoxes will be dealt with as the class is a space for critical reflection. "Meanwhile, politics soldiers on, claiming to defend what it has not enclosed, enclosing what it cannot defend but only endanger."[65] What is set out in More's class is "the communal project" and this is where things can even merge in radical ways that have not been thought of before. The spirit of commitment is made apparent by Ciccariello-Maher thus: "The commune *is* the plan, and the plan *is* the commune—and to decolonize one is thereby to decolonize the other as well."[66]

It is in More's class, according to Harney and Moten, "where the revolution is black, still strong."[67] The critical spirit that prevails in the class is one that creates a commune, and this, according to Harney and Moten, is a "prophetic organization." What informs this prophetic organization is the elevated sense of what is termed "political education" by Fanon which, by way of spontaneity, is intensified to "bring pressure to bear on the colonial administration."[68] The continuity of the colonial administration through philosophy is met with the decolonial might of the prophetic organization, and it coming as a result of what Harney and Moten call the "collective orientation" makes the class to be a space where another kind of thinking is produced.[69] Both Harney and Moten insist that before anything, "teaching happened" and it is still happening and will happen. In the way that More executed it through collective orientation, the making of political education to be the imperative is the way that ensures that critical practices come into being.

Whatever forms of impediments are imposed as rules and their edicts do not dampen the spirit of More, who knows that teaching will not be easy and it should be revolutionized. This makes it to be the act of antagonism, of struggle, of liberation. The way of thinking, knowing, and doing that More embodies is the commitment to students, and thus being responsible for them. Gordon writes: "How one lives in a community is not identical to the sort of knowledge involved in how one *studies* a community."[70] There is a different form of study that is supposed to be engendered. There are things that are there which cannot be seen and what is both seen and unseen should be studied. This means, according to Fanon, "to educate them politically and to raise the level of their struggle."[71] By having to be subjected to brutalities that come with all forms of dehumanization, and the denial of their capacity to think, know, and do, More radically insists to teach. This is what makes him the revolutionary teacher. The constant act of philo-praxis is, as More makes the class to be those who, according to Fanon, work things out "to clarify their ideas and strengthen their determination."[72]

It is through the political education of philosophy as executed by More that the revelatory drive means not only having a different perspective of the world, but being consciousness of one's own being. In the class, things begin to have a different meaning as what is deemed a canon is challenged. "Consciousness slowly dawns upon truths that are only partial, limited and unstable."[73] If philosophy parades itself as the absolute truth, this gets unmasked. Alain Badiou writes: "I am perfectly in agreement with the statement that philosophy depends on certain nonphilosophical domains, which I have proposed to call the 'conditions' of philosophy."[74] It is by challenging philosophy that More teaches philosophy. Gordon gives an illuminating account: "Mainstream philosophy has turned its back on education for a few decades now because, frankly, it's a field afraid of looking at itself."[75] The class becomes a space where philosophy is thought, known, and done differently. In short, More decolonizes philosophy. Being a revolutionary teacher means that More's philosophical craft and task is nothing "but discipline and prolonged work to find strategic means for victory."[76] It is clear that this is existential struggle and it demands radical commitment.

The way of teaching what is not supposed to be taught and those who are not supposed to be taught is what More radically insists upon. It is this radical insistence that makes him to be the revolutionary teacher who is in the class. This class, according to Moten, is one that is engendered by the "intellectual practice" where the phenomenological inscription is of "undermonasticism" that fuels the communal spirit that is away from purisms reign.[77] If philosophy is a monastic practice, that which is purist so that it is the exclusionary domain, it is, in More's class, unmasked for what it is. In a sense, it is not imposed as absolute, but a practice of thought done by thinking and living beings. Its posture has always been, as More shows, "the utmost logical rigor and coherence."[78] As a revolutionary, and criticizing the monastic practice of philosophy in class, More argues for "a philosopher of change."[79] The change is not only about how the monastic practices are changed, but the reality and the world in which this philosophy is lived and practiced. Philosophy is, in More's class, mobilized for what Moten's conception of undermonasticism. The kind of intellectual practice that Moten calls for is that of the "fleshly, unruly, flawed."[80] Moten presents illuminating ensemble of questions thus:

> Because what if intellectual practice is irreducibly chor(e)ographic? What if you have to move in order to map? What if reflection is a matter of reflex? What if the animation of the flesh is fundamental to reflection? What if reflection and reflexion and refleshment and refreshment are on in the same? Deeper still, what if the movement in question is, at once, collective and on concert, but also disruptive or deconstructive of the idea of a certain coherence or integrity of the single body/being?[81]

These questions are right at the heart of More's revolutionary teaching where the undermonasticism of philosophy is charged in class in order to dissolve philosophy's monasticism. This intellectual practice of the expression of form and content of philosophy is a way of becoming being in different ways that this being is lived and thought—that is, the denied being, the being who is even denied philosophy radically insisting on doing philosophy. Here is a mode of doing philosophy otherwise. This, by definition, is what the revolutionary teacher and the class are in the world that relegates the black to the status of non-thinking being, and the black not seeking validation and proving that there is thinking and the black is a thinking being. What is done is the class that is supposed to be done. "This means resisting the setting side of that place."[82] More's class is not only different, but deferral. It is the class that postpones ignorance of black thought. It stays on black thought in order to delay philosophy's monasticism that passes through black thought. Moten writes: "Then our class will remain open in defiant refusal of the (final) assignment, which administration designates as the end of our class but which is always only an assigned preface to the (next) assignment, which will have been the regulatory deferral of our class, our set, our jam."[83] It is this openness that intensifies the class to be engaged in the rigorous intellectual practice. By doing philosophy in this delay is not a tactic, but the tract whose influence makes students to see philosophy differently. Indeed, the revolutionary teaching will mean a delay, in that there has to be learning and unlearning at the same time. The learning that has been canonized through monastic practices is subjected to decanonization of undermonasticism. In class, the tract that comes in a form of marginal notes is what punctures what Gordon calls "epistemic enclosure" which has canonized and valorized philosophy as nothing that has to do with the black.[84] The absence of the black in philosophy is what More even challenges by making philosophy to be an intellectual practice that deals with the question of the human, and thus insisting on philosophy in black.[85] More, as the revolutionary teacher rails against philosophy's monasticism by insisting in what Gordon calls "epistemic openness" where the humanity of blacks is the rigorous practice of philosophy.[86] It is in this rigorous practice that what philosophy forecloses More ruptures, and philosophy is subjected to the black way of thinking, knowing, and doing.

The class is studying insurgent ideas in order to do philosophy. In More's class, philosophy is what Moten calls "insurgent study" whose animating force is the will for there to be fundamental change in ways of thinking, knowing, and doing.[87] What is being wrestled with in class is, according to Saidiya Hartman, "the tension between the facts of blackness and the lived experience."[88] It is in this tension that undermonasticism unmasks philosophy's monasticism in ways that engender philosophy in black which, to More, is the embrace of nonconformity. More writes: "Nonconformity is usually regarded as simply not mere eccentricity, but very often it is taken as symptomatic of some disease."[89] It is this rejection of nonconformity that comes from the sensibility of the idea of the one, the only way, the absolute. "An insight of phenomenological reflection is that one must it as a *radical* activity, and that condition of radicality paradoxically requires not engage it *as a condition*."[90] The class is a different kind of a workshop, a philosophical workshop.

The different and the deferral is the intellectual practice of the class where philosophy is done in ways that go against the grain. If monasticism is the devotional intellectual practice, so is undermonasticism. The class taught by the revolutionary teacher is the congregation of those, in thinking, knowing, and doing engender critique and fidelity to it is, in the spirit of undermonastic intellectual practice, philosophy in black as principality. This, to follow what Moten, makes the eruption that comes in a form of "the general structure of complaint."[91] This complaint is done in the spirit of critique, and there is no expectation that things will change by making this complaint. There has to be philo-praxis to create different conditions of possibility.

ON THE REVOLUTIONARY OPERATION

One way of teaching is what More is not up to. The love of teaching makes it clear for him how he should not only relate to students, but to know them in terms of their strength and weakness. Multiple ways of teaching are what the revolutionary teacher does.

> For example, in my early years of teaching, I had a female student (Mmakheni) who was so argumentative in class she had on occasion had a one-on-one with me to the exclusion of the rest of the class, which was predominately male. She was so articulate in her discussions that no one doubted her intelligence and knowledge of the subject. She taught me a great lesson, though, which I kept with me for the entire span of my teaching career; namely, that being articulate does not necessarily translate itself into a good writer. Mmakheni could not write! She found it very difficult to put her ideas on paper. She failed to produce good papers or write good essays in the tests. Recognizing her ability as a speaker and her weakness as a writer, I arranged that all her final examinations should be oral exams. I met her over thirty years later, and she was a successful motivational speaker.[92]

This undermonasticism made More's revolutionary teaching to be expansive and to break from the regime of examinations or knowledge as everything that has to do with written form. As Freire states: "The revolution is born as a social entity within the oppressor society; to the extent that it is cultural action, it cannot fail to correspond to the potentialities of the social entity in which it originated."[93] Revolution demands a different way of thinking, and this is what More demonstrated in Mmakheni's case. He knows what were her strengths and weakness. Teaching, for More, is the wholeness of learning. That is why he saw it fit to give Mmakheni an alternative form of assessment that is aligned to her strengths. More, as a revolutionary teacher, has to create different kinds of possibility. As Freire states:

> I have already affirmed that it would indeed be naïve to expect the oppressor elites to carry out a liberating education. But because the revolution undeniably has an educational nature, in the sense that it liberates it is not revolution, the taking of power is only one moment—no matter how decisive—in the revolutionary process. As process, the "before" of the revolution is located within the oppressor society and is apparent only to the revolutionary consciousness.[94]

More does not fear freedom and that is why he made it a radical task to make education to be a liberating force. This is a form of thinking and as Gordon warms, "where there is no thinking there is no distinction; and where there is no distinction, we collapse under the force of sameness or mandatory sameness (where thinking is indecent)."[95] This is the decadence of monasticism. The way examination is approached is different from the convention. Clearly, More as the revolutionary teacher thought with his students. That is why he saw a need for doing things differently. Here is what Walter Benjamin has to say:

> It is very easy to establish oppositions, according to determinate point of view, within the various "fields" of any epoch, such that on one side lies the "productive," "forward-looking," "lively," "positive" part of the epoch, and on the other side the abortive, retrograde, and obsolescent. The very contours of the positive element will appear distinctly only insofar as this element is set off against the negative. On the other hand, every negation has its value solely as background for the delineation of the lively, the positive. It is therefore of decisive importance that a new partition be applied to this initially excluded, negative components so that, by a displacement of the angle of vision (but not of the criteria!), a positive element emerges anew in it too—something different from that previously signified.[96]

More's undermonasticism is in line with the Benjaminian interruption and rupture of the status quo. Things have to be done differently, and this is the spirit of the revolutionary teaching that More is committed in. The undermonasticism of More made him to be a nonconformist, hence the revolutionary teacher. He chose to defy the status quo. In the antiblack world, monasticism will come with the act of not wanting to do anything with the existential condition and to be complicit by claiming to be singular and detached from reality itself. This can be an escape route of philosophy by it claiming not to be responsible for the existential maladies and it is just the domain of rational thinking, thinking for its pure sake, where problems are as just problems and them having nothing to do with the problematic existence of living beings. More, rallying against this trope, insists on philosophy's necessity to be preoccupied with being and specifically to the being of the black in an antiblack world.[97] According to More, philosophy is supposed to respond to the existential concerns of the time, and those who are affected are supposed to respond accordingly even if it means that they will be such efforts being denied. The status quo cannot stand. "That things are 'status quo' *is* the catastrophe."[98] It is at the expense of the black to be in defense of the status quo because the status quo is antiblack. In short, More finds it absurd for blacks to embrace antiblackness. This is captured clearly by Gordon who argues that black antiblacks exist as (self) denial.[99]

By being authentic, and not valorizing the status quo, More refuses to be in service of the status quo. He is the black qua black who stands in opposition to the antiblackness writ large, including black antiblackness. This undermonsticism is the interruption and rupture that Benjamin sketched earlier and taking this far, More mobilizes philosophy to critique philosophy to argue for metaphilosophical questions to question philosophy's self-justification.[100] Philosophy is complicit in dehumanizing blacks and by coming through the disposition of philosophy in black, the metaphilosophical questions unmasks the hypocrisy of philosophy. Here is More: "This being the case, how then can Black people fail to engage in existential and ontological self-interrogation?"[101] It is this question that brings the revolutionary attended feature which is resistance. This makes the politics of being of the black to be a project of difference. In the affirmative, More writes: "The politics of difference, therefore, functions effectively both as a critique of existing power relations and as a project of self-empowerment for marginalised groups."[102] This is undermonasticism, and it is from revolutionary teaching that difference will be made, as the status quo cannot stand as it is. What More affirms is what is denied—the denial of the black as philosophical—what, in turn, is affirmed as philosophical. This revolutionary act is to "reconfigure this difference in a different manner."[103]

What is different and deferral is clear in More's undermonastic practices of not only doing philosophy, but the manner of assessment in a form of examination. More argues for "dialogical transgressive teaching method."[104] But this, according to More, comes from having to know your stuff. It is by way of giving students confidence, and being on top of the subject matter. For there to be undermonastic practices, there should be a deeper knowledge of monasticism. In a way, More is the revolutionary teacher who knows teaching very well. He is a black philosopher who is well-rounded on philosophy. He is a revolutionary teacher who loves philosophy and that is why he gave himself the responsibility of being responsible for philosophy.

It is More's revolutionary teaching that makes philosophy, according to the sense of Badiou, to be there and "in a form of a particular philosophy."[105] In this different form of an inscription, there are knowledges intensified in struggle, the creation of a different ways of knowing, thinking, and doing.

> The act of seizing, such as an entity orients it, picks truths out from the dross of sense, *separating* them from the law of the world. Philosophy is subtractive in that it makes holes in sense, or causes an interruption I the circulation of sense, so that it may come that truths are said all together. Philosophy is a sense-less or mad . . . act, and by the same token rational.[106]

The modes of doing philosophy, a particular philosophy that to More is philosophy in black, the liberation of philosophy itself. This happens by what Badiou states as "philosophy induces every disaster in thought."[107] It is in this disaster where there is colonial victory, and philosophy is mobilized to propagate this image, this illusion, this dissimulation. Benjamin remarks: "And the enemy has not ceased to be victorious."[108] It is here that philosophy is a struggle against dehumanization, and it is the radical insistence on liberation. The inscription of philosophy is a document, and it is not only its materiality but the inscriptive force of its form and content. Here is the document of those who are refusing defeat, and who, at the same time, do not claim victories but continue to engender the existential struggle. They produce documents in what Badiou calls the "an underground printing press."[109] It is in this underground press where undermonasticism is the critical practice and the form of inscription that exists is that of what Harney and Moten call "bad documents" which are said to be produced out of love.[110] All this is the effort of subversion of what claims to be totality and authority. It is through bad documents that philosophy in black is the teaching that More engages out of love. Moten gives the following exposition:

> On a practical level, here's what's at stake: to take note of your intellectual movement/passage/practice. Open a file. You can call it your journal but let it also be your missal. Let it be the liturgical book prepared in/for celebration. Let it be your life plan, your projectile, your missile. It would not only be a record of but also a set of protocols for your intellectual practice. Here's a way to start: Find, take note of, an object—a movement, a passage, from a song, a movie, a memory, a dance, a sculpture, a word or phrase or sentence or paragraph from one of the books that we've been reading, something you heard from the bus, a billboard, a flash of unexpected color that falls in the corner of your eye. Copy it in your file the write your relation to that object informally. Then, through a

> (devotional/sacramental/ritual) practice of revision, let a form begin to emerge. Consider the relation between revising and remaining, between revision and the refrain (of a song), between revision and the break (the musical unit out of which hip-hop flows). To write your relation is not a matter of a report at the end of your thinking. It is not to offer a conclusion. It is, rather, an extension of your thinking, one that constitutes another method in disavowing the conclusion. Don't try to close it down; try to keep it open. Let your relation; let your relation change; let your relation fade into an entanglement that lets difference run even faster. Revision is keeping open, seeing it again, playing it again. Practicing. Practice thinking because that is the practice of thinking. So let's share our files, share our objects and some moments of our ongoing revisionary relations to them.[111]

The form of learning is not that of production but cultivation. This has to do with all there is with a lifelong project. Harney and Moten are for the cultivation of the students who are going to learn dangerous ideas and who will see themselves as the problem. "Later, these students will be able to see themselves properly as obstacles to society, or perhaps, with lifelong learning, students will return having successfully diagnosed themselves as the problem."[112] It is by recognizing themselves as the problem that students will begin to think, know, and do differently. Benjamin states: "The themes which monastic discipline assigned to friars for meditation were designed to turn them away from the world and its affairs."[113] But here is Moten who offers a counterstatement by means of undermonsaticism whose radical insistence is confronting and combating the world and its affairs.[114] There is nothing to adhere to, and what is principal is having to do study. Under the critical practice of undermonasticism, it is worth considering Benjamin's statement: "The great revolution introduced a new calendar."[115] More's revolutionary teaching has been a radical persistence of change and the teaching of philosophy in black means the new calendar. More's revolutionary teaching is articulated by Corey Walker as "a discourse derived from a rigorous, vigilant, and militant theoretical site of struggle."[116] Clearly, as Walker states, there is rupture, and the ongoing struggle will not be blind to what has been paraded as truth but the effort will be the continued unveiling of this truth. One way of doing that is through study, and Harney and Moten insist on the inscription of bad documents that embody the knowledge of struggle. It is in bad documents that there is a radical critique of what Chela Sandoval terms as the tendency that "continually reproduce an apartheid of theoretical domains."[117] The hegemonic structure of knowledge is challenged and it is clear that philosophy in black as accentuated by More is what, according to Sandoval, should be a differential form. By way of elaboration, Sabine Broeck puts forth the "de-enslavist transdisciplinary research and institutional pedagogy, because the abjection of Blackness is closely tied—in political, cultural, social, and philosophical terms—to the Europeans politics of white identity, of which European landscape is one of the remaining bastions."[118] It is urgent that things have to be fundamentally different. The negated black life is what is affirmed in philosophy's deliberate disregard—that is, de-enslavization is philosophy in black.

The revolutionary teacher refuses to be reduced to an administrator. The revolutionary teacher wants to do what has to be done—teaching. It is in this teaching that ideas are not instrumentalized, but they are put in service of revolutionizing ideas. This, in class, is creating modes of thinking differently and being in a state of perpetual questioning. This is the question of the absolutes. The refusal to be an administrator and to be a revolutionary teacher has been, for More, his definitional marker in his philosophical career. It is this refusal that Moten articulates thus: "What I am trying to do, as emphatically and absolutely as I can, is refuse the administrative function."[119] This is More's refusal to bow to the strictures and edicts that deny modes of thinking that are coming from undermonastic practices. These are the practices that do not allow epistemic rupture, but the solidification of the status quo. What Moten calls for is the "an open form of scholarship."[120] It is this radical openness that forms and informs More's revolutionary teaching and his meditation on philosophy in black. More's thought is the living thought in the time of crisis.[121]

To conclude, it is worth stating that More does not take revolutionary teaching as a polemical and comical dimension of thinking, knowing, and doing philosophy. More undertakes philosophy as the matter of necessity and that should be rooted from the lived experience of being-black-in-an-antiblack-world. If philosophy is pure abstraction of the universal, he brings it back to the concrete and materiality of the everyday life of the black. By this way of teaching, he makes philosophy real and what is within the firm grasp of the students. The terms in which philosophy is engaged in the arena of the everyday life is what revolutionary teaching is. In a way, this is the axis and departure point from which philosophy is done. The function of the revolutionary teacher is the prohibited one. It is the act of the figure denied, the one who, by the fact of nonconformity, is regarded as not being of the profession or being professions—that is, the one who is exteriorized from the constitution of the thing itself—the teacher. According to this decadent sensibility of what the teacher is, More breaks the mold and thinks, knows, and does things differently.

To be in class is to be in a life world. It is here that revolutionary teaching is not only transformative, but elevating in the sense of reaching the essence of things—that is, ideas, concepts, themes, propositions, questions, and the like are engaged in ways that they change the meaning of the way reality is perceived. Without any end of the absolute and knowing it all, More operates within the protocols of long-life learning where the quest for knowledge is value as opposed to a mode of instrumentalization.

It is the lived experience as the black that makes More to have a different philosophical project and that is the thing that he remains consistently to embody—philosophy in black. A teacher of many decades, More also has the attitude of a student as he is continuing to learn in passionate and rigorous ways. This makes the ideas that he is teaching to be living ideas. It is this disposition that takes philosophy as what should be opened up to critical investigation and exposition and what should not be there to be applied. There is no way that More cannot be intensive in his role as the revolutionary teacher, because he deals with tensions, intensity, and intentions. Meanwhile, within, there is that place that shutters because things cannot be accepted as they are and they have to be altered and become fundamentally different.

NOTES

1. Reiland Rabaka, *Forms of Fanonism: Frantz Fanon's Critical Theory and the Dialectics of Decolonization* (Lanham: Lexington Books, 2010). This is a dungeon that the black are thrown at so that they are kept out, away, at bay, in absence—the *exteriori* of the world buried deep in the abyss of existence. This is the place that the black did not choose as the racist tropes claim. The "dark dungeon" is there to make sure that whatever that is done to the black is done without anyone seeing. Those who are walking on top of the surface do so on top of those who are thrown in the dark dungeon. It is as if this is the place of those who are not there anywhere in the world. The only way of getting out of the dungeon is when the black climb up in their own effort. They are thrown there in order to remain there (to live and die there as they cannot be with whites. The dark dungeon is not a place of habitability, but one of struggle. To exist in the dark dungeon is to be in the life that was never was in the first place, but the place where the black is thrown at.

2. Nahum D. Chandler, *X—The Problem of Negro as the Problem for Thought* (New York: Fordham University Press, 2014), 3.

3. Rabaka, *Forms of Fanonism.*

4. Kwame Nkrumah, *Consciencism: Philosophy and Ideology for Decolonization and Development in Particular Reference to the African Revolution* (London: Heinemann, 1964), 86.

5. Ibid., 99.

6. Ibid., 104.

7. Ibid.

8. Reiland Rabaka, *Concepts of Cabralism: Amilcar Cabral and Africana Theory* (Lanham: Lexington Books, 2014).

9. Nkrumah, *Consciencism*, 86.

10. Rabaka, *Concepts of Cabralism*, 102.

11. Nelson Maldonado-Torres, *Against War: Views from the Underside of Modernity* (Durham and London: Duke University Press, 2008).

12. Chandler, *X*, 69.

13. Mabogo P. More, *Biko: Philosophy, Identity, and Liberation* (Cape Town: HSRC Press, 2017), 91.

14. Lewis R. Gordon, *Existentia Africana: Understanding Africana Existential Thought* (New York and London: Routledge, 2000), 33.

15. Ibid., 32.

16. Fred Moten, *Stolen Life* (Durham and London: Duke University Press, 2018), 183.

17. Ibid.

18. Gerald Raunig, *Factories of Knowledge: Industries of Creativity* (Los Angeles: Semiotext(e), 2013), 54.

19. Raunig, *Factories of Knowledge.*

20. Ibid., 53.

21. Stefano Harney and Fred Moten. *The Undercommons: Fugitive Planning and Black Study* (Wivenhoe and New York: Minor Compositions, 2013), 26.

22. Moten, *Stolen Life*, 186.

23. Ibid., 227.

24. Ibid.

25. Mabogo P. More, *Looking through Philosophy in Black: Memoirs* (Lanham: Rowman and Littlefield International, 2019), 58.

26. Moten, *Stolen Life*, 227.

27. Ibid.

28. Chandler, *X*, 1.

29. David Marriott, "The Ocular Truth: C. L. R. James's England," *Critical Quarterly* 57, no. 3 (2015): 35–50.

30. More, *Looking through Philosophy in Black*, 59.

31. Marriott, "The Ocular Truth," 37.

32. Ibid., 38.

33. More, *Looking through Philosophy in Black*, 59.

34. Marriott, "The Ocular Truth," 39.

35. Ibid., 41.

36. Ibid., 36.

37. Ibid., 46.

38. More, *Looking through Philosophy in Black*, 59. It is having lived out of this violated space that even breeds violence in turn that philosophical concerns emerge. Townships, segregated areas created for blacks, are meant to be camps. Townships are designed away from white suburbs, and they are meant to be far from towns and cities. Black people who live there are used as the surplus of labor, dispossessed and exploited. The dehumanized conditions of living in the township indeed raises philosophical questions that are existential in nature.

39. Frantz Fanon, *Black Skin, White Masks*. Translated by Charles L. Markman (New York: Grove Press, 1967).

40. Marriott, "The Ocular Truth," 35.
41. Nkrumah, *Consciencism*, 95.
42. More, *Looking through Philosophy in Black*, 59; emphasis in the original.
43. Marriott, "The Ocular Truth," 46.
44. Harney and Moten, *The Undercommons*.
45. More, *Looking through Philosophy in Black*, 15.
46. Ibid.
47. Enrique Dussel, *Philosophy of Liberation*. Translated by Aquilina Martinez and Christene Morkovsky (Oregon: Wipf and Stock Publishers, 1985), 16.
48. Ibid. This means not accepting everything as reality. But to question that reality, to really get into the booting of it, rooting it up, and seeing things differently.
49. More, *Looking through Philosophy in Black*.
50. Dussel, *Philosophy of Liberation*, 33.
51. Ibid., 34.
52. Paulo Freire, *Pedagogy of the Oppressed* (New York: Continuum, 1994), 55. Students are conscious beings who are in the world. They are not beings with no consciousness. They are not there as passive. By having an encounter with a revolutionary teacher, together they are in a setting where learning is, in a Freirean sense, mutual. There is no linear directionality of the teacher imparting consciousness, there is a transaction going on.
53. Ibid. More's teaching is intentional and he is influenced by Freirean pedagogical modes. This is the teaching that is not instrumental, it is one that is lived, his reality and that of the students.
54. More, *Looking through Philosophy in Black*, 98. More refused to be tokenized. White liberal universities have a tendency of making cosmetic changes and wanting a black face to be window-dressed in some nebulous name of "transformation." Sadly, even to date, nothing has transformed even when Rhodes Must Fall and Fees Must Fall have called for the decolonization of the curriculum. Cosmetic gestures are still the order of the day. When More refused the offer, it meant that the naming of the course will still stand as the banal trick that will make the black lived experience will vegetate in the margins and the Euro-North American centric canon will remain untouched. By refusing to be tokenized clearly shows that More takes his revolutionary teaching seriously.
55. Freire, *Pedagogy of the Oppressed*, 50.
56. Dussel, *Philosophy of Liberation*.
57. Freire, *Pedagogy of the Oppressed*, 48.
58. Ibid., 49.
59. Dussel, *Philosophy of Liberation*, 63.
60. George Ciccariello-Maher, "The Commune is the Plan," *The South Atlantic Quarterly* 119, no. 1 (2020): 113–132.
61. Ciccariello-Maher, "The Commune is the Plan," 114.
62. Harney and Moten, *The Undercommons*.
63. Ibid., 18.
64. Rabaka, *Concepts of Cabralism*.

65. Harney and Moten, *The Undercommons*, 18.

66. Ciccariello-Maher, "The Commune is the Plan," 129; emphasis in the original.

67. Harney and Moten, *The Undercommons*, 26.

68. Frantz Fanon, *The Wretched of the Earth*. Translated by Constance Farrington (London: Penguin Books, 1969), 85.

69. Harney and Moten, *The Undercommons*.

70. Gordon, *Existentia Africana*, 92.

71. Fanon, *The Wretched of the Earth*, 93. In terms of More's revolutionary teaching, it clearly means deepening the meaning of the world as lived, not as something that is out there, but the actuality of him and the students. Of course, this would mean having different interpretations. But the primacy is on the experiential mode of understanding the world. If there are abstract ideas, they are brought down to the level of the concrete. This, in a class, is the world that can be related to, the relevant world. This is one thing that will raise deeper existential questions and also shape the modalities of the existential struggle.

72. Ibid., 99. This is a constant exercise in class. Since this is linked to the mode of self-education, the ideas received are not a final determining instance. They are engaged, wrestled with, and exchanged. This is an unending process.

73. Ibid., 117.

74. Alain Badiou, *Philosophy for Militants*. Translated by Bruno Bosteels (London and New York: Verso, 2015), 2. What can be deemed nonphilosophical can also be philosophical. This is what More shows in his body of work.

75. Lewis R. Gordon, *Disciplinary Decadence: Living Thought in Trying Times* (Boulder and London: Paradigm Publishers, 2006), 28.

76. Badiou, *Philosophy for Militants*, 26.

77. Moten, *Stolen Life*.

78. More, *Looking through Philosophy in Black*, 16.

79. More, *Biko*, 58.

80. Moten, *Stolen Life*, 230.

81. Ibid.

82. Ibid., 231.

83. Ibid., 232.

84. Gordon, *Existentia Africana*.

85. More, *Looking through Philosophy in Black*.

86. Gordon, *Existentia Africana*.

87. Moten, *Stolen Life*.

88. Saidiya V. Hartman, "The Belly of the World: A Note on Black Women's Labors," *Souls* 18, no. 1 (2016): 166–173. Cited in 1.

89. More, *Looking through Philosophy in Black*, 11.

90. Gordon, *Disciplinary Decadence*, 7; emphasis in the original.

91. Fred Moten, *Black and Blur* (Durham and London: Duke University Press, 2017).

92. More, *Looking through Philosophy in Black*, 59. This is not a form of a favor as a result of being lenient. It is having to understand teaching as holistic. Here, again, Freirean pedagogy is very apparent.

93. Freire, *Pedagogy of the Oppressed*, 117.

94. Freire, *Pedagogy of the Oppressed*, 117.

95. Gordon, *Disciplinary Decadence*, 26–27.

96. Walter Benjamin, *The Arcades Project.* Translated by Howard Eiland and Kevin McLaughlin (Cambridge and London: The Belknap Press of Harvard University Press, 2002), 459.

97. Mabogo P. More, "Black Consciousness Movement's Ontology: The Politics of Being," *Philosophia Africana* 14, no. 1 (2012): 23–39.

98. Benjamin, *The Arcades Project*, 473; emphasis in the original.

99. Lewis R. Gordon, *Bad Faith and Antiblack Racism* (New York: Humanity Books, 1995). These are blacks who will deny the reality of racism and what they will do instead is to flee to whiteness which will then reject them. They will loathe their own blackness in love for whiteness which hates them. In living in bad faith, they will engineer the delusion that there is no race, of if they are faced with the facticity of their body, they will deny the blackness. But all efforts of evading their blackness are in vain. Even if they are throwing themselves in the canon where they cannot find themselves, they will be met by the racist epithets which they will try to brush off. If there is any canon that has to do with their reality, they will reject it and embrace what is still not there for them.

100. More, "Black Consciousness Movement's Ontology."

101. Ibid., 30.

102. Mabogo P. More, "What Difference Does Difference Make?" *Alternation* 6, no. 2 (1999): 332–349. Cited in 335.

103. Ibid., 347.

104. More, *Looking through Philosophy in Black*, 47.

105. Badiou, *Philosophy for Militants*, 29.

106. Ibid., 24.

107. Ibid., 25.

108. Walter Benjamin, *Illuminations*. Edited and with an Introduction by Hannah Arendt. Translated by Harry Zohn (London: Fontana Press, 1973), 247.

109. Alain Badiou, *Conditions*. Translated by Stephen Corcoran (New York: Continuum, 2008), 31.

110. Harney and Moten, *The Undercommons*. Bad documents, in the case of More, can be referred to the literature that is considered not philosophical in the mainstream realm of things. It is from these documents that serious thought emerges in class. Here, black study is

taken upon as a devotional practice.

111. Moten, *Stolen Life*, 231–232.

112. Harney and Moten, *The Undercommons*, 29.

113. Benjamin, *Illuminations*, 249–250.

114. Moten, *Stolen Life*.

115. Benjamin, *Illuminations*, 253.

116. Corey D. B. Walker, "'How Does it Feel to Be a Problem?' (Local) Knowledge, Human Interests, and the Ethics of Opacity," *Transmodernity* 1, no. 2 (2011): 104–119. Cited in 108.

117. Chela Sandoval, *Methodology of the Oppressed* (Minneapolis and London: University of Minnesota Press, 2000), 71.

118. Sabine Broeck, "Legacies of Enslavism and White Abjectorship," in *Postcoloniality-Decoloniality-Black Critique: Joints and Fissures*, edited by Sabine Broeck and Carsten Junker, 109–128 (Frankfurt and New York: Campus Verlag, 2014), 113.

119. Moten, *Stolen Life*, 22.

120. Ibid., 235.

121. Gordon, *Disciplinary Decadence*.

Chapter 2

The Phenomenology of Azania

Heavily pressed, erased, deferred, muted, disavowed, and all things that want nothing to do with the name Azania, the shakedown to be done is to evoke and invoke it. A rightful name for South Africa, Azania became everything wrong from the liberal consensus whose palates and sensibilities are nothing but a distain, extreme hate even. South Africa is the name of the country, and it is, in addition to its history and present, one name that is inconceivable in having to be changed. South Africa, that is it! Mabogo P. More charges the liberal consensus and the whole arrangement of the post-1994 South Africa—the Rainbow Nation.

There will be no contestation where the name South Africa comes from. Nor will there be exhaustion what is the idea that underpins this name. Suffice it to say that the name South Africa proves the long history of dehumanization, and it goes without saying that this will be defended at all costs, in that in the contemporary, the post-1994 era, South Africa is declared new and is seen as having severed from its past—that is apartheid, more erroneously so.

More's Africana existentialist philosophy is the radical confrontation with South Africa. It is from this disposition that he even goes to the extent of calling the country Azania. Since this is the name that has been used and defended by the Pan-Africanist Congress and also Black Consciousness Movement, South Africa is seen as not the name of the country but the geographic reference. Indeed, in its location, the country is at the southern tip of the African continent, and it is not like Zimbabwe (formerly Rhodesia), Malawi (formerly Northern Rhodesia), Namibia (formerly South West Africa), just to name a few. More specifically, these countries are settler colonies and they did, in attaining their independence, have their colonially imposed names altered. In 1994, under the charismatic and sainthood presidency of Nelson Mandela, the issue of the name change, like other fellow southern African countries just mentioned, did not happen. The name stayed as it is, and with a cosmetic touch which did not last longer—the "new" South Africa. Persistently, holding on to the post-1994, the aftermath, the country is referred to as a younger democracy, and it thus prides itself with having the most progressive Constitution in the world. South Africa, after apartheid, does not mean a radical break. As More shows, the country still stained by the long history of settler-colonialism. The name Azania was conceived in the continued battle against settler-colonialism, and more specifically, its advanced stage called apartheid which came in 1948. So, the dehumanizing history that More confronts is not between 1948 and 1994, but what should be traced back to the genealogy, trajectory, and horizons of black existential struggles that ensured from 1652 when settler-colonialism inaugurated itself through conquest.

More's Africana phenomenological exposition challenges the dehumanization project that underpins South Africa whose racist architectonics and fundaments are glossed over by the name South Africa and are fundamentally exposed by evoking the name Azania. By meditating on the phenomenology of Azania, the attempt here is made to account for the lived experience of the black in racist South Africa. Azania is the antidote of conquest, and it is ironic that post-1994 which claims to be the land of the free is the one that More exposes as being plagued by the black as the landless lot. This irony goes to the heart of bad faith because those who are claiming to be free are not free in their passionate allegiance of South Africa which wants nothing to do with dealing with racism but glossing it over with the cliché of non-racialism.

THE APPARATUS AS THE PROBLEM FOR THOUGHT

Azania is the name of the liberated people—the land of the free. What, then, is South Africa? The answer to the affirmative is that South Africa is a country. But, what kind of a country? It will be submitted here that South Africa is a country without a name.[1] Being a geographic reference, it is no irony that it is still a country that still battles not only with its own identity, but it lacks to express itself in the name of its own freedom. For More, South Africa, even after 1994, is still a settler colony.[2] It is the racist apparatus. More writes of its problem as one that demands the "most lucid phenomenological description of apartheid qua colonial and racist situation par excellence."[3] More has his finger on a pulse, thus hitting the nail of the coffin to critically engage South Africa in phenomenological terms in order to account for the project of Azania. From his position, South Africa is engaged from the point of view of being black, the phenomenological account of "the positionality of lived experience."[4]

South Africa is a racist apparatus, and to call it such is also something without specificity. What kind of an apparatus is it? But first, it is worth exploring Giorgio Agamben's operationalized description, and not definition, for it is a contested term, with multiple genealogies.[5] Thus, conceptually elucidated, the apparatus came to mean "a set of practices and mechanisms (both linguistic and nonlinguistic, juridical, technical, and military) that aim to face an urgent need and obtain an effect that is more or less immediate."[6] Even though this might not be satisfactory in having to account for an apparatus, it is clear that to say South Africa as the apparatus is acute in line with Agamben's investigative thought. The manner in which power is organized and operates, accounts not only to the meaning of the apparatus, but its very constitution as the thing that does not want to be seen or pointed at, should it be called out. There is a myriad of elements of what South Africa is, and as a country in itself, it operates in a complex way to solidify itself. Since the concept of power is evoked, what about power in the settler-colonial context? Since South Africa has been manufactured through settler-colonialism, its contours and infrastructural networks and relations have been marshaled to such an extent that they should serve the colonial project and they have to be in the way that has to ensure that it should be the country, and it should be controlled to serve the minority settler interests.

The apparatus here is not in the sense of Louis Althusser, whose conception is on the center of the subject and power being exercised through production and reproduction.[7] Althusser's statist view is not totally invalid, but it has some valence, however minimal, if the *longue durèe* of the apparatus is the subject of examination. How power works, or what are the works of power, is what both Agamben and Althusser handle well insofar as the concept of the apparatus is concerned. The apparatus has been, in relation to the State, the State itself (when reference is made in its modes of exercising power), the State, again, as the totality of that power or it being constituted by it to the point where its exercise is excess. In a sense, its distribution and how it is interpellating its subjects under the spell of ideology.[8] The apparatus, here, becomes a modality of power insofar as that power is intersected with knowledge. This view, which is taken further by Agamben, makes the apparatus to be the concretization of power relations, and it as a decisive problem, the operation of power.[9] According to Agamben, the specific operation of power in relation to the apparatus is capture. The apparatus as the constitutive element of the operation of power, it being a wholly strategic function as Agamben punctuates, it is clear that he departs from Althusser who emphasizes ideology as the operative. For Agamben, however, the apparatus is the constitutive element of the experiment. Since the apparatus can be seen as wholly negative, it can sever from such a characterization strategically to be viewed as positive, or conceal itself.

> The term "apparatus" designates that in which, and through which, one realizes a pure activity of governance devoid of any foundation of being. This is the reason why apparatuses must always imply a process of subjectification, that is to say, they must produce their subject.[10]

One thing is for sure insofar as the apparatus is concerned. It is the operation that wants to assume a concealed character. The apparatus is the secret operation of power. Since the secret is one of the possessive traits of power, it not wanting to be seen in what it is doing, or it not wanting to be seen for what it really is, the power of the secret is always concretized to intensify the manifestation of power. If power were to be an open phenomenon, it would not amount to any form of excess, as its limits will be too revealing. In fact, how far can power go, what it can do, and how its valor is accelerated, and what that has to do with it seeing itself as an experiment?

South Africa is an experiment in the racist settler-colonial imagination. This is the domain of perversion, and the idea of antiblack racism can be understood as the concrete manifestation of this experiment. It is through the exercise of power in its excess that makes racist fantasies to becomes real, and thus to be a legislative force. South Africa's history is part of that force of creation. It is this creation that will even be referred to as destructive creation, because the creation of whiteness can, through the destruction of blackness. Conquest is the creation of accumulation that is set out to destroy livelihood. The forms of lives of the black which were considered barbaric, idle, oversexed, and bestial were to be destroyed by what justified itself to be modern, progressive, civilized, restraint, and moral. This Manichean axis even went so far as to declare the language of the black as the *exterior*. As J. M. Coetzee states, "their speech is not like that of human beings."[11] What more of thought if not everything that has to do with bodily life is thrown out of the fold of the human. Licentious conceptual categories were invented through the settler-colonial episteme in order to justify dehumanization. These conceptual categories, in the Manichean axis, constitutes an apparatus, in that they are conjured up, replicated, propagated, internalized, and normalized, the absurd extent that they are even not only real, but scientific. The apparatus, as the operative force of power and knowledge, becomes solidified in the sense that all effort is made to close any means of refutation, or subjecting the racist claims to verification.

In fact, a whole discourse is fabricated in the name of science where even what Coetzee refers to as narratives and descriptions are thrown around in order to impose the fabricated conception of reality. By the apparatus, in this sense, it as knowledge and power as Agamben insists, it then becomes clear why the name, South Africa, becomes a standard.[12] This is what Coetzee does not even problematized (not that he is expected to) becomes pertinent insofar as the conception of the apparatus is concerned.[13] In other words, the apparatus should be understood here, in line with More's philosophical thought, as how white mythology has become a concretized reality that is there to create South Africa. Indeed, as the mythology, South Africa is white as it is discovered by whites who "worked hard" to save it from "darkness" and bestow "civilization." Consequently, South Africa is white. It was discovered and reinvented. There was no one life before settler-colonialists conquered. Everything started with them. So, the apparatus is, here, the logic of invention that is hidden in narrative and description under the name of discourse of science. To retort the apparatchik of this apparatus Frantz Fanon, indeed, with indignation says: "What a shameful science!"[14]

But still, what about South Africa as an apparatus? Indeed, South Africa came into being and continues to be what it is through the works of power in different idioms, forms, customs, and expressions. These are settler-colonial in form and content. The interest, here, in relation to More's existential phenomenological account, is having to think about South Africa, or having to account for his ideas on what Azania is. By focusing on the concept of apparatus, the interest lies in locating the source of antiblack racism which, in fact, came into being through myriad ways, but thus traceable to the inauguration of the conquest.

The apparatus, in effecting conquest, is a strategic function whose destruction is, in service of the settler-colonial project, instituting modalities of power that will even be made to be harder to resist. The apparatus, the South African settler-colonial project, just like elsewhere, is indeed, firepower. That is why this cannot be decoupled from destruction. It is a force that imposes itself. Its expansionist logic is driven by the impulses of not only control by accumulation and dispossession. At the base of this drive is the law whose regulatory function is not that of justice but the justification. If the law is fair, balanced, and impartial (justice), this is suspended in the settler colony because the law, whose jurists are the very settler-colonialists, is there to lubricate the operation of the apparatus. The law is, as a justificatory force, the imposition of misery to the black. South Africa's jurisprudence has been nothing but the settler-colonial apparatus. To be specific, the law of conquest is the judicial attitude, and this has nothing to do with justice.

Still even in the post-1994, South Africa's law is spirited in Roman-Dutch Law. This law of conquest is the one that idea of Azania is not spirited from. The law of justice, the law of the wronged, the law of the dead and the living anti-colonialists is the spirit that informs the Azanian jurisprudence. This marginally certified jurisprudence, the outlawed jurisprudence, the one which is what,the Roman-Dutch Law's protection of settler-colonialism will even murderously execute with impunity. The statute of the Azanian jurisprudence is the law underground, the law of resistance—that is, More's phenomenological inscription. It is the Azanian jurisprudence which is illegalized by the post-1994 Constitution which arrogated itself as the highest law in the land where the black are a landless lot. This is South Africa's tragedy. But this should not come as a surprise because the settler-colonial experiment which continues to date has been a tragedy without any comic mask.

The law that has always been against the freedom of the black has always been a tragedy. The birth of Azania has always been criminalized instead of this becoming an aborted mission. The intentional miscarriage of the law (not justice) has been the motif force of the Roman-Dutch Law. Indeed, it should be noted that this has been, is, and will still be the law as long as South Africa exists. The only end of this law is only if Azania is birthed through struggle. This struggle means, by all accounts, the destruction of the apparatus. The drive of his apparatus is whiteness, all there is to law is the protection of whiteness. This protection, under the complex that Agamben terms the "semantic sphere," the legal jargon is intensified in the name of the juridical order whose function is to make the language of the law as a sacred linguistic code whose criticism is tantamount to blasphemy. The semantic sphere becomes the law itself—that is to say, the law's absolute and final word. That is why there is so much vested interest, even in the post-1994 South Africa, to protect the Constitution as it is the imposter against any "desegregative imperative" which, to Fred Moten, becomes the antithesis of the "renewed privilege called 'whiteness.'"[15] The protection of whiteness, the apparatus called South Africa, is the force that will always stand to destroy the birth of Azania. The erect standing of the Constitution, as the highest law, is the strategic function of the apparatus to make sure that whiteness, the marker of settler-colonialism, remains untouched. It is for this reason that this juridical strategic function that deems the Constitution the highest law of the land to criminalize whatever that might appear as the Azanian jurisprudential inscription.

Here is Anthony's Farley who exposes the law as a myth that claims to be itself the absolute and the sacred.[16] Law is mechanized and weaponized, notes Farley, as both reason and desire. In its legislating and adjudicating, reason is pitted against desire. But then, this sanction gets lifted if the law does not want to surprise its inner-most desire, to a point where it will even justify itself by suspending reason. Reason and desire are, according to Farley, infused, in that the law is able to switch between it being law or lawlessness at will since there is nothing that will hold it accountable. There will not even be the question—What is the law? For, if this litigated question, which means that it must always be an unasked question, or should it be asked, it will be retorted with closed answer that masks itself absolute—the law is the law *tout court*. This retort imposes itself as reason, whereas it is the perverted desire of the law to always act in excess. Indeed, reason is a mask of desire. Or, if desire is exercised, it will be under the protection of the law. Even though prohibition or repression can be seen as the function of law, this gets suspended in the settler colony where the law is not the domain of the racially conquered blacks who are perverted by colonial desire masked as reason—law as a fundament.

It is clear that reason, in most of the time, is there to repress desire. This does not mean, however, that reason is immune from being perverted and it cascading to denigration or it being lawless compulsion and destructive drive. Since there is ethical suspension, or the suspension of all faculties deemed human when it comes to the black in the settler colony or in an antiblack world in general, law is, always, "an instrument of repression."[17] In the settler-colonial and in an antiblack world, the law is driven by what Farley calls the "perpetrators of law." Undeniably, the law's function is that of the apparatus, and its interpretation of statutes and ratification is the language of desire that veils itself as reason, whereas it is a labyrinth that Farley defines finely as "a network of lines that enlace."[18] The very fabric of the apparatus, the law is excess. It is the law that, according to Farley, erects walls that divide, cut, slice, break—say, the invention and investment of separation. "The wall separates *us* form *them*."[19] The law is there to impose. As the ontological weight, the law has the capacity to crush the black into objecthood. Truly, in the colony, the black is stripped everything that has to do with being a juridical persona. It is at this exposure, this nakedness that the law can serve, under desire masked as reason, to violate with impunity.

Naïvely so, or erroneous at best, Coetzee writes: "The law protects the law-abiding citizen."[20] This statement of guarantee suggests that the law is bound by its duty and obligation which, at any time, can be altered in all manner and in the name of authorizing the law itself. Even with those that the law protects, say settler-colonialists, the law can exercise its will and might upon them even though they are law abiding. Coetzee seems to be stuck in the binary of the law-abiding citizen and the outlaw. The law, in fact, can easily turn the law-abiding citizen into the outlaw, at will and justifiably so as the law deems fit. Coetzee correctly notes: "But there is no law to protect the outlaw, the man who takes up arms against his own state, that is to say, the state that claims him as its own."[21] However correct is this assertion, it is worthy asking: What about the outlaw who is just conjured up from the racist fantasies? Here Coetzee's binary schema of the law-abiding citizen and the outlaw suffers exhaustion, as it cannot account for the complex ways the law can just invent its subject. The outlaw does not come into being through one taking up arms against the state. In the settler colony like South Africa, the black has been the thing that is external to law, the outlaw. The weaponization of the law against the black has meant, it is the will of the law by might and decree to classify, index, categorize, rank in the sense of Farley's conception of the law and the law of us and them. The law can create, protect, and abandon protection in whatever side of the wall. The us and them, in this view, can, with reason and desire, one as the reinforcement, complement, replacement, and alternation the other, be in service of what the law wants in terms of it creating the law-abiding citizen and the outlaw. Coetzee should head this warning by Farley: "Signs can be turned against their meanings and then mean something else and then turn again and again."[22] In fact, the law-abiding citizen and the outlaw are not the automatic inventions of the self, but they are the invention of the law in its reason and desire depending on what the law feels. The outlaw is the excluded figure, the banned one in the domain of law whose exercise will be, in relation to this figure, the extra-legal one.

Gil Anidjar writes: "Law is where the enemy is identified and adjudicated upon."[23] The outlaw is identified as the enemy of the State and it is this construction that serves as the justificatory means of the extra-legal. The law, in its arbitrary operation, becomes absolute in its identification of the outlaw. In a sense, the outlaw is the invention of law. And then, the State must then hunt down this figure and eliminate with whatever punitive measures the law deems fit. In no way will the outlaw have access to justice, since this is already suspended. The invention of the outlaw is the immediate suspension of justice. The outlaw is the one exteriorized by law, "the outside of the law" as Anidjar notes, but one who is inside it only to be destroyed by its extra-legal means.[24] The outlaw is the hyperbolic expression of the law. The apparatus, which then expresses itself not only in legal terminology, then becomes the elaboration of exteriorization. In a way, the apparatus ensures that there is nothing that attaches the law to the outlaw.

With this exposition above, the question the apparatus becomes more pressing and thus forever urgent. In taking it up, Moten asks: "But what of the outlaw that prompts the apparatuses of exposure?"[25] The one who is outside thought, as Moten states, the one who, according to Farley, is the exclusionary character who is at the receiving end of law's lawless violation, seems to have no say if the Roman-Dutch Law and the Constitution are to be considered.[26] Well, this will obviously turn disappointing because these are the sites of the apparatus that More is waging his existential struggle against. Clearly, by this positionality, More is the outlaw, he is the advocate if not the paralegal *personalia* whose auxiliary function is not that of "the friends of the court," but the one who is on the accused stand judging the judge on the bench. More is, as this paralegal assumption of duty, this necessity, arguing for what Moten encapsulates as "the *un*reason of (thinking) things."[27] It is this unreason of those deemed the outlaw, those who have no standing as the defecate on the laws violating flux that bipolarly switches between reason and desire all in the interest on criminalizing black juridical thought. It is here that this defection will literally come to be the reality of shit hitting the fan—shit spattered everywhere.

More, in this capacity as Africana philosopher qua paralegal jurist, is linguistically fluent in speaking and rhyming from jurisprudence letters. His grammar is, as it is outlawed in South Africa's judiciary and its jurisprudential episteme, deemed "criminal, illegitimately criminalized capacity to make law."[28] But as More forever does in this necessity where he should, in dealing with the lawlessness of law, stick out his tongue and say things and not perfume the stink that the law is. In fact, the *longue durèe* has been so long, so long that it has been stinking and no one can take this shit anymore—right from More's forebears since the colonial encounter.

The apparatus has forever been stinking, and the black have been pathologized and criminalized as the outlaw when they stood up for themselves. The other language of the Azanian jurisprudential inscription is, to Moten, the "capacity to generate what shows up as the unagrammatical."[29] The making of language, here, is not reducible to the linguistic offering and uttering, but the spirit of rewriting the law itself. If the law stands to be the language in its edifice of reason, with it being a lettered spirit, pious as it claims and climbs to heaven, then it is decadence. As Farley writes: "Laying down the law, laying down one's arms, a frightening prospect, seems like heaven."[30] This, for More's Africana existential philosophy, qua Azanian jurisprudential inscription, does not evoke any fear, nor is this law held in the heavenly regard it arrogates itself to be. Thus, in this unagrammatical Azanian jurisprudential inscription, the law is yet to be written through the obliteration of the apparatus. This effort will come as a result of continuing the existential struggle. As More correctly notes, the unagrammatical Azanian jurisprudential inscription is not the effort of what he calls "pacifists" and "legalists."[31] Of them, More says the following with disappointment: "Afraid of the fire power of the colonialists, they preach nonviolence as a viable solution to the political problems they face; hence the negotiated settlement and the compromise and betray of the revolution."[32]

From where the Azanian jurisprudence will find expression, its language, is through its acts of liberation, what this jurisprudence is. Say, the Azanian jurisprudential inscription is/as liberation. For, in appropriating Agamben's liberatory inscription by the name of "profanation," which he also marks as the "counter-apparatus," there should be a bold critique of the Constitution that poses itself as the sacred text. Or if it is seemed to be such, More's Africana existential philosophical reading practices can be turned to be the critical exegesis, with the attitude of mounting criticism where profanity will not be a swear word. In this critical task, profanation as the counter-apparatus will be unflinching and not bow before any judicial bench that is inspirited the law of antiblackness, the Constitution notwithstanding. What serves as the operative in More is the diacriticism he mounts directly to South Africa which given to the black on a silver platter called a "negotiated settlement" rather than a revolutionary struggle where the black set their own terms of liberation.[33] This is diacriticism because More's philosophical project is a different accent, and it is not palatable to the vices of the liberal consensus, thus it not being a structured sensibility that sings praises for the post-1994 South Africa as a "new dawn." More's diacriticism, that different kind of criticism, stems from the existential cry for Azania, and its mounted, spirited, frontal, non-apologetic antagonism. It is not that diacriticism is the installation of the mark which makes the accent different or anything that has to do with the diction of the accent of the letter. It is, rather wholesomely, a different form of critique. Its disposition and exposition are passionate to mark not a cosmetic change but fundamental change. More's diacriticism makes it clear that post-1994 South Africa is the result of been birthed by the "flag freedoms." More does not fall for the trap that post-1994 was a liberation struggle that brought liberation. The concept of "flag freedoms," coming from Fanon, is a clear diacritical mark.[34] It clearly means that the black is acted upon and knows no cost of freedom. "One day the White Master, *without conflict*, recognized the Negro slave."[35] This, even sketched further, goes thus: "One day a good white master who had influence said to his friends, 'Let's be nice to the nigger.'"[36] This one day, one day out of the blue, that one day that Fanon states twice, is the day that got Nelson Mandela and all the blacks by surprise. More's diacriticism is enduring by amplification thus:

> More jubilation was to follow with 'declaration of emancipation' in April 1994 during the first democratic elections. President de Klerk has sprung a surprise on Mandela and all South Africa by first unbanning all previously banned political parties, realizing Mandela. . . . It is evident that Mandela and black people were all acted upon by de Klerk, that is, their freedom emerged from without and not within themselves.[37]

This is acute in terms of this being the operational logic of the apparatus that gives freedom while solidifying the logic of capture. This produces what Agamben calls the "penitential self" which, by the way, is the self that is clutched to the captive logic of the apparatus.[38] As the subject of the apparatus, and not the self of reinvention through the revolutionary struggle, this subject is, according to More, the black who is clutched in the colonial situation.[39] For, in coming into being through the logic of capture, this "penitential self," according to Fanon, heard the master saying: "From now on you are free."[40] This declaration is only in words as South Africa still remains a racist apparatus. For More, since there is no internal freedom of the black, the declaration of external freedom will always reproduce, through the apparatus of capture, the penitential self.[41] Or, in More's terms accurate to describe the post-1994 South Africa, "flag freedom." It is in this kind of a situation, as More points out, "neoslavery takes over."[42]

> The upheaval reached the Negroes from without. The black man was acted upon. Values that has not been born of the systolic tide of blood, danced in a hued whirl round him. The upheaval did not make a difference in the Negro. He went from one way of life to another, but not from one life to another.[43]

Neoslavery takes over precisely because being acted upon means not knowing the cost of that freedom that was just given. Directing his criticism to South Africa, More states that this freedom has been deemed a miracle transition for apartheid to liberal democracy.[44] This is in line with Fanonesque conception of having gone from one way of life to another, which, in the effect of capture by the apparatus, means no change at all. It is life as it were, the life of unfreedom. This condition, according to More, "still leaves the slave in bondage, albeit being upgraded to the status of a human being."[45] But this status is only honorary and can be rescinded at any time and at will depending on the feathery and weatherly feeling of the master is. The will of the master, as Jared Sexton states, is excess and the last word is that of the master, and no one else but the master.[46]

> The master in his brief dialogue is stuck in his dwelling, gripped by a structure of prevarication wherein he cannot decide upon any action whatsoever; the logic of the decision confounds him in the face of vanity. He encounters not only the ambiguity of the situation before him or the ambivalence of his feelings about the issue at hand, but also a certain undecidability and, more fundamentally, an opacity inherent to his own initiative in the most general sense. What, he seems to ask, do I have truly want? The slave's function as sounding board or echo chamber serves only to amplify the noise within the master's thinking, offering no guarantee of a clear and fixed signal. He contemplates, before his slave as captive audience, a myriad of issues in varying degrees of significance: faith and homage, hunting and dining, sex and marriage, industry and philanthropy, litigation and revolution, and eventually, life and death. As he works first to assert and then to negate each proposition in turn, the master finally arrives at a point of desperation (the slave's interminable patience, we note, is entirely presumed by the direct relations of force, but any such obligatory understanding has long been exercised). Then, in the penultimate lines, the master resorts to threat and assault.[47]

One thing is for sure, the humanity of the black will still be in question. Thus, this is the case in South Africa where black life is superfluous. That is why the master, in seeing the slave, always sees the object whom violent and unimaginable fantasies can be directed to, applied, and forced. The resultant death of this will not give the master any moral dilemmas because the slave is not human. Between the master and the slave, there is no "with" and "between". There is, in point of fact, no relation but non-relation due to the suspension of the humanity of the slave by the master. For there to be the master, there must be the slave. This parasitic arrangement is a paradigm through which the concept of the apparatus rests.

The post-1994 is the result of the transition from "apartheid" to "democracy" and that being misread as victory by the landless black lots is defeating to understand More's "flag freedoms" and thus defeating to understand "genuine freedom." The values of the struggle for freedom in South Africa are non-existent, as they are not carried through the post-1994 era.

> But the Negro knows nothing of the cost of freedom, for he has not fought for it. From time to time he has fought for Liberty and Justice, but these were always white liberty and white justice; that is, values secreted by his masters.[48]

The Constitution has created a condition that solidifies the captive force of the apparatus. That is why the black fought for what was white, and the result that comes as the Constitution, deemed the triumph of South African under the deceptive mantra of the "Rainbow Nation," with Mandela as a poster boy became apparent, absurdity at best. "The 'historic compromise,' while it handed out political power to the ANC, left economic power in the hands of the corporate white elite."[49] Freedom does not come for free, or from being acted upon. The Constitution is not, at all, any form of triumph.

> There are laws that, little by little, are invalidated under the Constitution. There are other laws that forbid certain forms of discrimination. And we can be sure that nothing is going to be given free.[50]

The Constitution in South Africa forbids racial discrimination but it does not say anything about racism. Not only that, the Constitution appears as if South Africa has no long history of racism. Words like "racism," "apartheid," "colonialism," "land theft," "conquest," and many others that shed light to the long history of 1652, the year which is not even printed in the Constitution under the pretext that the 1913 is the origin of all problems, marks a glaring absence that is not accounted for and something that is deliberately juridically censured. The Constitution, its idea of South Africa, supposes a *tabala rasa*. What the Constitution says, in a disavowing fashion is "injustices of the past"—a silly generality at best. The lack of specificity is deliberate. The gesture was closing the dark chapter of apartheid. Nothing is mentioned about South Africa as the apparatus, and also it being the *longue durèe*.

What is the apparatus in relation to South Africa as the *longue durèe*? South Africa can be coined rightly as the racist-settler-colonial-segregationist-apartheid-nonracial-constitutionalist-apparatus. This is the apparatus in its pure nature. It is a complex network, continuation, mutation, transaction, exchange, inter/penetration of power to maintain the fault line of the racist infrastructure. In this *longue durèe,* the operative function of the apparatus has been to ensure that there is white superiority and black inferiority, alas, with the black government in the throne since 1994.

The cosmetic changes that came as the solidification and sophistication of the apparatus in the post-1994 were based on values secreted by the masters that Fanon earlier decried. These changes were there just to mask the apparatus, to give it a black face—stated another way, the ANC regime to stand as the manager of the racist infrastructure. The apparatus with the black face is what South Africa is in the post-1994. This, according to More, is "incapable of delivering the fullest achievement of liberation and equality possible."[51] That is why the fundamental change is resisted because in South Africa the *longue durèe* wants nothing to do with the liberated ontology of the black. It is the attaining of this ontology that will come through freedom from within the rooted in the deeper annals of self-consciousness which is the potent possession of the being-towards-inner-freedom. This self-validated being is that of the one who "needs a challenge to his humanity" as Fanon states, one who "wants a conflict, a riot."[52] The one who does not get doomed and surprised on the rehearsed and choreographed "one day" where the master lays the proclamation of emancipation. The one who will exclaim "to hell with emancipation," "to hell with flag freedom," "to hell..." The one is in unison with what Aimè Cèsaire calls the colonized.[53] "They know that their temporary 'masters' are lying."[54] The one who cannot, anymore, be subjected to distraction and dissimulation. The one is who, indeed, possess self-consciousness and is not a captive object of the apparatus who will be duped, dumped, and dumbed down by cosmetic changes that claim "now you are free" which More abhors, at best, which means nothing but hot air. The one, just like More, who will say "there must be conflict, a battle, and a life-and-death struggle."[55] The one who knows that, just as Fanon writes: "There is a war, there are defeats, truces, victories."[56]

The internal freedom that should erupt from the black is the animative force of More's Africana existential philosophy that does not valorize South Africa that came into being through flag freedom but the cry of Azania that will come through true freedom that is rooted in the self-consciousness of the black. This freedom is one that the apparatus that pervades South Africa in all its sphere of life should be found, and as such, it should be infused with the force of rupture not to jam or slow down the apparatus but to obliterate it. Why? Fanon answers: "I believe that the fact of the juxtaposition of the white and black races has created a massive psychoexistential complex. I hope by analyzing it to destroy it."[57] The humanity that is fought for by the black, which More advocates, is one way of obliterating the apparatus.[58] This, for More, will not come as the result of the negotiated settlement but the deepening of the existential struggle. The apparatus, according to Fanon, is the "shameful livery put together by centuries of incomprehension."[59] That is why it is the *longue durèe* and it makes no sense to declare South Africa "new" with the "progressive Constitution," "non-racialism," "hard won freedoms," whereas antiblack racism is still a defining reality.

THE FOUNDATIONLESS MANDELA'S HOUSE

The reality is that cosmetic changes are not changes in a fundamental sense. The emphasis on "fundamental" has to do with reality that the black faces. It is this reality that cannot be denied by those who are affected by the weight of dehumanization, those who still hold on the faith of Azania to come. South Africa is, for More, a neo-colony, with the spirit of "neoslavery" being the ruling order.[60] The foundation of South Africa is the one that structures what More calls Mandela's House.[61]

This is the house where secret negotiations with the apartheid regime will continue as they began before his release from prison. It should be noted that Mandela was the only black in those secret talks. His comrades whom he was imprisoned with did not get the opportunity to form part of these meetings. So, it was one black meeting with all whites. The apartheid regime incubated and cemented what would become the spirit of what More calls "Mandela's House." Indeed, the secret talks even went to be held at Mandela's House nearing his release by De Klerk. Mandela writes: "The first formal meeting of the secret working group took place in May 1988, at a posh officers' club within the precincts of Pollsmoor."[62] Still, to date, there are no minutes of these meetings. These are secret meetings; there is a veil in everything that has to do with their form and content. Mandela's narrative does not, in fact, reveal much. Mandela only states that these meetings continued, but were stalled on the issues like the armed struggle, the Communist Party, and majority rule. It appears, misleadingly so, that he was the one who was in charge by being somewhat rebellious. The frequency of these meetings leaves more questions than answers. In Mandela's House, there are secret talks with the apartheid regime, and this is even outside the intimate knowledge of Mandela's comrades, and the oppressed that he is accountable to. The talks are between Mandela alone and his oppressors in the capacity as apartheid senior officials

(Kobbie Coetsee, General Willemse, Niel Barnard, and Fanie van der Merwe) whom Mandela affectionately referred to as "my new colleagues," also fellow victims who fell prey to the propaganda of apartheid.[63] The committee that was formed was called the "secret committee." Mandela even went so far as to call this "our secret committee meeting" as if this is the secret that is shared by all without considering the secrets about him. The asymmetrical constitution of this secret committee is telling—four against one.

> The initial meeting was quite stiff, but in subsequent sessions we were able to talk more freely and directly. I met with them almost every week for a few months, and then the meetings occurred at irregular intervals, sometimes not for a month, and then suddenly every week. The meetings were usually scheduled by the government, but sometimes I would request a session.[64]

Of interest, still, is the frequency of these meetings. They cannot just be talks over tea and biscuits. Mandela says: "Tea was served and we began to talk. From the first, it was not as though we were engaged in tense political arguments but a lively and interesting tutorial."[65] These meetings serve as the brick and mortar of Mandela's House. More states clearly that the comforts given to Mandela might seem like dignified ones, but they are not.[66] There is no fundamental change in relation to the cause that Mandela is jailed for. "This state of affairs leads to a situation of massive discount among the hungry unrecognized masses, who begin to sulk."[67] The building of Mandela's House led to this discontent.

What is said of Mandela's twenty-seven incarceratory hardship is often emphasized on Robben Island, without mentioning the fact that it was only twenty-two years spent there, and Mandela was smuggled out of prison to meet his apartheid generals under the tag of "secret talks." He did not go to these secret talks in a prison garb but wore a tailored suit. As Mandela says, "a short while later a tailor appeared to take my measurements."[68] How unthinkable for a political prisoner. So many unthinkable gestures will be made by the apartheid. The political prisoner even sat with his main jailer—the apartheid Prime Minister Pieter Willem Botha under the same roof. Mandela recounts:

> The meeting was not even half an hour long, and was friendly and breezy until the end. It was then that I raised a serious issue. I asked Mr Botha to release unconditionally all political prisoners, including myself. That was the only tense moment in the meeting, and Mr Botha said that he was afraid he could not to that.[69]

Mandela even states that he has been constantly warned that he should not raise any "controversial issues." As the slave, cordially as this might sound from his masters, he is emphatically told to toe the line and to know and stay at his place. Mandela would continue to insist on his demand and Frederik Willem De Klerk, who succeeded Botha, and the last apartheid president came to power, and political prisoners were released in 1989. "De Klerk has lived up to his promise, and the men were released under no bans; they could speak in the name of the ANC."[70] Mandela admits that De Klerk brought reforms to apartheid. "De Klerk began a systematic dismantling of many of the building blocks of apartheid."[71] It is Mandela who congratulated de Klerk when he became president. He even wrote him a letter to express his gratitude.

> I told Mr de Klerk how impressed I was by his emphasis on reconciliation, enunciated in his inaugural address. His words had imbued millions of South Africans and people around the world with the hope that the new South Africa was about to be born. The very first step on the road to reconciliation. I said, would be complete dismantling of apartheid and all measures to enforce it.[72]

The meeting happened, and Mandela says:

> On the morning of 13 December I was again taken to Tuynhuys. I met de Klerk in the same room where I had had tea with his predecessor. He was accompanied by Kobie Coetsee, General Willemse, Dr Barnard and his colleague Mike Louw. I congratulated Mr de Klerk on becoming president and expressed the hope that we would be able to work together. He was extremely cordial and reciprocated these sentiments.
>
> From the first I noticed that Mr de Klerk listened to what I had to say. This was a novel experience. National Party leaders generally heard what they wanted to hear in discussions with black leaders, but Mr de Klerk seemed to be making a real attempt to listen and understand.[73]

The worrisome thing for More is that Mandela's House is built on bad faith. Is it the sincerity of Mandela to have a Stockholm syndrome?[74] Not only is Mandela appealing to the moral conscience of his oppressors. He claims to know how they feel, or even, their perceptions. The sentimentality of focusing on the human and humane side is so totalizing that the "secrete committee" meetings are not seen as the inner workings of psychic warfare. Having met Botha and de Klerk should not be seen as triumph but the strategic function of figuring Mandela out and putting him at the compromising situation. Everything is as a result of a compromise. For Deborah Posel, this "itself as an element of De Klerk's own symbolic capital as a leader attempting to marshal his constituency in support of negotiations with the ANC."[75] Whatever change the apartheid regime makes in those meetings is not (wittingly or unwittingly) at its own expense.

It is Mandela who is in the powerless situation, the power of the master and his extension on the slave. The faith of Mandela is astonishing in another encounter where he met whites who raised their clenched fist to salute him as he was just released from prison and being driven to the Grand Parade. "At one point I stopped and got out of the car to greet and thank one such white family and tell them how inspired I was by their support. It made me think that the South Africa I was returning to was far different from the one I had left."[76] But before that encounter, there is a more troubling one. Mandela wanted, more than anything else, to meet his white jailers and their families before he could meet the black masses who were eagerly waiting for him outside prison gates. But before he could get out of the prison gates, he thanked Swart "not only for the food he had provided for the last two years but also the companionship."[77]

> There was little time for lengthy farewells. The plan was that Winnie and I would be driven in a car to the front of the gate of the prison. I had told authorities that I wanted to be able to say good-bye to the guards and warders who had looked after me and I asked that they and their families wait for me at the front gate, where I would be able to thank them individually.[78]

The black masses are the ones who are at the gate waiting for their hero. Will their hero thank them individually? Do they know that their hero said his white jailers "looked after" him? The euphoric expression of those who are outside the prison gates, and not his white jailers and families is described as "a noise that sounded like some great herd of metallic beasts."[79]

> When I was among the crowd I raised my right fist, and there was a roar. I had not been able to do that for twenty-seven years and it gave me a surge of strength and joy. We stayed among the crowd for only a few minutes before jumping back in the car for the drive to Cape Town. Although I was pleased to have such a reception, I was greatly vexed by the fact that I did not have a chance to say good bye to the prison stuff.[80]

Mandela's House, in its spirit of race eliminativism as More shows, should be understood in relation to the sentimental attachment to his oppressors than his fellow oppressed.[81] The kind of gestures he was willing to perform, thanking them, and thus having to be worried about those who jailed him and not being overjoyed by the embrace of his very own is the matter of concern. Susan Sontag writes:

> We seek his freedom because we seek the freedom of the majority of the inhabitants of his country. His freedom is theirs. He has made it so. (He could not

> have lived his imprisoned otherwise.) We demand his freedom. And the freedom of those for whom he is imprisoned.[82]

It is this punctuative declaration by Sontag that would give a disappointing account of Mandela who is, upon his freedom, would want to pay gratitude to his jailers. Indeed, for Sontag to argue for the freedom of those whom Mandela is imprisoned, she did not refer to the jailers that Mandela is gesturing to. The suffering of Mandela in Robben Island is captured by Sontag as being harsh and she compared that with being in any other Gulag.

The thoughts of escaping, says Mandela, have always been there. However, they became the aborted mission. After gaining trust of his apartheid generals, Mandela was rewarded with privileges, and the last subsequent prisons he was housed became different from Robben Island. It is in 1982 where Mandela is transferred from Robben Island to Pollsmoor Prison to Victor Verster Prison. In the latter, he was in the cottage, a house more comfortable than a prison cell. The moving of Mandela to different houses disguised, as "prison" was a deliberate strategy by the apartheid regime to give him some sort of comfort. Mandela, the slave, recounts what he is told by his master thus: "He told me that the cottage at Victor Verster would be my last home before becoming a free man."[83] This is the home that was prepared to be, as Mandela notes as "a place where I could hold discussions in privacy and comfort."[84] These are the words of one of his masters, Kobie Coetsee. Mandela notes that "there were other signs that the government was preparing me for a different kind of existence."[85] With regard to the cottage, Mandela says the following:

> The cottage did in fact give one the illusion of freedom. I could go to sleep and wake up as I pleased, swim whenever I wanted, eat when I was hungry—all were delicious sensations. Simply to be able to go outside during the day and take a walk when I desired was a moment of private glory. There were no bars on the windows, no jangling keys, no doors to lock or unlock. It was altogether pleasant, but I never forgot that it was a gilded cage.[86]

It is clear that preparation for Mandela's freedom has to start with giving Mandela a master's house so that he could be cushioned to the illusion of freedom. The privileges that are extended to him mean that he is the exceptional black, and him, by that him alone, is different and will be treated different. This level of preferential treatment to a political prisoner known as terrorist and being imprisoned on the charges on treason is dazzling. Mandela is known to have been one who thought about others and could not accept any privileges unless others are also afforded them in equal measure. This is a good measure of selflessness. It is the spirit of being with/as/for/in others.

Chris Sanders attests: "He repeatedly refused privileges that were offered to him and not to other prisoners."[87]

However, as More shows, this is the deliberate strategy of creating Mandela to be "Mr Nice Black."[88] He is treated differently, and this does not leave the apartheid regime, which Steve Biko judged as evil, to be in good faith.[89] Cushioning Mandela to comfort, uprooting him from a prison hole to a plushy House, the standards which are so to Mandela considering where he has been confined to for more than two decades, is a testament to what Mandela says: "The prison service provided me with a cook, Warrant Officer Swart, a tall, quite Afrikaner who had been once a warder on Robben Island."[90] Just like Mandela claimed his apartheid masters to be colleagues and fellow victims, Swart was not even spared of Mandela's affection.

> I did not remember him, but he said he sometimes drove us to the quarry and purposefully steered the truck over bumps to give us a rocky ride. "I did that to you," he said sheepishly, and I laughed. He was a decent, sweet-tempered fellow without any prejudice and he became like a younger brother to me.[91]

This is really concerning. In just this account, Mandela claims that Swart is without prejudice. What informed his actions while in Robben Island? It is what is beyond prejudice—hate! Mandela's House is a prison. He is isolated from others, and how does he know that Swart, in his absence, is the same person whom he claims to be. Well, he can claim him to be his brother because the rehearsal and performance are scripted only for Mandela's House, the backstage and not the stage where there is public spectacle.

> In early December 1988, security on my ward was tightened and the officers on duty were more alert than usual. Some change was imminent. On the evening of December 9, Major Marais came into my room, and told me to prepare myself to leave. Where to? I asked him. He could not say. I packed my things and looked around for some of my loyal nurses; I was disappointed at not being able to thank them and bid them farewell.
>
> We left in a rush, and after about an hour on the road we entered a prison whose name I recognized: Victor Verster. Located in the lovely old Cape Dutch town of Paarl, Victor Verster is thirty-five miles northeast of Cape Town in the province's wine-growing region. The prison had the reputation of being a model facility. We drove through the entire length of the prison, and then along a winding dirt road through a rather wild, wooded area at the rear of the property. At the end of the road we came to an isolated, whitewashed one-story cottage set behind a concrete wall and shaded by tall fir trees.

> I was ushered into the house by Major Marais and found a spacious lounge, next to a large kitchen, with an even larger bedroom at the back of the house. The place was sparsely but comfortably furnished. It had not been cleaned or swept before my arrival, and the bedroom and living room were teeming with all kinds of exotic insects, centipedes, monkey spiders, and the like, some of which I had never seen before. That night, I swept the insects off my bed and windowsill and slept extremely well in what was to be my new home.
>
> The next morning I surveyed my new abode and discovered a swimming pool in the backyard, and two smaller bedrooms. I walked outside and admired the trees that shaded the house and kept it cool. The entire place felt removed, isolated. The only thing spoiling the idyllic picture was that the walls were topped with razor wire, and there were guards at the entrance to the house. Even so, it was a lovely place and situation; a halfway house between prison and freedom.[92]

Why is this Mandela's House following More's diacriticism? Mandela writes: "That afternoon I was visited by Kobie Coetsee, who brought a case of Cape wine as a housewarming gift."[93] This, indeed, is Mandela's House—a master's house. Mandela, after his release, and having going back to Qunu (in former Bantustan, Transkei), Eastern Cape, the village he was born, built a house—Mandela's House. This, for Mandela, as he states, is a dream home.

> I have always believed that a man should have a home with sight of the house where he was born. After being released from prison, I set out plans to build a country house for myself in Qunu. By autumn 1993, the house was complete. It was based on the floor plan of the house I has lived in at Victor Verster. People often commented on this, but the answer was simple: the Victor Venter house was the first spacious and comfortable home I ever stayed in, and I like it very much. I was familiar with its dimensions so at Qunu I would not have to wander at night looking for the kitchen.[94]

Sarah Nuttall and Achille Mbembe remark on this house thus: "Mandela's Qunu house is built on the model of the warder's house at Victor Verster Prison, where he spent his last period of captivity."[95] Why would Mandela build his house just like his jail? No matter how this might be justified in terms of the house being better in terms of space that Mandela has been deprived in many years of his incarceration, the argument that Nuttall and Mbembe state that Mandela was "subverting the logic of the system that sought to contain and break him" still holds no ground in justifying this slave mimicry. There is nothing revolutionary by Mandela in building the house like this. By replicating the prison means that he wanted to be in it. This is not a mode of Mandela making a "counter-intuitive move" as Nuttall and Mbembe claim by embracing the house of his jailer.

The problem of replication will go insofar as the *longue durèe* of the racist-settler-colonial-segregationist-apartheid-nonracial-constitutionalist-apparatus is the critical marker of South Africa and it having no radical break. Mandela is in the grind of systematic, systemic, and continuous apparatus of antiblackness that still continue to haunt Mandela's House.

Mandela's House that More is referring to is indeed the post-1994 regime: he was a president. But it is important to remark that this house is preceded by what the apartheid regime gave Mandela as a house in the last years of his imprisonment. Mandela's House, contra More, predates 1994. It is worthy examining what happened when Mandela left a prison cell to house imprisonment. It is worth stating that More should have gone back and gave an account of the idea of the house as the ante-1994 phenomenon. This would give a richer account of showing that there is no radical break as More insists.

> Indeed, as president and despite the huge compromise he and the ANC made, Mandela spent years of his tenure trying to assuage white fears by attending the Rugby World Cup in Springbok Jersey (Springbok is a symbol of Afrikaner sporting power), visiting and having tea with Betsy Verwoerd—the wife of arguably the architect of apartheid, Hendrik Verwoerd—who claimed that blacks stink; paid the arch conservative former president, P. W. Botha a visit, assured whites that the ANC will protect their property, took the concerns of the conservative White farmers seriously, made certain gestures of reconciliation to the neo-Nazi racist AWB, endorsed the Truth and Reconciliation Commission, never said a word against the numerous brutal attacks on blacks by conservative white and wholly heartedly embraced neo-liberalism's economic policies after initially threatening that the ANC would nationalize high industries.[96]

On the contrary, Posel deems Mandela's actions as a miracle.[97] "Throughout Mandela's tenure as president and beyond, his extraordinary persona was also scripted through a series of more ordinary encounters equally replete with symbolic meaning and tradition."[98] One that was punctuated as the result of the above mentioned is the fact that Mandela is a unifier, a messiah. But one thing is clear: South Africa is an untransformed land mass, the land where the blacks are suffering as the landless lot. It is, for More, a country of suspended revolution, where neoslavery reins.[99] The spirit of neoslavery was enchained in Mandela. It went insofar as deep as not him questioning his olive branch gestures to whites which were flung back to his face. "Immediately after Mandela's presidency, the reality of extant apartheid racism dawned on most Black people, their euphoria about freedom notwithstanding."[100]

Mandela's iconicity as the most famous prisoner is undisputable. However, this iconicity is fueled by the liberal consensus and liberatory mythology that prevails at the time, and thus memory being weaponized in favor of forgetting others who, in their dream of Azania, will not feature as conduits of the existential struggle for liberation. The myth is that Mandela, heroically so, liberated South Africa from the clutches of apartheid. He is a prisoner who fought for freedom, indeed, the freedom for/of all. A messiah *tout court*.

Upon his release, and addressing the people, Mandela's mythological construction is that he is the humble servant. But the authoritarian character of Mandela as a charismatic patriarch will betray this characterization. Sabelo Ndlovu-Gatsheni writes: "When Mandela presented himself as 'a humble servant of the people' he was announcing a new conception of politics in which the exercise of power is not for the self but rather on behalf of the people."[101] The myth of being a humble servant, the myth that Mandela will, by himself construct, did not last as he was more serving to white sensibilities as opposed to black aspirations insofar as the question of racism is concerned. Posel notes: "In the case of the 'new' South Africa, the early ingredients of Madiba magic were distilled during Mandela's years in prison, when he began the role of crafting himself as principal magician."[102] The new conception of politics that Ndlovu-Gatsheni points out to is the one that has to do with the politics of life as opposed to what he calls the "paradigm of war." Mandela, according to this line logic, struggled to promote the "paradigm of peace" which is predicated on "decolonial ethics of liberation."[103] Indeed, Ndlovu-Gatsheni does not agree with Posel with regard to the myth of "magic." It is on this that, as Posel insists, the work of mythologization has been done and this even went beyond Mandela himself. Mandela, a symbolic capital couched as myth, became a sort of insurrectionary figure, one who emerged from the prison tomb to the world—the second coming of some sort. "If apartheid ended in part because of the myth of Mandela, it must be remembered that that myth was only partially of his own making."[104]

The whole economy of signs has been evoked in mythologizing Mandela and declaring the choreographed negotiated transition being dubbed, fallaciously so, a miracle. Everything came with the pressure that was mounted by a myriad of anti-apartheid forces and the modern colonial world and its racial capital which has imposed sanctions on the regime that is not even far different from its racist operations. The force was exerted so that the struggle should be waged at the negotiation table. It is worth pointing out the fact that the negotiations did not start in CODESA, but while Mandela's House was being cushioned in prison—"secret talks." So, dubbed miracle is not the result of the revolutionary struggle. The negotiated settlement resulted in the ANC taking political power and land, capital and resources remained in white hands—thus, racial inequalities deepened—the crown of it all being that South Africa is now the most unequal society in the world along racial lines. What, then, is miraculous or magical about this? Posel writes: "The production of what would become known as Madiba magic emerged through a series of high- and low-profile performances of statesmanship and their widely (even if not uniformly) ecstatic reception within the polity. The first was the global spectacle of Mandela's release from Victor Verster Prison on February 11, 1990."[105]

Definitely, this economy of signs is nothing but dissimulation. The symptomatic play of euphoria is what is made to be apparent, and Mandela is paraded as a symbol. According to Ndlovu-Gatsheni, Mandela is a decolonial humanist, and he argues that this is an appropriate label because it is open-ended.[106] Contesting the fact that he cannot be pigeon-holed into one ideological label, this means that he is a complex phenomenon. Better still, the label of being a liberal, which Ndlovu-Gatsheni disavows him from, is what sticks out insofar as his mythologization, political thought, and statesmanship goes. For, he struggled for a liberal constitutional democracy, and this is the regime that he presides over as the president. It is Mandela's liberalism that encapsulates his conception of "long walk to freedom." This long walk means having reached it in 1994 euphoric inauguration—the "new" South Africa, the Rainbow Nation.

> Mandela articulated the struggle for freedom as a "long walk." The concept of a "long walk" captures how the struggle involved expenditure of human energy. In the concept of a "long walk" there is the element of sacrifice and commitment towards reaching a certain destination. To Mandela the "long walk" included "walking in the shadow of death" in search of freedom. It would seem from the allegory of the struggle of freedom as a "long walk," Mandela understood freedom as a form of "arrival."[107]

Indeed, freedom is not a moment of arrival as Ndlovu-Gatsheni illuminates. However, to Mandela, who has taken this "long walk," 1994 marked the arrival of that freedom. The spirit through which this "long walk" is embodied, as stated by Mandela, is worth noting.

> I have walked that long road to freedom. I have tried not to falter; I have made missteps along the way. But I have discovered the secret that after climbing one great hill, one finds that there are many more hills to climb. I have taken a moment here to rest, to steal a view of the glorious vista that surrounds me, to look back on a distance I have come. But I can rest only for a moment, for which freedom come responsibilities, and I dare not linger, for my long walk is not yet ended.[108]

These are Mandela's closing words in his freedom narrative. But then, the symbolic economy and the post-1994 euphoria suggest, affirmatively declare even, that freedom has been won. It is liberal constitutional democracy and it must be defended. What, then, is the radical continuity of the struggle? The long walk has been suspended. What took cause is having "opted for a non-racial liberal democratic model but not for true independence."[109] What has been entertained is what is far from what is at stake—antiblack racism. The declaration of non-racialism does not, at all, mean the absence of antiblack racism. After the euphoria has evaporated, the nightmare that scandalizes the "Rainbow Nation," the falling of the mask called a unified nation, the "new" South Africa, all the myths of Mandela's House, the reality sets and it is still that long past that is still a continued haunting. The long walk to freedom has not reached the destination if this freedom meant the end of dehumanization of the black. But the persisted arrival of this long walk due to the perversity of the myth of miracles, the pathological lies of Mandela's house, is nothing but iconicity of play. Everything is just symbolic. The mythology of Mandela just came as the result of the "deliverance" of the saint as the persona, but he came with nothing in hand insofar as the freedom is concerned, because this is the freedom he was given by his jailers and oppressors.

The sainthood of Mandela came as a result of him transforming from a black revolutionary to a liberal humanist.[110] To be such a figure means being palatable to white sensibilities and to model oneself as "reasonable." Posel marks Mandela's change from "a locus of his personal transformation from anger and aggression to a more controlled, if still commanding presence—without forgiving and of his stature as a heroic and forceful black leader."[111] Sontag even shows how a single figure can be singled out, set as exemplary, and constructed into a symbol.[112] This construction can even be extended to corrupted means. Thus, the symbolized figure might be complicit in this—Mandela that is. Here is a liberal Mandela, the one who, to be deemed reasonable, sensible, rational, likable and all things liberally induced, must renounce his blackness as the desire is nothing but to be a symbol. By maintaining sainthood and the imagery of "Mr Nice Black" he must, at all costs, be on the side of the human and not black which is deemed to be taking the country back to the "dark days" of apartheid. The only way forward, the one that is liberally palatable, the white-liked-black Mandela is made to be, is for him to be a liberal humanist. The dehumanization of black people is a concern for a black revolutionary and of a lesser concern to a black revolutionary turned a liberal humanist.

> The reappropriation of land and the nationalization of the main industries of the main industries project that Mandela announced when he walked free from Victor Verster Prison in February 1990 was abandoned during the negotiatiations. Restitution, reparations, and the reappropriation of the confisticated land from the whites were abandoned in favor of a policy of economic growth as a prerequisite for the redistribution of resources.[113]

The law in Mandela's House is that of the liberal consensus. It is the one that rules, and this is the script that Mandela choreographed, and thus being in unison with white liberals under the notion of being "progressive." This project is the one that guaranteed the safety of whiteness and Mandela's House became the site where the command to silence black aspirations and frustration came from. The law in Mandela's House is that, as More rightfully states, race becomes muted. For More, the climate of race eliminationists project found ground. This is what More says of Mandela:

> No human being in the late twentieth and early twenty-first centuries has been deified, glorified and constructed into a universal iconic figure as Nelson Mandela, the first black President of the "New" South Africa. He even attained unprecedented and unparalleled saintly status partly because of his portrayal of himself as an icon of race-transcending South African leader and moral excellence.[114]

Just because Mandela is liked by whites, even the racist conservatives felt safe that they could do as they please because blacks will be reprimanded by Mandela for being out of line with regard to the spirit of the reconciliation, rainbow nation, and in a silly way, not having the spirit of Ubuntu. The discourse of raise was just blackmailed under the banner of political correctness. "The death of apartheid and the introduction of liberal democratic constitution therefore meant that talk, writing or any discourse on race should stop in order to combat any semblance of racism."[115] This would become the rule of Mandela's House where non-racialism is paraded while glossing over the antiblack racist plague that is directed and affecting the black. The white racists even used Mandela as a weapon against any criticism of racism. In Mandela's House, More asserts, there is no racism as South Africans are all human in the Rainbow Nation.

As what More calls "Mr Nice Black," Mandela is liked by whites because he claims race insignificant.[116] He is even used as the exemplar in black faith where whites will, with arrogance and condescension, say "you must be like Mandela." This is the only figure they can refer to. Even when racism is called out, it is this line of defense that will be pulled. "Behaving like Mandela is a euphemism or code for deference, patience, forgiveness, reconciliation and absolute love of whites."[117] Mandela is liked by whites because he makes racism to be a silent scandal. It is not that he is genuinely liked by whites; he is their good weapon to make the race elimination effective. When it comes to dealing with racism and Mandela's reluctance to do so, or his mode of silencing, whites rally behind him as they parade him as the unifier of the nation as if there is anything like a unified nation in the racist South Africa.

Mandela's House is not built on his rules. The illusion is that post-1994 South Africa is a united nation, one and nonracial South Africa, while this is a lie. Whites like Mandela insofar as he panders to their sensibilities and does not rock the racial boat or cross the racial fault line. More emphatically asserts that "Mandela is the white world's darling and hero."[118] Mandela knows this, and this is what he has been using in his self-mythologization. By wanting not to be seen as a terrorist but a reasonable man, he wanted to be loved by whites, even that would mean at the expense of blacks who suffered the antiblack racism. The praise that Mandela got is the one that ruled Mandela's House. Indeed, his house but not his rules.

FOR AZANIA: ON CRITICAL CONJUNCTURES

Azania, in answering to its own name, and it being taken up by those who want to bring it to being without being concerned with what others say it was, is given a new name. It is, as a sematic drift, exercised upon to illuminate a concept—the rightful name for a country. In what emerges as praxis, the politics of naming taken upon as the transformative force, or what More calls "transformative power," naming is not only a semantic injunction but a semantic drift.[119] By rebelling against any command, the command which sematic injunction is, the semantic drift not only injects meaning but also comes with the inscriptive power, a declaration that answers in its own name. It is the politics of naming that makes it possible to then think about the Azania, and it being the transformative power that More gestures toward in accounting for philosophical anthropology of those who have even been denied to name anything, even themselves.

For the fact that Azania originates in the annals of the Pan-Africanist Congress and Black Consciousness Movements, transformative forces that cannot be housed in Mandela's House, forces loathed as irrelevant by Mandela himself due to them not having the hegemonic muscle of the ANC, it is of interest to note that the philosophical anthropology that comes from these marginalized sites of the black liberation struggle for Azania. Being rooted and footed in Black Consciousness—a philosophical medium and expression—More even calls it the "transformative philosophy of Black Consciousness in a world which is fundamentally still gripped by antiblack racism not dissimilar to invidious apartheid racism."[120] The semantic drift of Azania is symbiotic to Black Consciousness as a transformative philosophy. Why the sematic drift qua Black Consciousness? Biko has this to say: "In stages during my life I have managed to outgrow some of the things the system taught me."[121] The system that taught Biko that the country that he is born, living, and struggling to live in as South

Africa is what, together with his Black Consciousness Movement comrades, and their elders in the Pan Africanist Congress, they are subjecting to a semantic drift and calling for Azania. The semantic injunction called South Africa, which became Mandela's House as More states, is what has led to decadence.[122] Not moving from the semantic injunction is what, for Biko, is illuminated thus:

> This is the first truth, bitter as it may seem, that we have to acknowledge before we can start on any programme designed to change the status quo. It becomes more necessary to see the truth as it is if you realise that the only vehicle for change are these people who have lost their personality. The first step therefore is to make the black man to come to himself; to pump back life into his empty shell; to infuse him with pride and dignity, to remind him of complicity in the crime of allowing himself to be misused and therefore letting evil reign supreme in the country of his birth. This is what we mean by an inward-looking process. This is the definition of "Black Consciousness."[123]

The semantic drift of Azania in the annals of Black Consciousness not only assumes a different meaning and expression, but it becomes the living embodiment of Azania. That is also the case even in the Pan-Africanist Congress roots where Black Consciousness draws the phenomenon of Azania from. The definition of Black Consciousness, which comes as the result of the black coming back to the self, and not wallow in the alienation that the idea of South African has been orchestrated to be, is the transformative force that More has been insisting upon, the force which does not agree to the liberal consensus whose structured sensibilities are reigning supreme in the mythology of Mandela's House.[124]

In Azania, there will be no way that white supremacy will be allowed to reign supreme, and the transformative force that infuses this philosophy is the one that uproots antiblackness, and thus makes a radical break with the past that still haunts the post-1994 South Africa—Mandela's House.

Athi Joja states clearly that South Africa is not only a country without a name, what he calls "a geographic designator" which, in the lack and absence of its name "but also a settler colony."[125] The post-1994 which More has been referring to as flag freedom is foregrounded, and thus illuminated by Joja who dubs it a "nonevent of freedom." It is in this condition that there is no freedom to speak of even though there is that noisy orgy about its attainment is just the carnivalesque orgy is nothing by "Madiba Magic." The nonevent of this freedom also bears relevance to Azania. The conquered blacks, in the name of South Africa, are subjected to sing the staccato chorus of the songs of freedom (chief among them being the botched *Nkosi Sikelel iAfrika*). This bastardized anthem is the cocktail with the apartheid's national Anthem *Die*

Stem—the song of the Rainbow Nation—Mandela's House anthem whose sainthood cannot be criticized as this is tantamount to blasphemy.

The name Azania has been contested at the level of not only its meaning but its etymological root. John Hilton has been one of the most formidable figures in this etymological project stating its allusions, iterations, alterations, trajectories, and genealogies but one thing for sure being the contestation whether it has Hamito-Semitic rather than Negroid roots.[126] Joja writes: "All these heightened interests in its historical, etymological and to demythologized perspectives, index a certain panic."[127] One thing is for sure, even under Hilton's careful investigation that Azania "therefore may have been a blend of Arabic and the indigenous African language in the region."[128] Even though Hilton somehow is hesitating to submit that Azania is rootedly black, and giving credit to Greece as the origin, a typical philosophical and classical gesture. Hilton, along this line, writes: "The name has since been given other interpretations and modern interpretations of the name reflect the ideological importance currently attached to it in South Africa."[129] It still stands that Azania is everything in reference to blackness.

Azania, for Joja, is a decisive site of antagonism.[130] For, it is rooted in the revolutionary praxis of Jafta Masemola (the aforementioned long-serving political prisoner who did time in Robben Island more than Mandela from the Pan-Africanist Congress). The installation of the concept of "the master key," the one that, as Joja notes, Masemola cloned while he was in Robben Island, is the freedom key. This master key's function is to open the bars that incarcerate Azania. Moreover, this master key, to extend from Joja, is not operating within Mandela's House, but the jail that Mandela's House is confined into. Masemola's master key will open the whole jail, which is South Africa to free Azania from conquest, capture, control, and occupation. This key, which results from Masemola's own formation will, according to Joja, solidify ideas that continually open their formations.

From the political project of the Pan-Africanist Congress, and the philosophical elucidation and cementation of Black Consciousness, Azania is taken not only at the different meaning that is non-contextual as Hilton claims. It is, in fact, foregrounded in the lived experience of being-black-in-an-antiblack-world. It is this semantic drift that also resurrects the word from its shallow burial whose obscurity was rendered to be the fall in history that will never rise. It so happened that the raising of consciousness from the annals of anti-colonial resistance made this name to be retrieved and it was injected with a soul, a black one at that, the soul that is no longer the possession of whiteness and whose instrumentalization is subjected to be an artifact, the thing that cannot be in the black bodily possession. The black soul is embodied and everything is claimed by the black. The word Azania underwrites the drive of what More insists to be a transformative force.[131]

This force is the change of the word Azania. It is this force that will not fall from the etymological fancy of Hilton which presents itself as the final say, and thus rendering the use of the word Azania in South Africa is erroneous.[132] Nor is the contest made to claim that Hilton is right or wrong, except him being dead wrong, to wrong the black using the name Azania to rename the country that has been taken away from them through conquest. Not only they have the right and duty to name the country, they have named it anyway. The transformative force of this naming was not exerted by firstly having to consult with the etymological accuracy of the word Azania. They found its meaning resonating with their lived experience, and thus the name being the spirit through which the transformative force of what More what-ought-to-be being engendered.[133] Azania emerged—in a politicized fashion of the anti-colonial struggle—within the ranks of organizational framework called Pan-Africanist Congress. The outlook and expression of this organizational framework was the effort of strengthening the identity through which the broader struggle is enunciated, and in no way will that be taken from a rootless position of alienation and ambivalence.

For those who are in the quest of the self-that-knows-thy-self, More's imperative of what-ought-to-be is well fitting. Thus, they should, in the pursuit of their struggle, name themselves in the ways that are identical and fused with their struggle *to be*. Here, Azania should be understood, in the philosophically anthropological sense of More, as the politics of being driven by the imperative of having to account for the black lived experience, the being of the black in the world that denies the humanity of the black.[134] In the light of this context, Azania is the generative force. It is the name that has nothing to do with the worshiping of the past, but subjecting that past to the transformative force that will give it the revitalization. This has been the stance of the Pan-Africanist Congress, and Black Consciousness Movement gave this a philosophical expression, and with the elevation of consciousness to make the self-that-knows-thy-self, and in what Biko captures as the self-coming-back-to-the-self—say, Black Consciousness.[135] Biko amplifies:

> Blacks are not out to completely transform the system and to make of it what they wish. Such a major undertaking can only be realized in an atmosphere where people are convinced of the truth inherent in their stand. Liberation therefore, is of paramount importance in the concept of Black Consciousness, for we cannot be conscious of ourselves and yet remain in bondage. We want to attain the envisioned self which is a free self.[136]

The genealogical connection of the Pan-Africanist Congress to Azania, it being radically invented through critical black *poeisis*, that effort being philosophically experimented by Black Consciousness, gives Azania not only a contextually fitting account, but it becomes a necessity (not only at the level of a claim being made or any sort of a declarative intent)—More's ought-to-be as the result of putting the transformative force to its rightful use.[137] It is the intentioned action that makes the semantic drift necessary. In this semantic drift, taking from Biko's illumination above, Azania as the land of the free will also means the land of the free self. This is the antithesis of Mandela's House which is in the bondage of the *longue durèe* of the racist-settler-colonial-segregationist-apartheid-nonracial-constitutionalist-apparatus. Azania, the radical break, the *tabula rasa*, is what the African National Congress has been resisting and wanting the cushioned route to liberation.

It has to be stated, more than Hilton, the African National Congress has been the one resistant force against the word Azania.[138] The use of the name Azania, the sparked criticism it elicited from the African National Congress became the subject that Hilton commented upon to say that the uses to which the name Azania has been put is subject to many interpretations, and this deserves the comment and contextualization of the scholarship of the nineteenth and twentieth centuries[139] Truly, this is the task that the Hilton took and where the African National Congress criticism left of, Hilton did make a commentary, sketchingly brief, however.

The name Azania as the new name for a new South Africa was, according to Hilton, embraced by the Pan-Africanist Congress in All-African Peoples Conference at Accra, Ghana, in December 1958. This was a platform which meant, for the Pan-Africanist Congress, the right to name oneself, and that being the right to name South Africa. Continuing with this, Black Consciousness Movement took the name as a right proposition. According to Hilton, the name Azania "become more popular, with the formation of the Azanian People's Organization (AZAPO), the Azanian Students' Organization (AZASO), and many other Black civic organizations."[140] This is necessary as the name made sense with the struggle.

The only reason, which the African National Congress does not want to admit, is that Azania is not the name it came about. If it did, it would have embraced the name. If fact, in the radical elements of the African National Congress—the radical Africanist tradition who do not embrace the liberal Freedom Charter—there is no *ad hominen* rejection of Azania. This is the tradition that is skeptical and critical of liberal and communist influence within the movement. But as it is known, its traction is not powerful and it is marginalized just like the Pan-Africanist Congress and Black Consciousness, outside the African National Congress, of course. Due to the interpellation of liberalism's progressive politics and communist influence of the South African Communist Party (whose Stalinist Soviet names and tendencies go unchecked), the African National Congress have even gone to the extent of rejecting the word Azania and calling it a myth that must be abandoned, the spirit of the title of the anonymous article in its periodical *Sechaba*. The rejection of Azania goes like: "It would not only be politically misleading and dangerous, but historically quite wrong to think of renaming South Africa, or any part of Southern Africa, as 'Azania'."[141] This appears as the alarm, and read in another sense, or understood from the white liberal influences aforementioned, this is plausible. The African National Congress has done the job of their white masters. "Things remain as they are; South Africa is a country without a name."[142] The African National Congress denied the name Azania and still continues to hold on to the name of oppressors. This alarmist stance can even be mistaken as the *swaart gevaar* (the black peril). This alarm reads as if it is also the apartheid propaganda. With a condescending tone, the alarmist African National Congress goes on at some length to say:

> Politically, it is objectionable for a progressive national liberation movement to give any importance at all to name changing at this stage of the struggle. Recent history, in Africa and elsewhere, has shown what false trails and dead ends people can be led to by unrepresentative small groups or regimes which try to capture popularity by changing names—without a broad consensus—to sound more "authentic," then wave them aloft as a substitute for slogans with real political content and meaning. When embarked upon as a form of self-gratification for misdirected intellectuals, and in the place for a proper analysis of the real issues this kind of practice can be a useful tool of imperialism, which likes to lay false trails for people to dissipate their militancy.[143]

In this scathing attack against the Pan-Africanist Congress and Black Consciousness, in this utter disdain of the word Azania, the alarmist stance of the African National Congress is leaking. For, it claims that it is the progressive national liberation movement and speaks lesser if not in imperialistic terms by liberally labeling these movements as being led by "misdirected intellectuals." The slander goes further to suggest that they are, in calling for Azania, tools of imperialism. To retort, George Wauchope writes: "The term 'Azania' carries with it an essentially anti-imperialist content." [144] The name was key in helping to situate the struggle in Africanist terms, the terms which are not alien to the black lived experience. But then, why is the passionate insistence on the alarmist stance and disavowing the radical expression if not the reappropriation of the term Azania? Is this alarmist stance not a useful tool of colonialism—the divide-and-rule tactic which the African National Congress is out-rolling *en-masse* in its disdain for fellow blacks who are oppressed like them? Is this *swaart gevaar* not, paradoxically, evoked by the African National Congress?

The criticism continues, however, though:

> Whatever the name is to be chosen for a free South Africa when the time comes, it is for the people themselves to choose, and not for a small group to foist synthetic labels on to the struggle, the cause or the goal. If there is ever to be a new name for our country—or for any part of southern Africa—it should certainly not be Azania, because (a) it is riddled with connotations of cultural aggression towards blacks, going back to ancient times, and of imperialism, colonialism and slavery, and (b) it was the name used for a different part of Africa altogether.[145]

Of course, the justificatory reasons, two which are chief, is that Azania's connotations. But what about the connotations of the African Nationalist Congress embrace that still riddle liberalism and communism (the ultra-Stalinist one for that matter) and that not being a matter of concern for the African National Congress? Indeed, the recent and persistent history of liberal and communist shenanigans is what the African National Congress mutes. The second justification borders on xenophobia, if not ultra-nationalism who autochthony is absurdity at best. What is wrong with using Azania even if it was the name used in different parts of Africa? Just like Hilton study shows, the African National Congress goes on to write: "First ancient Greeks, then the Persian colonists of the east coast applied the name to parts of Eastern Africa which are much further to the north"[146] The African National Congress is correct on this classic-historical note, and it is not as if the Pan-Africanist Congress and Black Consciousness Movement do not know the etymology of the concept. Do they use the concept in the sense that it has been classic-historically inscribed? Of course, the African National Congress knows that this is not the case. By admitting that Azania means black, and it thus being used in a pejorative sense to mark different ontologies, and that being weaponized against blacks, there is a different way that the name is being used by blacks.

Surely, the African National Congress knows this better from its liberal and communist influences—that is, the proponents of its ideological formation and expression. Also, liberalism and communist being the African National Congress critical embrace because it has synthesized these influences to fit their context. Indeed, the question cannot be: Why not cut Azania some slack? This, indeed, is not the responsibility of the African National Congress but solely that of Pan-Africanist Congress and Black Consciousness who must answer in their own name, Azania. Why? "The word, in all its forms, has connoted racial contempt for over a thousand years, and is an unsuitable name for any part of Africa."[147] The African National Congress, again in bad faith, does not say the same with liberalism and communism. The two do not have any roots in Africa. The two are laced with the long and continued history of antiblackness. But they are used, rightfully, with modified inflections that are rooted with the black experience as the primary force. Is the African National

Congress not accusing the Pan-Africanist Congress and Black Consciousness for what it is doing far worse? Is non-racialism not an imperial force of race denialism? Is the name South Africa not a colonial name?

It is of interest that the African National Congress refers to the name Azania as a myth. Is the liberation struggle of the very same African National Congress not found on myth? The Pan-Africanist Congress and Black Consciousness Movement are found on myth, and which also serves the calibrating force that makes the struggle to continue. Myth, in the black existential struggle is not trapped in the logical positivist empiricist terms just like the African National Congress, which will just reject the concept because "it makes no sense." From the black radical thought tradition, which the African National Congress is part of myth has been foundational. Why, then, the disavowal? Myth is political and the political is myth. This is clear in the existential struggle—the clash of myths. The myth of the colonization is challenged by the myth of the black existential struggle. The myth of colonization, backed by psychic power, fire power, technical power, technologized power, forms of power which are far accelerating and fundamentally racist, turn things into reality because they inform the modern colonial world. The dissimulation of the world is intensified because it does not want its myths to be seen.

Myth, in its affirmative and pejorative sense, is what will not be belabored on. Suffice to say that myth is real, in that it can be drawn from to bring reality into being or it can be turned out to be reality. The African National Congress, despite this irreducible nature of myth, insists that Azania is a myth and it should be abandoned. This is propagated with the ferocious passion of alarmist nature. This alarmist nature of the African National Congress, which is the claim that the name Azania will be "political misleading" and, at best, "dangerous" is what not substantiated at all. It is not clear, from this spirited criticism, what are the consequences that comes with such alarmist force. Also, there is no effort made to distill the mythical nature of Azania except for referring to the classic-historical facts, assumptions, assertions, claims, narratives, and the like.

In an acute response to the criticism by the African National Congress, and in defense of the name Azania, George Wauchope writes: "There often exist an undeclared state of war among people involved in the struggle for liberation as between those who support and those who are against the use of the name Azania as an alternative name for a liberated South Africa."[148] It is the name that will come, and which, in every sense, it should stand for what it means—the land of the free. It is, in this sense, imperative to take More seriously who says that land is the base—say, the fundamental basis through which the conception of Azania is predicated.[149] The Pan-Africanist Congress and Black Consciousness are clear on this, and they are so identical in this firm position. There is no way that the landless can claim Azania, just like the African National Congress has claimed victory while land dispossession reigns. The importance of land is Azania is key, and for More, "land is the most essential requirement for life."[150] Wauchope's conception of Azania, it being tied to land, is one of his expressive points of his criticism against the criticism that the African National Congress has launched against those who are for and of the name. "Those who oppose the use of the name Azania often argue that it means 'the land of the slave'."[151] Directing this to the African National Congress' criticism, and exposing it for its liberal attachments by waning to do nothing with those fellow blacks who have been subjected to and subjugated by slavery, and thus painting everything "progressive," the name Azania if it had to do with be fitting since those who are in the liberation struggle are identical to slaves. The rejection of the name Azania has everything to do with the space inhabited by slaves or slaves themselves, borders on the absurd, that being a ludicrous rejection. Since the African National Congress claims to be direct in its intellectual acumen and it being informed by "proper analysis," Wauchope retorts: "This is a contradiction in terms, for slaves are by definition people who are owned; they can hardly own a thing, let alone land."[152] This damning clarification, which then states the condition of landlessness of the slave, and the landless that still haunts post-1994 South Africa, is the scandal that wrecks the African National Congress as it fails to conceptualize the land question. It is this failure which, in its criticism of Azania, that clearly shows that it did not take the land question very seriously. As More states:

> Given the disparity in land ownership, property, citizenship, voting rights, and so on that came with the oppressive apartheid regime. We need to ask the question: Was there any significant transformation after Mandela became president on April 27, 1994? I think the initial appropriate question to be asked in order to put things into proper perspective is: What kind of means led to Mandela's presidency? It is well known that the transition from apartheid to Mandela came about not through a revolutionary break or complete discontinuity with the past, but through a negotiated settlement commonly dubbed the "South African Miracle."[153]

The Azania that the African National Congress venomously criticized, which would bring humanity to the dehumanized black, makes the "new" South Africa to be a sham. For, there is, in the "new" South Africa, the pathology of landlessness. Since land is life, as More firmly asserts, this life is denied in the "new" South Africa. In Azania, land is, first and foremost, the imperative.

Its meaning, resolves Wauchope, goes like: "There, Azania mean the land of Black people."[154] It is for this name being powerfully inscribed, and its use being to properly to re-situate it in the annals of the slave rebels who were resolute in their pursuit of being free—the *Zanj*. Woachope here is in synch with More's philosophical formulation: what-ought-to-be. Accordingly, Wauchope calls for "Azanians to resume their position as pace-setters in the world."[155] It is this position that serves as a foundation through which More's philosophical anthropology is enunciated insofar as the politics of naming are concerned. As for Biko, this "expresses group pride and the determination by the blacks to rise and attain the envisaged self."[156] It is through this effort, on this operative basis, that the notion of ought-to-be is inscribed through the transformative force that yearns for fundamental change that Azania is as opposed to it being just a shell decoration by what More calls flag freedom which is not freedom at all because the ought-to-be has been abandoned.[157]

The ought-to-be, as More is relevant in the politics of naming, and Azania as the case in point.[158] Here, in terms of Azania, More says: "To use the word to name is to bring something into existence and reclaiming of a word also constitutes a decisive aspect of the struggle."[159]

Azania as what-ought-to-be, should, as More insists, what should be brought into existence. For More, this is what "matters most." It is that thing which cannot be done without. As the matter of dealing with the lived reality, what-ought-to-be is a response to what denies this possibility, and it thus comes as a fundamental response in a sense that it necessitates that possibility, however denied. Azania is what should be realized, what-ought-to-be. In its name, the existential struggle is defined—say, named. Azania is the land of the free, the struggle being launched to bring its reality into being. Azania is a problem for thought; it is the problem that is through the existential struggle in order to bring into being different conditions of possibility.

For More, the naming of Azania is imperative. This naming did not come just as the arbitrary expression by deep philosophical engagements whose encounters have been to face dehumanization. For the fact that Azania comes as the radical expression of those who speak, think, write, and struggle in their own name, it is in no uncertain terms that Azania is nothing but the politics of life that is livable. Azania came as a result of intentioned moral deliberation in the face of dehumanizing antiblack world.

Averting the risk of being too hasty, the fundamental error on the concept Azania, and its bastardization so to say, it is worth paying brief attention to the use of the name by Barry Buzan and H. O. Nazareth as what will originate from a "political deal" (say, a negotiated settlement).[160] They even forecast:

> There are two main alternative routes to the emergence of Azania. The first is based on sustained white intransigence, a long and bitter cycle of violence and repression causing massive economic damage, the eventual defeat of white rule, the imposition of an extremist black government, and the driving out of other

> races. There are all the markings of this scenario, and it is widely held to be the most probable one. That belief may tend to act as a self-fulfilling prophecy. But when the spectre of all-out civil war which it promises begins to become a daily reality, attitudes may change sufficiently to open up an alternative, less catastrophic outcome.[161]

Again:

> The 'decolonization' process that produces Azania will be unique. Three factors stand out: first, the period of white rule has been very long; secondly, the period of the blacks' struggle for power has been protracted; and thirdly, the urban and industrial experience of a substantial portion of the black population has been considerable and long-lasting. No other sub-Saharan state has been forged in conditions like this, and they will give Azania some tremendous advantage.[162]

The name Azania, as erroneously deployed by Buzan and Nazareth, instead of South Africa, is the very basis of criticism. For, in this account they give, they are not referring to the political project of the Pan-Africanist Congress and Black Consciousness, but the project of the African National Congress, and also the United Democratic Front. Indeed, there are slight differences in rendering South Africa ungovernable by both the African National Congress and the United Democratic Front. This was not done in the name of Azania as Buzan and Nazareth falsely claim even if they say "we can sketch some of the main features of Azania quite clearly."[163] The Azania they both propagate is the name that has nothing to do with its major drivers—the Pan-Africanist Congress and Black Consciousness Movement. That is why the two are glaringly missing. It is for this reason that Buzan and Nazareth continue with great error to say:

> If Azania is to come into being as a result of a deal, without destroying its assets in a protracted civil war, then a new social coalition will have to be created as the basis for the country's political life. The obvious vehicles for this coalition are the African National Congress (ANC) and the United Democratic Front, which already cross the racial divides of apartheid between blacks, Indians, and whites. The widely circulated 1955 Freedom Charter supported by these groups contains a blueprint for a multiracial state. The existence of long-established, non-tribal, multiracial organizations is one of the greatest assets that Azania will have in sustaining a modern state. Both Indians and liberal whites—and the capital they command—will have every incentive to support such a coalition.[164]

The use of the word Azania is fundamentally wrong in the light of Buzan and Nazareth's prognosis. It is so wrong that even though it does not make reference to the heirs of Azania, it is foreign to the political project of the concept which means no compromise but the total seizure of power and complete eradication of antiblack racism. By pulling both the African National Congress and United Democratic Front as the only key forces, one which are tied with Azania that they reject, the tenants of Azania get glaringly missed if not corrupted.

> A broader coalition based on the ANC and UDF is probably the only hope for reaching a stable deal with the main group of conservative whites. The whites are in a strong enough position to resist the establishment of Azania if they see it as going the way of most other black-ruled states. Indeed the main question about the emergence of Azania is whether the South African government will allow a new social coalition to emerge. If they do, then there will be hope for a negotiated transition and stable Azania.[165]

The less said about Buzan's and Nazareth's grave errors, the better. What they say has nothing to do with Azania, but perhaps Mandela's House, but still, these grave errors stand to some extent. Worth noting is that nothing is said about racism in their erroneous conception of Azania. Well, they cannot be expected to as this will not help matters as they got it all wrong. For More, what they stand for is the "compromise" which they erroneously dub as the "decolonization process."[166] Their decolonization process is not decolonial at all. Theirs is just a "legal declaration" which to More is just like a declaration of emancipation. Indeed, in Buzan and Nazareth, everything insofar as the spirit of Azania as encapsulated by Pan-Africanist Congress and Black Consciousness is what More calls "flag independence." Their perverted Azania is the one that wants the status quo to be entrenched. They write: "We assume, therefore, an Azania that is majority-ruled, but in which whites retain a protected status much more entrenched than in Zimbabwe."[167] This is not a Freudian slip, it is as it is. Here is the imperialist expression of this perverted Azania:

> Economically, Azania will inherit the international interests of South Africa. It will find willing trading partners in the West, and will have every interest in maintaining and expanding existing patterns of import, export and production. Indeed a negotiated Azania would have such tremendous advantages in terms of economic and political goodwill that this factor alone should be a major influence on the reasoning of those now preparing to fight to the preservation of South Africa.[168]

Evidently, Buzan and Nazareth know nothing about Azania. It is the erroneous use of the name that is at stake. It is the name that they should have abandoned. Their imperial spirit has everything to do with South Africa—Mandela's House which More states clearly that it is a "neo-apartheid South Africa" in its post-1994 foundation.[169] The perversion of Azania has, ironically, found its way through the very own tongue of the African National Congress. In line with Buzan and Nazareth, the ranks of the African National Congress are starting to flirt with the word Azania. But of course, this is a nonevent. This is nothing but a flirt—bad faith *tout court*. Joja intimately recounts:

> In the wake of Minister of Arts and Culture Nathi Mthethwa's 2017 controversial remarks, made in a closed meeting, that it is high time that South Africa consider changing its name—to Azania, sparked a national but relatively short-lived dispute. Mthethwa had seen this intervention as continuous with the government's ongoing attempt to *Africanize* the South African landscape, by replacing colonial and apartheid commemorative imagery strewn across the country, with those that invoked heroic struggle memories. But the orientation towards Azania couldn't be more of a surprising ice cake. The uncanny familiarity of it all should have alerted us of the elasticity of white supremacy and its contemporary iterations. What prompted this newfound fondness for Azania in the Congress movement and its defecting iterations, bearing in mind the unflinching rejection of the past? The fingering of black radical nationalism as the force that prevailed over the recent student protest, which called for the falling of the colonial infrastructure and its props, might have sublimely conjured this code switching.[170]

The Azania of Pan-Africanist Congress and Black Consciousness is what More evokes, and that is the imperative of the politics of being. This is the inseparability of ontology and politics.[171] Azania is the articulation and expression of the resurrected being (the being of a new beginning) and not the resuscitated being (the being of continuity). It is in these two conceptions of being that the transformative force that More enacts will have to do with Azania as the total end of dehumanization.[172] The resurrected being is the one who emerges from the tomb of dehumanization and comes to the polity through the existential struggle whose transformative force is what-ought-to-be. This does not come as a result of a compromise but as More says, "without struggle there can be no freedom."[173] This is what Azania is as opposed to South Africa where the resuscitated being will still wake up to the same nightmare of bondage in a form of the *longue durèe* of the racist-settler-colonial-segregationist-apartheid-nonracial-constitutionalist-apparatus whose brick and mortar is Mandela's House. "In such a racist world, 'all is permitted' when it come[s] to White actions towards Blacks."[174] In South Africa, even if it is called "post," "new," "democratic," or whatever cosmetic concept, the infrastructure of racism continues which, in Azania, is something that will not see its living continuity. "Azania is the signifier. It is the politics of becoming and of possibility of uncertainty."[175] Indeed, this fitting rhetorical question by More amplifies it all in terms of Azania: "This being the case, how then can Black people fail to engage in existential and ontological self-interrogation?"[176]

Azania, in the spirit of philosophical anthropology, is predicted on the politics of being. This, in other words, is the critical engagement with the condition of being toward freedom. But this is a protracted struggle as the birth of Azania is denied. This is the being of the black in Azania, the land of the free. Clearly, the coming into being of Azania will not be the continuity of the Mandela's House which is in the bondage of the *longue durèe* of the racist-settler-colonial-segregationist-apartheid-nonracial-constitutionalist-apparatus. The dismantling of this apparatus is More's philosophical anthropology, and with what-ought-to-be, means a different mark of the conditions of freedom, which cannot be negotiated on the table of the oppressor. The African National Congress in favor of a negotiated settlement "already acquiesced to the disavowal of the settler-colonial debt."[177]

To conclude, the phenomenological understanding that More brings into being, a philosophical anthropology whose transformative force does not mean being palatable to colonial and liberal sensibilities, being affected by race and racism intensifies the call for Azania since fundamental change must be in place. The problems of existence has been antiblack and it is the transformative power that is deployed in the name of Azania that makes More's to be a potent inscription that will bring the grammar of Azania as the modality of expression of the world that is here and now, even though it is denied. Azania, in this anthropological philosophical installment that More installs, is phenomenology's gift for the world to come—Azania.

It is clear that Azania is not a name. It is, it in manifolds, a political project—that is, the necessity of what-ought-to-be. It is the becoming of the possibility denied but which does not dissipate as the result of this denial. It is the radical insistence whose tenacity is the very essence of the existential struggle itself. Those who fought for Azania, who fight for it, and will continue to fight for it, are imbued with the restless spirit that does not concede to the liberal lies and its easy exists from the "long walk" to freedom. Mandela's House has been the place of not only rest but also lull. The abandoning of the ideal of freedom, and claiming easy victories, is yet to see antiblack racism being a force that still haunts like in its longer yesteryears.

NOTES

1. Tendayi Sithole, *Steve Biko: Decolonial Meditations of Black Consciousness* (Lanham: Lexington Books, 2016). This is also drawn from Zim Nqawana's track titled "Säd Afrika (A Country Without a Name)" in Zim Ngqawana. *Zimphonic Suites*. Sheer Sound. *SSCD 072*, 2001.

2. Mabogo P. More, "Locating Frantz Fanon in Post-Apartheid South Africa," *Journal of Asian and African Studies* 49, no. 6 (2014): 1–15.

3. Ibid., 2.

4. Ibid.

5. Giorgio Agamben, *What is an Apparatus? And Other Essays*. Translated by David Kishik and Stefan Pedatella (Stanford: Stanford University Press, 2009).

6. Ibid., 8.

7. Louis Althusser, "Ideology and Ideological State Apparatus (Notes towards an Investigation)," in *On Ideology*, edited by Louis Althusser, 1–60 (London and New York: Verso, 1971).

8. Ibid.

9. Agamben, *What is an Apparatus?*

10. Ibid., 11.

11. John M. Coetzee, *White Writing: On the Culture of Letters in South Africa* (Braamfontein: Pentz Publishers, 2007), 23.

12. Agamben, *What is an Apparatus?*

13. Coetzee, *White Writing?*

14. Frantz Fanon, *Black Skin, White Masks.* Translated by Charles L. Markman (New York: Grove Press, 1967), 120.

15. Fred Moten, *Stolen Life* (Durham and London: Duke University Press, 2018), 123.

16. Anthony P. Farley, "Behind the Wall of Sleep," *Law and Literature* 15, no. 3 (2003): 421–434.

17. Ibid., 242.

18. Ibid., 245.

19. Ibid., 248.

20. J. M. Coetzee, *Diary of a Bad Year* (London: Harvill Secker, 2007), 4.

21. Ibid.

22. Farley, "Behind the Wall of Sleep," 422.

23. Gil Anidjar, "Terror Right," *CR: The New Centennial Review* 4, no. 3 (2004): 35–69. Cited in 38.

24. Ibid., 41.

25. Moten, *Stolen Life*, 53.

26. Farley, "Behind the Wall of Sleep." The law is there, in thought, by way of thinking the black outside thought, and writing the black outside the law, a way of dehumanization. The law, in its own name, operates through the violation of the black.

27. Moten, *Stolen Life*, 54.

28. Ibid., 125.

29. Ibid.

30. Farley, "Behind the Wall of Sleep," 423.

31. Mabogo P. More, "Fanon and the Land Question in (Post)Apartheid South Africa," in *Living Fanon: Global Perspectives*, edited by Nigel C. Gibson, 173–185 (New York: Palgrave Macmillan, 2011).

32. Ibid., 177.

33. Ibid.

34. Fanon, *Black Skin, White Masks.*
35. Ibid., 217.
36. Ibid., 220.
37. Fanon, "Fanon and the Land Question in (Post)Apartheid South Africa," 175.
38. Agamben, *What is an Apparatus?*
39. More, "Fanon and the Land Question in (Post)Apartheid South Africa."
40. Fanon, *Black Skin, White Masks*, 220.
41. More, "Fanon and the Land Question in (Post)Apartheid South Africa."
42. Ibid., 174.
43. Fanon, *Black Skin, White Masks*, 220.
44. More, "Fanon and the Land Question in (Post)Apartheid South Africa."
45. Ibid., 175.
46. Jared Sexton, "Affirmation in the Dark: Racial Slavery and Philosophical Pessimism," *The Comparist* 43 (October 2019): 90–111.
47. Ibid., 91.
48. Fanon, *Black Skin, White Masks*, 221.
49. More, "Fanon and the Land Question in (Post)Apartheid South Africa," 179.
50. Fanon, *Black Skin, White Masks*, 221. The Constitution is not the liberatory document for the black. It is lauded as progressive, but this is as far as it is a liberal consensus.
51. More, "Fanon and the Land Question in (Post)Apartheid South Africa," 179.
52. Fanon, *Black Skin, White Masks*, 221.
53. Aimè Cèsaire, *Discourse on Colonialism.* Translated by Joan Pinkham (New York: Monthly Review Press, 1972).
54. Ibid., 32.
55. More, "Fanon and the Land Question in (Post)Apartheid South Africa," 174.
56. Fanon, *Black Skin, White Masks*, 221.
57. Ibid., 12.
58. More, "Fanon and the Land Question in (Post)Apartheid South Africa."
59. Fanon, *Black Skin, White Masks*, 12.
60. More, "Fanon and the Land Question in (Post)Apartheid South Africa."
61. Mabogo P. More, "The Transformative Power of Lewis Gordon's Africana Philosophy in Mandela's House," Unpublished Paper, 2019.
62. Nelson Mandela, *Long Walk to Freedom* (London: Abacus, 1995), 640.
63. Ibid.
64. Ibid.
65. Ibid., 659.
66. More, "Fanon and the Land Question in (Post)Apartheid South Africa."
67. Ibid., 177. The black have been met with disappointment. When things are supposed to change, they are still regressing. The change that was expected never came.
68. Mandela, *Long Walk to Freedom*, 657.
69. Ibid., 659.
70. Ibid., 661.
71. Ibid., 662.

72. Ibid., 662–3.
73. Ibid., 663.
74. More, "The Transformative Power of Lewis Gordon's Africana Philosophy in Mandela's House."
75. Deborah Posel, "'Madiba Magic': Politics as Enchantment," in *The Cambridge Companion to Nelson Mandela*, edited by Rita Barnard, 70–91 (Cambridge: Cambridge University Press, 2014), 74.
76. Mandela, *Long Walk to Freedom*, 674.
77. Ibid., 672. The gesture of Mandela is like that of the emancipated slave thanking the master for being nice.
78. Ibid. This is a very troubling account which shows Mandela's affection to whiteness. This is not the popular feeling of the black masses who were still in the clutches of apartheid. For Mandela to thank his jailers is something that, even from a humanist compassion, still baffles logic.
79. Ibid., 673.
80. Ibid. This is troubling indeed. Mandela is still expressing the worry of his jailers.
81. More, "The Transformative Power of Lewis Gordon's Africana Philosophy in Mandela's House." Mandela has been intolerant of what he often referred to as "race talk."
82. Susan Sontag, "For Nelson Mandela," *The Threepenny Review* 28 (Winter 1987): 27. Cited on 27.
83. Mandela, *Long Walk to Freedom*, 650.
84. Ibid.
85. Ibid., 632.
86. Ibid. 650.
87. Chris Sanders, "Reflections on Mandela's Role in Ending Apartheid and Promoting South African Democracy," in *Nelson R Mandela: Decolonial Ethics of Liberation and Servant Leadership*, edited by Busani Ngcaweni and Sabelo J. Ndlovu-Gatsheni, 203–216 (Trenton: Africa World Press, 2018), 206.
88. More, "The Transformative Power of Lewis Gordon's Africana Philosophy in Mandela's House." This is the image of the black who is presented and paraded as the civilized one, the exemplary, and one who can be trusted by whites. This is the black that must be emulated, the model. But it is known that such a black is pandering to the whims of whites and is also the one who will want to be the only individual black among whites.
89. Steve Biko, *I Write What I Like* (Oxford and Johannesburg: Heinemann, 1978).
90. Mandela, *Long Walk to Freedom*, 650.
91. Ibid.
92. Ibid., 649–50.
93. Ibid.
94. Ibid., 728. The will to freedom is, to Mandela, with attachment to oppression. By having to take memories of prison and replicating them in the condition that is supposed to be lived in freedom is, as a matter of fact, very troubling.

95. Sarah Nuttal and Achille Mbembe, "Mandela's Mortality," in *The Cambridge Companion to Nelson Mandela*, edited by Rita Barnard, 267–289 (Cambridge: Cambridge University Press, 2014), 274.

96. More, "The Transformative Power of Lewis Gordon's Africana Philosophy in Mandela's House," 10.

97. Posel, "'Madiba Magic.'"

98. Ibid., 82.

99. More, "Fanon and the Land Question in (Post)Apartheid South Africa."

100. More, "The Transformative Power of Lewis Gordon's Africana Philosophy in Mandela's House," 10.

101. Sabelo J. Ndlovu-Gatsheni, *The Decolonial Mandela: Peace, Justice and the Politics of Life* (New York and Oxford: Berghahn, 2016), 25.

102. Posel, "'Madiba Magic,'" 73.

103. Ndlovu-Gatsheni, *The Decolonial Mandela*, 27.

104. Sanders, "Reflections on Mandela's Role in Ending Apartheid and Promoting South African Democracy," 206.

105. Posel, "'Madiba Magic,'" 78.

106. Ndlovu-Gatsheni, *The Decolonial Mandela.*

107. Ibid., 68.

108. Mandela, *Long Walk to Freedom*, 751.

109. More, "Fanon and the Land Question in (Post)Apartheid South Africa," 182.

110. More, "The Transformative Power of Lewis Gordon's Africana Philosophy in Mandela's House."

111. Posel, "'Madiba Magic,'" 80.

112. Susan, "For Nelson Mandela."

113. More, "Fanon and the Land Question in (Post)Apartheid South Africa," 182.

114. More, "The Transformative Power of Lewis Gordon's Africana Philosophy in Mandela's House," 7.

115. Ibid.

116. Ibid.

117. Ibid., 8

118. Ibid.

119. Ibid.

120. Ibid., 2.

121. Biko, *I Write What I Like*, 26. The internalization of self-hate is what is exorcised. The coming into consciousness will demand the black to be liberated from the racist fabrication of the black.

122. Mabogo P. More, *Looking through Philosophy in Black: Memoirs* (Lanham: Rowman and Littlefield International, 2019).

123. Biko, *I Write What I Like*, 29.

124. More, "The Transformative Power of Lewis Gordon's Africana Philosophy in Mandela's House."

125. Athi Joja, "Jafta Masemola's Master Key: Experimental Notes on Azanian Aesthetic Theory," Unpublished Paper, 2019.

126. John L. Hilton, "Azania—Some Etymological Considerations," *Acta Classica* 35 (1992): 151–159.

127. Joja, "Jafta Masemola's Master Key," 3.

128. Hilton, "Azania," 154.

129. Ibid., 156.

130. Joja, "Jafta Masemola's Master Key."

131. More, "The Transformative Power of Lewis Gordon's Africana Philosophy in Mandela's House."

132. Hilton, "Azania."

133. Mabogo P. More, *Biko: Philosophy, Identity, and Liberation* (Cape Town: HSRC Press, 2017).

134. Mabogo P. More, "Black Consciousness Movement's Ontology: The Politics of Being," *Philosophia Africana* 14, no. 1 (2012): 23–39.

135. Biko, *I Write What I Like*.

136. Ibid., 49.

137. More, *Biko*.

138. Hilton, "Azania."

139. John L. Hilton, "People of Azania." *Scholia* 2 (1993): 3–16.

140. Ibid., 6.

141. ANC, "A Time to End the Myth," *Sechaba* 11, no. 3 (1977): 64.

142. Sithole, *Steve Biko*, 121.

143. ANC, "A Time to End the Myth," 64.

144. George Wauchope, "Azania = Land of the Black People," *Frank Talk* (1984): 7–8. Cited in 8. One thing that is clear from Wauchope is that there is no liberation without the return of the stolen land. The colonial conquest that led to the territorial formation has been about land theft. The existential struggle for liberation and in the name of Azania is never complete without land.

145. ANC, "A Time to End the Myth," 64.

146. Ibid.

147. Ibid.

148. Wauchope, "Azania," 8.

149. More, "Fanon and the Land Question in (Post)Apartheid South Africa."

150. Ibid., 180.

151. Wauchope, "Azania," 8.

152. Ibid.

153. More, "Fanon and the Land Question in (Post)Apartheid South Africa," 181.

154. Wauchope, "Azania," 8.

155. Ibid.

156. Biko, *I Write What I Like*, 68.

157. More, "Fanon and the Land Question in (Post)Apartheid South Africa."

158. More, *Biko*.

159. Ibid., 46.

160. Barry Buzan and H. O. Nazareth, "South Africa Versus Azania: The Implications of Who Rules," *International Affairs* 1 (Winter 1986): 35–40.

161. Ibid., 35.

162. Ibid., 36.

163. Ibid.

164. Ibid., 37.

165. Ibid., 38.

166. More, "Fanon and the Land Question in (Post)Apartheid South Africa."

167. Buzan and Nazareth, "South Africa Versus Azania," 39.

168. Ibid.

169. More, "The Transformative Power of Lewis Gordon's Africana Philosophy in Mandela's House."

170. Joja, "Jafta Masemola's Master Key," 1–2.

171. More, "Black Consciousness Movement's Ontology."

172. More, "The Transformative Power of Lewis Gordon's Africana Philosophy in Mandela's House."

173. More, "Fanon and the Land Question in (Post)Apartheid South Africa," 176.

174. More, "Black Consciousness Movement's Ontology," 27.

175. Sithole, *Steve Biko*, 127.

176. More, "Black Consciousness Movement's Ontology," 30.

177. Joja, "Jafta Masemola's Master Key," 3. The rightful demands that are supposed to be articulated and actualized did not and still do not find traction in the post-1994 era as the obsession is building liberal democracy. The structural destruction of black life is even treated as if it is something that does not have the historical narrative of the settler-colonial debt that must be settled. The land question is even treated as if it is just a controversial matter and with nothing that bears any historical memory.

Chapter 3

Shifting the Geography of Reason

The ground from which thought is engaged is the presentation of reality, and this has nothing to do with the totality of truth or the banality of universalism. From where thought is enunciated, philosophically speaking, has nothing to do with it being the exactness of reality, or it being fixed and that calling for the abdication of responsibility as everything is empirical and it is the absolute fact as to how things are and nothing can be done about that. But there is another account—say, what can be done is what can be done and it is what must be done. Truly, thought, in itself, is a way of doing it. Thus, this depends in the modes of its framing and modes of inquiry and inscription. The modes of justification have to do with thought come through reason, and there is no finality to what is deemed reason. In its origin, intent, and purpose, and in particular, the concern being a different set of condition through which reason is taken to be not only the level of closure, but rupture, this gives reason a different conception. The call for the shifting of the geography of reason is what is at stake and this is what cannot be disavowed.

Mabogo P. More is intrinsically linked with the shifting of the geography of reason which is the motto of his philosophical home: the Caribbean Philosophical Association. It is this philosophical community that More found a home. Put ironically, a home outside home. What was supposed to be a home, The Philosophical Society of Southern Africa, became a hostile place for him, and he could not identify with it because of the problem of racism. The shifting of the geography of reason is acute description of More who had to shift his body from the South African philosophical community to one that take seriously the question of humanity and one that aims to create a better world.

Philosophy in black is More's disposition and it is the arena where reason, as a philosophical trope, is engaged in ways that are different. Reason, propagated as white, and with philosophy parachuting it as the paragon of whiteness, has been a discipline that does this arrogantly but fears to face its ugly head—racism. The problem of racism in philosophy in black is not a matter that can be avoided, including the critique of philosophy in South Africa which has the history of detaching itself from the reality that still haunts the existential landscape. It will be more expected, in South Africa, a country that is plagued by the long history of antiblack racism that philosophy will grapple with reality as it is.

More's philosophical anthropology is grounded in the lived reality that demands that reason be in service of this reality and, thus, there is no room for complicity where the racist reality cannot be dissimulated in the name of reason being universal, and philosophy is paraded as universal as if it is not situated in the reality that it is in. In philosophy in black, a clear radical stance, a mode of philosophizing that becomes a thorn on philosophy's racist flesh, becomes a way of not only articulating the world, but that of being. The reality that More is in demands philosophy to stand up to its task. As in most racist situations, philosophy in South Africa is not the exception in masking itself as reason while it is unreasonableness by virtue of not facing the racist reality that is also perpetuated in the name of philosophy. So, shifting the geography of reason, as More's philosophy in black, will show how reason in the domain of the black scandalizes what claims to be a paragon of virtue in the name of philosophy.

LOCATION AND DISLOCATION

More is dislocated in the condition where he was supposed to be located. By right of being a philosophy in the land of his birth, it is ironic that this is the location that dislocated him, but he did not, in any event, choose to be of the philosophical community that dehumanizes him. Dehumanization dislocates. The rightful place of being has to do with the very fact of being located.

Dislocation is what More took a decision on. He dislocated himself from what dislocated him. There is no way that he could be part of the philosophical community that does not recognize the being of the black. By being marginalized as the black, More took his blackness as a rallying point of his philosophical choice, and he could not ingratiate himself in The Philosophical Society of Southern Africa.

Finding a place in an antiblack world that denies the ontological presence of the black is an extraordinary affair. But the issue is not finding a place by ingratiating oneself in what misrecognizes, undermines, denies, and obliterates the self. It is clear, then, that the reality that informs More's philosophical practice is having been dislocated and he then took it upon himself to locate himself elsewhere. The way of asserting his humanity and the manner of his philosophical practice stems from not conforming to the legibility claims that are driven by the question of being recognized. Where he is doing philosophy, South Africa that is, More is a philosopher on the margins, if not a philosopher at all. The landscape which is the country of his birth sees philosophy as having nothing to do with the concerns of a black philosopher and this also includes the conditions that this philosopher (if focusing on race and racism) has to deal with. The immediacy of More's philosophical themes can be easily dismissed as nothing philosophical and thus not being relevant to philosophy itself. More, in his disposition, takes philosophy along the reality of antiblackness, and he states clearly that this is the reality that philosophy in South Africa refuses to confront and deal with.[1] More remarks: "Racism refused to die."[2] This is what he deems as the matter of philosophy, what philosophy should not disavow, what really haunts philosophy insofar as his location is concerned. More goes on to state: "Methodologically, philosophy regards the questions of 'race' and 'racism' to be questions outside the conventional realm of philosophical discourse."[3] The disavowal of race in the South African philosophical discourse clearly means More's disposition, and his location as a black philosopher, is what does not matter even though what really matters is a country that is plagued by the long history of antiblack racism.

More stands and stems from the existential fact of being-black-in-an-antiblack-world. In fact, his consistency on the matter of philosophy has, by way of it being a meta-discourse, being at the expense of his dislocation. Worth stating is the fact that he could not allow himself to be deterred. More, a nonconformist of note, philosophizes against the grain.

What has remained the racist enclave, the chamber of silence, and where the exclusionary vices and devises are operated in strenuous ways against the black, More becomes a thorn on the side by exposing South African philosophy for what it is.

> Despite the increase in race consciousness, philosophy in general, but South African philosophy in particular, have generally, sadly, ignored discourses on racism where analytic skills and philosophical reflection are most needed. Some of the reasons for the silence have to do with the fact that some philosophers, philosophy itself, and its practice have been complicitous in racism.[4]

Sadly, in South Africa, philosophy is racism's partner. More points out how philosophy has not been in good faith in confronting reality. By not asking philosophy to entertain the question of racism, More instead argues against the muzzling practices against the reality of racism in the name of philosophy. By charging against the grain, More does not cease to philosophize, he continues to do philosophy from the lived experience of being-black-in-an-antiblack-world. The nature of philosophical discourse in South Africa is what More finds very hostile to the question of race and the problem of racism, thus its antiblack make-up and posture. The embodied nature of the black, under the clutch of antiblackness, is the very idea that makes the strictures and edicts to be in standing. The way More philosophizes, therefore, is not conterminous with the supposed South African philosophical discourse. No more is philosophy a holy grail whose criticism is tantamount to what might be deemed irrelevant or irrational. The reality of the black is a point of meta-reflection and More takes that reality seriously. This reality, then, makes More to do philosophy differently. But there is nothing exceptional about this, except to state clearly that it is different because it is something that is treated differently by the South African philosophical discourse.

The dislocation that More is put at, one that makes him not to be home at home, a philosophical hobo so to say, is what individuates the annals of philosophy in South Africa. It is this reality of exclusion and being relegated to nothingness that intensifies the grip that will eliminate More and which, with the unintended consequence, will make him not to, at all, want to fit in dislocation and for him to be located elsewhere. The dislocation of More has been a mark that will even make him not, at all, to force himself to belong where he is not wanted. It is his sense of dislocation which, ironically, did not make him to even pursue being a philosopher as opposed to relinquishing what he wants to be. The location of philosophy in South Africa did not become his home since dislocation made him not to belong. His effort has not been to force matters, but to pursue his love—philosophy. It means that he is doing philosophy at the realm of dislocation as opposed to that of location where he will belong to a philosophical community. To be in a community is to be in a relationship or its plural sets. To be in a community is to belong, to be one among many, one of others, one with others, one in service of others. It is not a matter of whether there are agreements and disagreements. It is about being together. But there was nothing of togetherness in The Philosophical Society of Southern Africa as More was set, put, and torn apart.

By not being one of others, to be without, outside—it is far from convincing that More can be said to matter not only as a philosopher, but as a human being. In an antiblack world and its apartheid vortex, he was in a location where he was not supposed to be. He was not only at the wrong place at the wrong time, but at a place that he was not supposed to be at from any time. That is a place of philosophers who are deemed white qua white. He cannot *be there*. Him being there meant that it was justified for him to be dislocated. To locate More there is to really engage in an act whose outcome will be nothing but dislocation. To be there is to be made not to be there by virtue of the fact that More, a black philosopher who is not supposed to be one at that, is not supposed to be there as the black. A black philosopher cannot be there in the philosophical community but he is not supposed to be in the location of whiteness (even if such a location will be deemed inclusive and not use any criteria and category of racial exclusions). To be among whites who are doing philosophy and who do not see the black as a philosopher (or one who is not able to philosophize in "rigorous ways"), the long-held attitude has been that a black philosopher is an oxymoron. There is no such a thing as a kaffir philosopher! The dislocation of a black philosopher is justified on these silly grounds. That is why the racist question is at the crux of the matter of philosophy, and that being informed by antiblack discursive structures that do not want anything to do with black.

So, then, what is it that More is concerned with? At no point, More was going to continue to be a member of a philosophical community that does not want him and he made an honorable choice of not subjecting himself to further humiliation by manner of dislocation. By being located at the interiority and exterior of his being, his totality of being that is militated against, More claims location by making a choice. The choice he made is what he chose to live with. As such, he does so knowing that he is responsible for his choices, his location even.

More declares: "The oppressed are mainly responsible for transforming the situation they found themselves in without excuse."[5] The situation they are in has to be radically changed so that it is different. Even if they do not succeed, they still have the responsibility to go on insisting at changing it. With the concern on philosophy in South Africa, More contends that philosophy is doing what is not supposed to do by choosing to stay out of politics. More asks: "What is the social, political and moral responsible of the philosopher in South Africa or anywhere else?"[6] What philosophers are supposed to do, urges More, is to be mindful of the fact that philosophy is a political matter. Philosophy has to speak of the lived reality of the society it is in. Even though his is not reducible to it, there is no justification for philosophy to claim to be non-political. In South Africa, More avers, philosophy is in crisis. It is not that philosophy has to solve this crisis, but to, in its commitment, "redefine and breach the dimension of this challenge."[7] In this line of view this, philosophy is, according to More, implicated in politics. It cannot be out of politics. However, with a high sense of irony, More states that "to stay out of politics persists," and this is the state of affairs.[8] More declares: "South African philosophy definitely had no difficulty staying out politics."[9] This is attitudinal stance smacks not only of bourgeoisie academicism, but it stems from the very fact of avoiding the race question which is the plague that haunts South Africa and a white elephant in the philosophical landscape. Since the lasting of philosophy in South Africa has been of exclusion, those patterns of exclusion even remain gripped in the content of the philosophical script. It is not irony to find philosophy in South Africa being concerned with matters that are, under the mask of being nowhere, empiricism, and universal, being the replica of bourgeoisie academicism. The philosophical common is on that claim to be philosophy proper and that being nothing to do with the antiblack reality that South Africa is in. The continually violated life of the black is what, in South Africa, should not be philosophically marginal but central. That, as a political question, is what cannot be shoved out of politics. There is no way that philosophy can be distant to its reality and claim to be philosophy.

More has this to say about South African philosophers: "(a) a certain loyalty to certain (foreign) philosophical tradition, (b) the abdication from social and political responsibility and roles, and consequently (c) the indifference and insensitivity to suffering."[10] But going further than this, More points out the problem lies elsewhere and this, in particular, is having to be detached from reality. The claim, then, will be the insistence that philosophers in South Africa are supposed to be neutral and value-free. This, for More, does not also address the entirety of the problem which is that philosophers are invested in dissimulation. They do not want to come into contact with the reality they are in. What appears, as More shows, is "'indifference;' 'abandonment,' 'detachment,' or loyalty to certain traditions.'"[11] As if this is not enough, More charges further to note: "The paradox in philosophy is the adoption of a particular definition or conception of philosophy is simultaneously an expression of one's ideological position."[12] In this context, it is clear that there is no way that philosophy can claim to be apolitical. Philosophers are political beings who are socialized and ideologically informed by the reality they are in. They are engaged, by matter of appearance, in what More calls "anti-politics politics." This is the very legitimation of their detachment. That, at the same time, is their ambivalent position which they have deliberated, orchestrated in order not to be held accountable. Therefore, the insistence of anti-politics position has meant to save face. By lamenting on the depoliticization of what is supposed to be infused in politics, More accuses South African philosophy of nothing but sophistry. And, also, More points to something else, wherein the apolitical stance of philosopher is, in fact, a political one. There is a way that there can be the staying out of politics since those who are in a polity are political beings and by virtue of their existence, they are in politics. In going to another extent, it is worth mentioning but politics is the social activity. As More states, "there is no exit from politics anything, especially in a crisis-ridden and highlight politics society such as ours."[13] But can it be that the insistence of staying out of politics is still held on even in the face of its impossibility? More responds: "The point is, philosophers in this country have been neither apolitical nor indifferent and it becomes, as I have mentioned above, mere sophistry to even claim that they should be political; they cannot escape from politics, since the very profession of philosophy itself is already a political domain."[14] In South Africa, More states that philosophy has never been of value for the oppressed as it militates against the existential reality. The question of suffering, which has plagued the black who are the majority of location where philosophy is done, have not factored in the philosophical agenda, let alone the fact that suffering has to be, without any question, a major philosophical preoccupation. Since this is the political reality, the matter is highly political in the same manner that it is highly philosophical.

More is still in a country that never changed its stance of antiblackness and the same can be said about philosophy, which has been hell-bent to stay as it is—pure. Pure in a sense that philosophy is high in the command of humanities (the cliché of being mother of all disciplines). What is a matter of concern is that, as More argues, philosophy does not want to deal with the reality it is in. South Africa is a racist society and it is also without irony that this racist reality will be avoided as a matter of philosophical concern.

What Mogobe Ramose points out is that philosophy in South Africa does not entail whatever that can be deemed to be anything of South Africa.[15] As Ramose notes, philosophy can yield identical or different insights, as well as insights that can be "contradictory" and "contentious." In the name of objectivity, Ramose further points out that philosophy has been able to import its logic and normalize the practice of exclusion. This is done in order to legitimate "suppression, oppression and exploitation of the other."[16] Philosophy in South Africa has been, for Ramose, the "academic and practical exclusion of the longest segment of the population of the country."[17] More, in the same breath with Ramose, expresses how the systematic exclusion of philosophy has been its own justification.[18] As Ramose states, "the future of philosophy in South Africa lies in dialogue of philosophies found in the country."[19] More is of the view that philosophy should be, by way of being political, one that has to deal with the reality of South Africa.[20]

One important thing that More states is the following: "There are as diverse philosophies as there are traditions."[21] In South Africa, philosophy has been the exclusionary domain. The exclusionary domain of philosophy has meant that there is no place for the black in the philosophical discourse. More, then, asks: "What does it mean to be a philosopher of African descent in South Africa?"[22] This is an important question in the contemporary moment and the manner in which it has been asked is still, as it were, just like the yesteryear of More's philosophical life. What does it mean to do philosophy in South Africa has been a question that is troubling in the light of the exclusionary domain of philosophy itself. There has been no space in South

Africa to do philosophy as black—or, black philosophy, which is also to say, philosophy in black. Ramose states that *South African Journal of Philosophy* published for the first time a journal article by a black person in the year 1994.[23] "The result is that it took more than two decades since its inception to have an article by a South African published in the *South African Journal of Philosophy*."[24] The absence of the black in the annals of philosophy speaks volume. It means that since More chose to leave The Philosophical Society of Southern Africa, which the above journal is its mouthpiece, the structural exclusion kept on persisting right until 1994. The exclusion of the black in philosophical discourse has been a norm. More is with Ramose in terms of pointing out the systematic exclusion of the black and this has been the limit of philosophy in South Africa. Both expose philosophy for what it is. More writes: "The two journals of philosophy in the country—obviously under white authorship and editorship—until very recently, hardly published a single piece on African philosophy during their long history, even located within the geographical space of Africans."[25]

More states that philosophy does not occur in a vacuum, but it is rooted in the social milieu it is in. "Academic philosophy in South Africa has always been the terrain of whites, particularly white males."[26] It means that there is no black to think of and there is no black there. The absence of the black has been ensured by the Afrikaner (Calvinism) and English (liberal)—what More calls the ideological strategy. The two philosophical spectrums that still perpetuate racism and also disavow it. "Therefore philosophy before apartheid was fundamentally and ideologically no different from philosophy during apartheid."[27] In these aforementioned philosophical spectrums, there is nothing that has to do with the lived experience of the black except to write about the black, in most cases, in demeaning if not dehumanizing ways. But what is essential is that there is the erasure of the black. What is not reflected as well is the existential reality of South Africa. The philosophical traditions as More characterizes them are as follows: English (analytical) and the Afrikaner (continental). More amplifies: "Both philosophical traditions—the Anglo-Saxon and the Continental—therefore, in varying degrees, may have been used to provide justification for racial and cultural discrimination before official apartheid in 1948 and during apartheid in the years that followed."[28] During apartheid, More states that there are three types of philosophers that emerges, namely: "defenders, neutralist, and dissents."[29] Indeed, in the annals of philosophy, these three types do not include black philosophers. Apartheid was wholly defended by most Afrikaners philosophers. "Moreover, philosophical traditions function not only as ideologies but as particular political agendas."[30] Even though there was a dissent tradition in philosophy, the fact still remains that it was white. Black exclusion has been a motif. The racist trope has been that there is no way that there can be rationality from the black. Philosophy in South Africa is structured in the complicity of racist exclusion. This is the domain of philosophy that More critiques, one that he, himself, suffered exclusion. What More stands for, in principle, is a different conception of philosophy. In South Africa, More is on a different philosophical location—"a philosophy born of experience and struggle."[31] The kind of philosophy that More argues for gives him a critical and living voice in the black intramural space. More is trying to "also bring back the humanity of black philosophers."[32] Why is More's philosophical project different?

> The black experience is not incorporated into the philosophical experience despite philosophy's putative universality and generality. In other words, the peculiar features of black experience such a racism, apartheid, oppression, colonialism, slavery, and more are part and parcel of the expenses represented in the abstraction of white philosophy. Philosophy stays away from messy issues such as racism, slavery, colonialism, phenomena that beget poverty, crime, pain, death and more to African people.[33]

The black experience is made to be what is not important. But it is More's task that has to do with the black experience. By confronting exclusion, More did not see the necessity for him to be complicit in what crafts and maintains itself as an exclusionary domain. The exclusion of the black is what More cannot stand for and nor can he afford to be paraded as "the only black"—the syndrome that is deliberately induced to create exceptionalism, a false gesture, at best, bastardization and dehumanization. Philosophy in service of mediocrity is what More subjects to criticism. This is what has been philosophy under apartheid where mediocrity has been a mask and the very fact of black exclusion and not claiming that there is no rationality in the black who are excluded based on *a priori* assumptions—the very evidence of that mediocrity indeed.

Where More is supposed to be located, that becomes the opposite. The Philosophical Society of Southern Africa could not be his home. Here is what really made More to shift the geography of reason.

> In 1976 the annual Philosophical Society of Southern Africa's conference (dominated by Afrikaans-speaking philosophers) was scheduled to be held at the University of Pretoria. The head of department of philosophy at that university, a certain Professor P. S. Dreyer, who, incidentally was our external examiner at Turfloop, on learning that two black philosophers (me and Mr [Tintswalo] Mashamba) were scheduled to attend the conference, refused to have it held at his university. Black people were not welcome at the University of Pretoria Philosophy Department even though they were members of the Philosophical Society of Southern Africa. To accommodate us, the conference

> was moved to the University of South Africa, also in Pretoria. On learning about Dreyer's position and the subsequent late-minute shifting of the conference, Mr. Mashamba and I decided not to attend.[34]

By standing on principle, and not wanting inclusion, More could not be where he is not wanted. In recounting another incident, More recounts:

> In January 1977, I attended the Fourth Congress of the Philosophical Society of Southern Africa held at Potchefstroom University for Christian Higher Education, one of the most conservative Afrikaner domains. Again, I was the only black in attendance. This was problematic precisely because I became a phenomenon, a kind of happening. For some reason other than philosophical reasons, I became the center of attraction. No one discussed any philosophical problems or issues with me. Indeed, there was hardly any discussion except interrogation. Since that was immediately after the 1976 Soweto student revolts, I suddenly was assumed to be an expert on black political aspirations and intentions. The Soweto students had shocked the white establishment, especially because for a change there were one or two white casualties in the process. I had to field a number of questions posed by my white colleagues about the future of the country and the political developments in the townships.[35]

It is clear from the above that More's blackness was seen and not his philosophical status. So, he is made to be answerable to his blackness. His blackness is made to be a liability. More writes: "Being the only black person at the conference, the hostile and unwelcoming gaze of the ordinary Potchefstroom white people was dehumanising and piercing to the bone."[36] In emphasis, More writes: "My blackness was so extremely visible that the speaker noticed my presence and never forgot me and remembered me even when I met him twelve years later."[37] More is in a lily white and racist domain. Below is what sums it all up.

> The crowning part of my stay at the Potchefstroom Congress was on day three when, during tea break, I together with everybody else went into a hall with a cafeteria to have tea. Since I did not want to have tea but Coca-Cola, I then went to the counter to purchase one. The white woman cashier behind the counter told me straight to my face—in the presence of white philosophers, including the head of philosophy at Unisa, René Meyer, who knew me because I was a registered MA degree student in his department—that 'kaffirs' cannot buy inside but have their small window counter outside the hall. None of these philosophers really made a fuss about this except to mumble some few embarrassing words to the cashier that I was part of the group. I didn't attend the following sessions and went home.[38]

Form the incident above, More is not only being refused to be served. His humanity is militated against for having being denied in the first place and it could not be in the place that it is barred from in the first place. It is not a matter of him being only present in the racist town like Potchefstroom, but being in the community of philosophy, a white domain. He cannot be there since he, as the black, is excluded in the domain of "thinking beings" (read white qua white philosophers). The barring of thought in the black existential milieu does not reside in thought, but the whole conception of the denied being of the black. The black is made not to have a place, but to be dislocated.

Here is a principle. The venue where The Philosophical Society of Southern Africa held is what is known as the central places of racism (even today in the post-1994)—Potchefstroom—but the philosophers who cannot live up to the spirit of thinking beings who are seeing wrongs of apartheid (however this will be a naïve expectation as they are justified by apartheid and are benefiting from it). So, what More is subjected to might just be a pure "isolated incident." It is clear for More that there is nothing to expect from his alleged colleagues. More was not served and was refused—say, ejected to feel dejected and subjecting him to the rejected status. To white philosopher who were in his midst that encounter, he deserved the humiliation and dehumanization he got. It is, then, clear to More that these white philosophers are in the same racist consciousness and they are allied with the cashier at the cafeteria.

By standing on principle, More writes: "That was the last time I attended the South African philosophy conference."[39] By leaving for good and not compromising but making a clear choice, More's leaving is what marked his shift of the geography of reason. More cannot be where he is not wanted. The Philosophical Society of Southern Africa has a history of not being a home for the black.

The amount of self-respect that More accorded and afforded himself allows him to take himself very seriously. This stems from the disposition of being Black Consciousness and that is all there is to it for the self that cannot be humiliated and still act as if nothing happened. By standing for the self, there is no choice for More but to leave the Philosophical Society of Southern Africa for good. It could not be his philosophical home anymore. By paying fidelity to the principle, More did not even return to The Philosophical Society of Southern Africa even after the post-1994. He took "never again" very seriously. More reiterates: "Tired of being a lone 'school kaffir' among white men with an attitude and constantly insulted me in more ways than one, I stopped attending these annual philosophy conferences from that year."[40] He chose not to be humiliated in what he calls a philosophical community. Still to date, "never again" still stands.

The Eurocentric outlook of The Philosophical Society of Southern Africa has been a stance that More criticizes, what became a philosophical community that is divorced from the lived reality it is in. The persistent plague of antiblackness even endured in the post-1994 in nuanced liberal forms. The Philosophical Society of Southern Africa has been shouting transformation since its post-1994 posture. "This gesture does not even attempt to address the fundamental problem facing not only philosophy but also South Africa as a whole; namely, racism. In the 2016 conference, The Philosophical Society of Southern Africa, More states, even had the audacity to host a panel under the theme "South African Identity" and it was a lily white panel.

> A group of young black philosophers and students calling themselves the Society for Black Philosophers in South Africa found this objectionable and raised their concern by threatening to boycott the 2017 PSSA conference if a special session or panel was not arranged to discuss the following issues:
>
> 1. Racism and the marginalization of African philosophy
> 2. The caricature of African philosophy by South African white philosophers who have no pretension to an interest in the study of African languages and culture
> 3. The enlisting of African American philosophers in the project of supposed transformation of white the same time marginalizing local blacks
> 4. The wisdom/folly of leaving the job of changing a problematic situation to its architects or heirs.
>
> When these issues were not satisfactorily addressed by the PSSA, the Young Black Philosophers organized a huge inaugural conference of the Azanian Philosophical Society from August 28 to August 31, 2017. Clearly, the question of racism within philosophy and the larger South African society has not been resolved.[41]

The events above are the reality of South Africa. What demands to be attended to will always be disavowed. The Philosophical Society of Southern Africa saw a mass exodus of its members (both black and white, albeit for different reasons). What is of interest in cosmetic politics raising its head where those who remained resolved to elect a young black woman Mpho Masebe as a president and after her being paraded as the first black woman to have earned a doctorate (one which she has just obtained). Clearly, The Philosophical Society of Southern Africa has abdicated responsibility.

The racist treatment that More experienced during apartheid still raises its ugly head in The Philosophical Society of Southern Africa. The overhauling of the racist infrastructure is what is being called upon and there is nothing that can be deemed an incident, but the deliberate re-anchor and re-elaboration of that racism. No wonder why The Philosophical Society of Southern Africa remains untransformed even if having to be faced by the scandal brought before it by the exodus it saw. The Philosophical Society of Southern Africa has been a domain of white philosophers, and blacks who were there were treated as tokens. It has been, to draw from Leonard Harris, the "evidence for white supremacy" and a marker of exclusion.[42] If the matters that were raised by the Young Black Philosophers are to be considered, then, it is apt to say that the Philosophical Society of Southern Africa remains untransformed and it is a stage for cosmetic performance where black minstrelsy is required. More left the Philosophical Society of Southern Africa which is still the same as it was.

HOME AWAY FROM HOME

By choosing to belong to the Caribbean Philosophical Association and Philosophy Born of Struggle as a member, More located himself in the Africana existential tradition with his roots stemming from the Azanian existentialist school. By this, he assumed a mantle of a distinct philosopher—Africana existentialist philosopher. "Africana existential philosophers, therefore, deal with issues of the emergence of black selfhood, black suffering, embodied agency, freedom, slavery, racism, and liberation."[43] In the Caribbean Philosophical Association and Philosophy Born of Struggle, these are issues that are dealt with head-on.[44] In the struggle against dehumanization, it is not only necessary for Caribbean Philosophical Association and Philosophy Born of Struggle to deal with these questions, but natural.

More writes: "The inaugural conference of the CPA, under the motto 'Shifting the Geography of Reason' was held in Barbados (2004), where I was one of the keynote speakers."[45] The founding of the Caribbean Philosophical Association is what has always been aimed at making things anew, possible, necessary, and to say the least, valuable. Clearly, this is a new world of endless possibilities. For More, it has been a totally new experience to be in a philosophical community where other modes of philosophizing are possible. It is a totally different experience which the idea of a philosophical community is one that is turned into a home where there is not even a feeling of being away from home. More's keynote address means that he is tasked to be at work with other philosophers, an invitation to have the Africana existential conversation that will create a livable world. More states: "As the conference title indicates, these philosophers are intent on shifting the geography of reason from the presumed place to another."[46] With More in particular, philosopher shifted from annals of philosophy as antiblackness to philosophy in black is a livable world. This means that he is together with other philosophers in the Caribbean Philosophical Association where the existential struggle to fight for liberatory possibilities is foundational and fundamental.

> This is done by debunking racist myths about the superiority of whites and promoting Africana philosophy. The latter embraces a whole range of philosophical discourses and traditions such as African philosophy, African American philosophy, Black philosophy, Africana existential philosophy, Africana Phenomenology, Black philosophy of existence, Afro-Caribbean philosophy, and other such traditions that have emerged from the socially transformative discourses and shared concerns of persons African and African descended in their resistance and struggle against slavery, imperialism, colonialism, racism, and oppression in general. The list of subsections of Africana philosophy just mentioned above makes it quite evident that such a philosophy is concerned with issues that across a wide range of philosophical and social topics. What unifies all these traditions under the umbrella field called Africana philosophy is fundamentally the shared concern about the dehumanization or the denied humanity of African and African-descended people by systems such as slavery, colonialism, and racism, which are given philosophical justification by the philosophical anthropologies of the dominant figures in philosophy.[47]

More again:

> In addition, the CPA has close partnerships with other professional organizations such as the Afro-Jewish Studies Association, American Society for Aesthetics, North American Sartre Society, Collegium of Black Women Philosophers, Merleau-Ponty Circle, The C. L. R. James Society, Simone de Beauvoir Society, Society for the Advancement of American Philosophy, PhiloSOPHIA, Philosophy Born of Struggle, and Roundtable on Latina Feminism.[48]

Another home for More is Philosophy Born of Struggle.

> Since its inception in 1993 the conference that brought together a sizeable number of African, African American, Latino, Caribbean, and other black philosophers in the world. Philosophy Born of Struggle is a site of struggle and resistance against the European insidious belief that black people don't have the intellectual capacity to philosophize, and as a consequence, the phrase *black philosopher* is an oxymoron. Black liberation and struggle against white supremacy became the philosophical *leitmotif* of the group. While PBOS is primarily a philosophical organization, it is, however, not exclusively philosophical but inclusive of other disciplines as well.[49]

In both the Caribbean Philosophical Association and Philosophy Born of Struggle, More finds home.

> The issues dealt with in both the PBOS and the CPA are definitely issues that the South African philosophical circle will would not dare engage. As a matter of fact, such issues should be considered nonphilosophical by the South African mainly white philosophical community, according to which philosophy should not primarily be aimed at a wider public but should be an in-ward looking theoretical discipline that has nothing to do with the concrete, social, political, and cultural realities surrounding it.[50]

What is supposed to be home is not, at all, what More deems homely. So, he cannot be there. More cannot be where he is not wanted. In his long span of philosophical carrier, More was not invited at the land of his birth to give a keynote address, but the invitation came from elsewhere—the Caribbean and the United States. It is this home that his work is read, taught, and engaged. But this is not an issue since More severed his ties with The Philosophical Society of Southern Africa. What is clear is the idea of being valued by another home away from home. In the case of having two homes elsewhere—the Caribbean Philosophical Association and Philosophy Born of Struggle. Here is what More has to say: "These organizations not only provided me with an academic networking resource but were also emotionally comforting because they constituted a socially friendly community without the fear of degradation I suffered at South African conferences where antiblackness is still a fact in the profession."[51] There is no feeling of neglect as More chose not to be a member of The Philosophical Society of Southern Africa. Nor is there any feeling of regret for having left for good in 1977. More tells: "I have had a very tenuous and problematic relationship with the South African philosophical community, which, of course, is overwhelmly white."[52] The white South African philosophical community, according to More, will not dare deal with racism and will not even allow the philosophy that exposes the racist scandal of philosophy. Any dossier or discourse that deals with this matter will be deemed not only non-philosophical, and the not-so-uncommon banal reaction is what More articulates as follows: "The normal defense mechanism of a racist white is to call the black victim of racism racist."[53] The formations of black philosophical alternatives are always haunted by this banal charge.

> It is such a social and institutional milieu that produced me *qua* philosopher. My work focused progressively in the problem of racism, especially as it manifests itself in philosophy in South Africa. I think I am not the darling of white philosophers in South Africa, and since the power relations haven't changed as institutions of higher learning such a universities and certain government

> research departments, and in other places, my chance of being employed in the traditionally white universities are almost nil. I do not blame any other person for this precisely because I chose to play the racial game the way I did. A free individual blames only him/herself for his failures; he or she assumes responsibility for them. But sometimes, most things happen to black people through the agency of others, and therefore these others are responsible for their woes.[54]

More is in a situation where he is surrounded by forces of exclusion. Since whiteness does not forgive, he dared to touch the honest nest.

> Within the context of racist hegemony such as South Africa, any other black person who says, writes, or does something that upsets whites runs the risk of being put in his own place. Blacks who utter *beyond the pale* remarks about white racism are never forgiven, nor are their statements or remarks forgotten.[55]

The banal trick done by most racist organizations is to get a black person who naively or opportunistically be put in the position of "prestige" to become the spokesperson of whiteness. The stock of these antiblack blacks come from being well-groomed by whiteness and thus fed with all its spoils and rots. This is the black person who will come from liberal persuasion and he or she is the one who will be strategically positioned to attack any other black person who raises the questions of racism. In defense of antiblackness, such a person will be paraded as the voice of reason. In South Africa, such a black will be in defense of non-racialism and will even dare call other blacks racist when they raise matters of racism. When racism hits such a person in the face, they evade it or suffer in bitter silence. Whitely "protected," this will be instantly withdrawn when the black-antiblack black is no longer of use. History is littered with such antiblack blacks and the script is the same—the spell of the banal trick.

By finding philosophical home away from home still keeps More foregrounded and the existential encounter he had are not unique as he is with other philosophers who experienced, and still continue to experience, racism in its many forms and guises. Being animated by the question of what the role of philosophy out to be in the struggle for liberation, More has made it part of his project since he began his career as a philosopher. It is a question that is inseparable from his being. By being invested in the midst of philosophers who vow that they will stand up to face reality as it is, More is at home. It is a home where the haunting question is asked again and again in order to keep the existential struggle going. It is a question that could not find a place at his home. By leaving The Philosophical Society of Southern Africa, More found a home that this question is not a silent scandal, but what is freely engaged without restraint, fear, intimidation, and as such, without the dissimulation of racism. The rigorous engagements that form the lifeblood of the Caribbean Philosophical Association and Philosophy Born of Struggle is where this question reigns. As Harris states, philosophy born of struggle has an interest in "social problems facing the black community and this in the long history of struggling against dehumanization."[56] This question does not mean philosophy works, but rather philosophy is put to work by working philosophers grappling with what philosophy ought to be qua liberation.

In More, philosophy is put to work, in that it gets exposed to other dimensions that are dismissed as non-philosophical. It is from this spirit of radical commitment and dedication to the cause of liberation that makes philosophy to be at work. This means the luxury of its canonization is no longer an edifice but a dissolve. But to make philosophy what it is—a human study by humans in a lived world—clearly, there emerges a living thought about the question of liberation. By putting philosophy to work clearly means it is put through what comes by the haunting question that animates More, a question that is fundamental in service of philosophy, a service that does not canonize philosophy but lives it—philosophy of existence. More will not find it an obligation to do what is required in terms of the question that haunts him—the labor of thinking—philosophy demands hard work and putting it to work even demands working harder. Philosophy is put to work through thinking and this is the work that is done by philosophers who are engaged in the concrete and materiality of an antiblack world that they seek to radically change. Therefore, the transformative force that comes with the labor of thinking demands the world to be fundamentally changed from being an antiblack world to a livable world. Thinking is put in the project of liberation and this could not be compromised for anything.

More, as a result of being troubled by dehumanization, made a choice to belong to philosophical communities that affirm his humanity. It is where his presence is also justified not only as a philosopher but as one who has a contribution to make in building a philosophical community. By being under the umbrella of what Lucius Outlaw calls Africana philosophy, which is defined as a gathering notion of black people as beings in the world, the question of philosophy as a mode of existence in the midst of dehumanization is a fundamental task.[57] As Outlaw states, the purpose is "conditioned by a critically informed sense of shared identities, shred histories, and a need to work together to help realize possible shared futures of enhanced liberation for ourselves and others, to develop refined, shared agendas and practices to guide structure our work."[58] It is in the Caribbean Philosophical Association where Africana philosophy, in its various stands, and also other liberatory practices of philosophy, finds home. More declares that Africana philosophy is a shared space, a home for various Africana existentialist formations and black struggles.[59] Being in a community that is homely makes More's philosophical project necessary.

A philosopher with an agenda, one who is doing philosophy in black, More is doing philosophy with those who have the same agenda. By the common experience of being affected by racist and exclusionary practice of philosophy in the name of this reason, they come together to wage the existential struggle. It is in the actualization of these agendas that philosophizing emerges. This, from various lived experiences, unity is called into being and the actualization of agendas that make philosophy to be liberatory are formed, developed, and sustained. Africana philosophy, argues Outlaw, is what is "created in service to contemporary needs and projects."[60]

The question of race, which has been avoided in the South Africa's philosophical corridors, is what finds expression in the abovementioned philosophical homes that More chose. More's land of birth, which is racist, still has a philosophical community that does not want to take the question of racism seriously. So, philosophy of existence, as a matter that has to do with life, becomes a serious one for meta-reflection. In the Caribbean Philosophical Association and Philosophy Born of Struggle, More is doing philosophy as a form of life, a living philosophy, philosophy of a different form of life. This is a way of doing philosophy out of bounds. It is doing philosophy without having to bow to the racist infrastructure that is imposed, but doing philosophy from the spirit of being free to philosophize about the conditions of freedom.

The motto of the Caribbean Philosophical Association is "shifting the geography of reason." This motto, according to Jane Gordon, can be said to be "the not-so-humble motto" as it is bold and it takes the sacred domain of reason head-on.[61] It is here that reason is dethroned from its proverbial high horse. Its sacredness is desecrated. Its authority is disobeyed—that is, what Mignolo calls "epistemic disobedience."[62] Reason is not worshipped at the altar of the Euro-North-American-centric canon, it is engaged radically from the lived experience of those who are deemed (by way of colonial fabrication) to be the exterior and interior of reason. It is motto that does not seek assimilation and accommodation in the exclusionary domain of reason that is falsely claimed to be sole domain of thinking beings who are in the Euro-North-American-centric canon. The shifting of the geography of reason is a radical effort and not a moderate one. It is a shift that demands fundamental change. The situation has to change and what reason has always been will be radically changed as a result of a challenge that comes from those who are creating a livable world and not serving a deadly civilization that is valorized by the Euro-North-American-centric canon.

In the Caribbean Philosophical Association and Philosophy Born of Struggle, More is not only in a place where he is able to do philosophy freely, but a community where he can live freely. It is where philosophy is located in the community that uses it in the service of creation. Here, it is demanding that the hard work of thinking be in the service of a living thought as opposed to epistemic ego. It is a place where it is justified and necessary to think from the existential struggle for the life of freedom. It is a place where, as a matter of fact, one is at the right place with others who are creating a place in the world that is fundamentally and structurally antiblack. By the agenda of ending that world, philosophy is also put in service of having the responsibility of constructing another world of the human since an antiblack world is antithetical to the black human, or any other project that has to do with the politics of black life.

In the Caribbean Philosophical Association, the mode of doing philosophy is transparent because the liberatory project in hand is the one that exposes what philosophy hides. As Mignolo states, the geo-political configuration propagates the logic of the so-called "divine truth" where there is one universal world and there are people who are racially ranked and their regions are marked as those which are outside the domain of philosophy proper.[63] The conception of the world is different, and shifting the geography of reason is having to come from not having to be the fabrication of purity that philosophy masks itself to be. Shifting the geography of reason is tied to what Mignolo declared thus: "Geo-politics of knowledge goes hand in hand with geo-politics of knowing."[64] Shifting the geography of reason means that reason is not replicated, but it is totally reconfigured by way of "de-linking" from the racist discursive structures. It is to come to recognize the fact that there is nothing universal, but epistemes are situated in their own "geo-historical" and "bio-graphical" locations.[65] This, for More, is thinking from being-black-in-an-antiblack world.

What Mignolo insists on is "waking up from the long process of westernization."[66] It is this continual awakening that elevates the necessity of the existential struggle. More as having de-linked from The Philosophical Society of Southern Africa, the reason is because of what Mignolo calls the "colonial wound." It is from this wound that More revitalizes the Africana existential conversations with philosophers who have, like him, suffered this wound. The terms of what is a conversation are radically different when those who are speaking from the wound are healing each other as opposed to the speaking to those who wounded them and still deny them their own pain and tears. More is engaged in the Africana existential conversation and this is the conversation of the existential struggle.[67] It is going to the heart of the matter—reconfiguring geo-historical and bio-graphical ways of knowledge it surges on. In short, the Africana existential conversation is a changed conversation. Mignolo adds:

> Changing the terms of the conversation implies going beyond disciplinary or interdisciplinary controversies and the conflict of interpretation. As far as

> controversies and interpretations remain within the same rules of the genre (terms of the conversation), the control of knowledge is not called into question. And in order to call into question the modern/colonial foundation of the control of knowledge, it is necessary to focus on the knower rather than the known. It means to go beyond the very assumptions that sustains that locus of enunciation.[68]

In is clear, from Mignolo, that a place that can be called a philosophical community encourages philosophers to think from where they are and the meaning of their Africana existential conversation is one that is situated in the language of their struggle—for, they are situated and embodied. The outlook determined by identity and liberation, both informed by lived experience, are what More terms the "existential dimension."[69] These become the hallmark of his philosophical preoccupation. More then becomes part of philosophical communities that are informed by this existential dimension. Maldonado-Torres notes: "From the very beginning, these movements, and the thought of the colonized people as a whole, tended to accentuate problems of identity and liberation."[70] The Africana existential conversation that More engages in happens in a dialogical manner where the separation between identity and liberation are rejected but enjoined.[71] The enjoined nature is what informs the content of the Africana existential conversation. "The problem of liberation is as central to the project of decolonization as it is that of identity."[72] The two, argues Maldonado-Torres, are not enough if there is no epistemic decolonization as the imperative. This is key in enriching the content of the Africana existential conversation which finds expression in the intramural spaces that are created and cultivated to be in service of liberation. By foregrounding the existential struggle in human reality, this then allows "a decolonial force in philosophy, theory, and critique that asks for and anticipates an-another kind of intellectual space."[73]

The dialogic nature of the Africana existential conversation is an ongoing practice. "This is a framework that focuses on the primacy of liberation and that highlights the relevance of questions that emerge from the colonized world."[74] The question of More's selfhood emerges not from the site of the individual subject, but the black who are in the existential struggle against dehumanization. This, as More puts it, is "the lived experience of black folks in a racist world that attempts to deny their humanity."[75]

Coming from a Black Consciousness tradition, More is clear that philosophy is a way of life. So, shifting the geography of reason is, then, not a matter of sophistry. The mark of the colonial wound is what generates different ways of understanding the world and dwelling at the place that wants nothing to do with assimilation and accommodation. It is a place of the intramural relations of those who are at the receiving end of dehumanization. Those who affirm their being in the state of its dehumanization. Those who vow to emerge again in the name of the existential struggle. More, in this fold, is not concerned with the Africana existential conversation as a basis for comparison or the conversation for its own sake, but the deepening of philosophical insights that reconfigure the world.[76] By philosophizing from the colonial wound, the Africana existential conversation becomes different as it engages, all the time, a different set of questions. Here, no answers are absolute; the conversation deepens as it is held in the midst of the existential struggle.

The Africana existential conversation is of those who are shifting the geography of reason and thus having to engage in thought that does not originate from epistemic privilege. It is here in the place of the existential struggle where thought originates, in the struggle where the colonial wound in being inflicted and the modes of healing are ones that nurture and sustain the liberatory project at hand.

There is no need for More to succumb to dehumanization. His refusal, by choosing the Caribbean Philosophical Association and Philosophy Born of Struggle as his home, means that he cannot find home in the philosophy that is Euro-North-American-centric fold that the Philosophical Society of Southern African is trapped in. For, there is, according to Mignolo, "nothing new and remarkable here."[77] There is nothing that can set More to deepen the Africana existential conversation there. As Mignolo states, what is important is "then to engage in shifting the geography of reason—in unveiling and enacting geopolitics and body-politics of knowledge."[78] By doing this, More, accordingly, moves to have the conversation with those whom, by being geographically unmapped in the world, are engaged in knowledge that emerges from their racialized bodies. It is those whom knowledge is confronted as a weaponized force, and they engage in discursive practices that know how the racist discursive frames are formed and continuing to dissimulate.

The Africana existential conversations that More engages in opens vistas of knowledge which are not enriched by philosophy but which enrich philosophy. What Paulo Moya calls the "interpretive horizon" is what More subjects to even further interrogation as everything in deepened and nothing in the surface is worth one look but it is necessary to re-look, again, having a different look.[79]

More's Africana existential conversation is a set of interlocutions where the existential struggle is set apace. The deepened nature of the Africana existential conversation is deepened. It has never been a place of More to be in the Philosophical Society of Southern Africa in the first place because even to date the nature of these conversations is not the agenda. The irony is that this is the country where these conversations are urgent.

The biography of reason, as Mignolo installs, is an embodied place where philosophy is a living project where the dialogue of living being is engaged on how to live a livable life.[80] The biography of reason is the embodiment of the Africana existential conversation that is necessary to actualize the shifting of the geography of reason. There is all there is with the Africana existentialist conversation as it is re-affirming as opposed to what Moya points out as the commodification of subjugated knowledges which are treated as the nothingness of value but mere raw data.[81] There is nothing seen as the coming out as the production of knowledge, and whatever that is produced is denied any form of a philosophical status.

In the Caribbean Philosophical Association and Philosophy Born of Struggle, More is in a place "working with other progressive scholars who are themselves committed to changing, and not simply playing, the academic game."[82] The project at hand is, More radically insists, what militates against the constraints.[83] The enabling environment that the Caribbean Philosophical Association and Philosophy Born of Struggle allow creates different possibilities to what is deemed impossible. The effort that marks More's body of work has been taking the Africana existential conversations to places outside the Philosophical Society of South Africa to other places unimaginable and thus creating more and more alternatives. This is necessary. Moya writes: "Such alternative perspectives call to account the distorted representation of people, ideas, and practices whose subjugation is fundamental to the maintenance of an unjust hierarchical social order."[84] This is the prevailing status quo that can no longer be what it was as it is subjected to the interruptions of the Africana existential conversation and the existential struggle that informs it. Shifting the geography of reason is a whole change of things.

By dedicating his life to philosophy, in service of philosophy by putting philosophy to work, through philosophy in black as a living philosophy, More's project is a living entity that will not be in service of decadence. Being in the generative community of living thought, the Caribbean Philosophical Association and Philosophy Born of Struggle intensified More's philosophical project, and this re-energized in him the necessity to do more—selflessness. It is clear that more than purpose, what became primary is More's life. It is the life that is intensified by the will to be alive. It is the lease of life that the spirit of living thought continues to be a priceless gift. The decadence of dehumanization under the guise of the discipline in fixation is what is confronted. In the radical insistence of life, philosophy as a way of life, as what More affirms, is what is re-affirmed in the philosophical community he is. This re-affirmation is in the following account that More gives:

> Early in January 2015, I received the most exciting news of my life, a message that would change my professional life considerably. The message was from the chairman of the Caribbean Philosophical Association Awards Committee, informing me that I was the winner of the 2015 Frantz Fanon Lifetime

> Achievement Award. I looked at the message in disbelief! What? Not only was I pleasantly surprised, but I was also deeply shocked. This not because I did not think highly of my work, but that it never occurred to me that people so far away and with so much international standing and credibility can find my work worth honoring. It was an act of validation that philosophers in my country steadfastly refused to accord.[85]

Here is a validation of life: Frantz Fanon Lifetime Achievement Award. This is fitting to More who has been doing a philosophy of existence and thus embodying his writing with the thought of Frantz Fanon. By continuing to engage in living thought, the award is his steadfast commitment in putting philosophy to work, and that being many years of the existential struggle. Even in the conditions that discouraged him, More continued to put philosophy to work. It is this necessity of living thought that makes the existential struggle to be the cultivation and nurturing of life. Frantz Fanon Lifetime Achievement Award puts him with other laureates like Paget Henry, Enrique Dussel, Molefi Kete Asante, Abdul JanMohammed, Leonard Harris, Grace Lee Bogs Hortense Spillers, María Lugones, Catherine Walsh, Souleymane Bachir Diagne, and many others. The recognition of More's life work is given recognition in the community of many others who are doing this life work.

Being valued, More feels valued and it is this value that he must generate back to others who value him. It is this value that made More to get messages of warms and congratulations from near and far. It is this value that made him to be counted among many others in recognition and honor of their work. In recounting what he experiences after being named a laureate, More recounts: "For the next three months and so, I suddenly found myself an unwilling celebrity, with invitations from radio stations for interviews and messages of congratulations from diverse people, some of whom I never thought knew me."[86] This, for More, is indeed overwhelming in a humble sense of the word. More even goes on to note: "The irony is that I received congratulatory messages even from the philosophers of universities that refused to consider me for a post in their department."[87] This is not surprising and it is with wonder if he was going to be "celebrated" should he was not a laureate. Well, it is known that he was not going to be. More writes:

> I subsequently received a number of invitations to contribute papers in edited books, to present papers as a keynote speaker at conferences, seminars, and memorial lectures, or to offer lectures at certain universities' departments. Certain organizations also sought my participation in their projects and events. Frankly, because I was not used to this kind of attention, I was overwhelmed with work and my personal projects took a backseat. By then I was completing a manuscript on Steve Biko with the tentative title "Steve Biko: Philosophy,

> Identity, and Liberation." I had to decline some invitations in order to finish my project.[88]

Truly, More received an outstanding award. There is no way that he will not get this kind of attention. With many awards that the Caribbean Philosophical Association gives to a community of thinkers who are doing life work, and who are continuing to do selfless work in various ways, there are awards such as The Frantz Fanon Award for Outstanding Book in Caribbean Thought, The Stuart Hall Award, The Nicolás Guillén Award, The Anna Julia Cooper Award, and The Claudia Jones Award. What is honored is what is appreciated and this is in line with the work of the figures whom these awards are named. They lived, fought, and thought for the livable world. More is still continuing to do what he has been doing, and this is based on the obligation of doing what is necessary because the existential struggle is necessary and it is a selfless struggle. By doing what has to be done, and doing it without minding for scorn and approval, More continued that hard work paid off.

The Caribbean Philosophical Association and Philosophy Born of Struggle are a place where work is done by those who philosophize (not limited to analytical and continental traditions as it was the case with the Philosophical Society of Southern Africa but an ongoing rigorous practice of thinking, knowing, and doing that makes Africana existential conversations possible). In the Caribbean Philosophical Association, the shifting of the geography of reason is the making and unmaking of the world and in Philosophy Born of Struggle, the existential struggle is waged in for the insurgency of keeping the struggle going. Both Caribbean Philosophical Association and Philosophy Born of Struggle are there in making philosophy possible. It is here that discursive impositions do not have the last word, since the site of generativity, and what is it to philosophize, is the meaning that is informed by the collective experience that stems from being dehumanized, and the claims of liberation are made in the name of those who philosophize in the service of liberation.

A CRITIQUE OF DECADENCE

Since there is everything to life, it means that there is everything to live for. The denied life, one that is subjected to dehumanization, is one that is made to be in decadence. It is the life that is the antithesis of life. The imposition of decadence to the black is what the black cannot live with. In More's philosophical life, decadence has been the phenomenon of the surround, entanglements, and shackles that restrain his body, but which he fought on to refuse. Still, even now, More departs from the stance that there is no single but multiple meanings of philosophy.[89] "There are as diverse philosophies as there are traditions."[90] It is having to recognizing the fact that if there are multiple meanings of philosophy, so is the practice of philosophy itself. More asks: "What, then, is philosophy?"[91] By having mapped out multiple definitions, since there are multiple philosophical traditions, some which are unknown (which will be known and some not), More shows clearly that there is nothing definitional in the absolute sense. This question, according to More, is "the most important philosophical question."[92] Therefore, in definition philosophy, More argues for a "phenomenological suspension" and this means he recognizes the fact that there is no universally declared answer. But then, the decadence that he faces is one that imposes the singular and absolute meaning of what philosophy is. As such, whatever that contradicts this meaning is regarded not as operational in the sense of the definition. This is what Gordon calls "disciplinary decadence" and it has to be mentioned that, in its own name, philosophy is not definitional in the absolute sense.[93]

Philosophy, More states that "is a discipline with the capacity to define everything except itself."[94] In its disciplinary decadence, it will claim to be the most critical, if not rigorous—the singular-absolute *tout court*. "Its complexity, breadth, with, and nature render it extremely difficult if not impossible to define."[95] What is philosophy is also a philosophical issue. It has been unresolved ever since inception. "The greatest controversy has hitherto been its definition."[96]

The claim of the singular-absolute definition borders on decadence. For, that is carelessly imposed under the pretext of the universal. It is the universal that claims to be the center of the world, and those who are erased from its cartography are deemed to be nothing worthy of being identified with matters philosophical. The definition of philosophy, More states, is a matter of a philosopher's disposition. What More argues is the fact that "a number of definitions have been attempted in the past and will continue to be offered in the future."[97]

What is philosophy, contra decadence, More argues for it as the human affair. Philosophy is a human practice, philosophers are human beings. On this fact, More partakes in the philosophy that deals with the human question, and as such, he calls that the humanization of philosophy. From More's disposition, contra decadence, philosophy is what is concerned with the acts of liberation in the decadent condition of antiblackness with the effort of creating a liberated world that is livable. His philosophy is philosophy in black. Undoubtedly, it will (as it is and has to be) have a different meaning. The problems of a black philosopher, as More states, are not the same with that of a white philosopher.[98] This, then, leads to More's stance against decadence which departs from the point of view that philosophy as a point of view should be reflected from the point of view of the one who philosophizes.

This does not mean that that point of view is absolute as the decadent imposition has been hegemonically imprinting itself, but rather there is no universal point of view where the Euro-North American-centric point of view is the singular-absolute point of view. There are points of view, and More's philosophical disposition of philosophy in black is such a point of view. This, according to More, is having to articulate philosophy as a way of life—say, philosophy of existence. A philosopher, More punctuates, "should start from her own experience of the world and not from abstract problems."[99] This is even more necessary to the black where the stakes of the question of life are very high. The problem of existence, which has been imposed and perpetuated by dehumanization, is one that is chief in philosophical practice.

Philosophy in black, as a matter of the shifting of the geography of reason, is when the black philosophizes from the concrete and materiality of being-black-in-an-antiblack-world. This is the decadent world that is invented and imposed to the black as reality while that is not the reality. By philosophizing on the everyday life of being dehumanized, More's philosophy in black departs from two existential groundings—identity and liberation. He is a black philosopher who is engaged with his experiential lifeworld that has been decadently rendered a deathscape through the structural imposition of antiblackness. Therefore, the task at hand is putting philosophy at work by engaging with the fact that "there exists concrete knowledge of the black situation" as More states, identity and liberation should be the embodiment of what has to be done unapologetically from philosophy in black.[100] By putting philosophy to work, More shifts the geography of reason. The shift from abstractions and universalistic totalities to what is fundamentally at stake and what ought to be is what makes philosophy to be a living practice, practices of living otherwise.

Putting philosophy at work through the shifting of the geography of reason is an effort that radically pushes against and away any form of decadence. This is a radical effort indeed that comes from the day-to-day lived struggles. Mignolo amplifies: "It requires an act of humility to realize that there is no longer room for abstract universals and truths without parenthesis."[101]

The shift of the geography of reason in confronting decadence is the spirit of generativity where the black is infused with the effort that gives primacy to confronting the structurally imposed existential misery in a form of dehumanization. Those who are shifting the geography of reason, according to More, are "to start giving serious thought to the reality of their identity."[102] The primacy to thought, thinking from one's own being, which is essentially thinking from one's own situation is the principal motif. This is the grounding which, against decadence, the question of life is central—philosophy of existence. The existence that is violated is one that has its own conception of philosophy, and philosophical themes are generated from that experience as opposed to being applied from pure abstractions that are alien to the lived experience of that reality.

Philosophy in black is mobilized by More in ways that anchor the concerns of the everyday life as the materiality of philosophy itself. That is why the shift of the geography of reason from the closures of the disciplinary decadence of philosophy makes More to put philosophy to work by engaging in "a phenomenological description of being black in an antiblack world."[103] The encounter with an antiblack world demands the shifting of the geography of reason from the universal category of being-in-the-world to being-black-in-an-antiblack-world. Philosophy has been concerned with being-in-the-world where the question of being is not a matter of life and death, but a philosophical muse. To More, this is a totally different reality where, dehumanization has raised the stakes so high and the concrete and materiality of the black situation makes the question of being-black-in-an-antiblack-world to be a matter of life and death; that said, philosophy is put to work through its shift from philosophy to philosophy in black. The matter of existence, which has everything with identity and liberation, becomes the philosophical motifs that really shift the geography of reason. It is in this shift that the dissimulation that has engulfing philosophy to be the edifice, is beginning to crack—say, cracking a code, a shell, a wall, a glass—(infra)structure.

If philosophy is seen through modernity, More seeks it from what Mignolo refers to as the darker side of modernity. More does not see philosophy from the side of its epistemic privilege, but it being the colonial script that valorizes and at the same time glosses over dehumanization. More's geopolitics of knowledge, according to Mignolo, comes from his dehumanized position of being racialized and the racial logics that inform philosophy in the project of modernity is what militates against the being of More. That is why the absenting of the black in modernity can be the positive presentation of the black in the modernity that does not want anything to do with the black. Modernity, in its darker side, is what is seen as having been at war with black life. It is important to note that the very same modernity has been built through the sweat, tears, and blood of the black. Philosophy, in the name of modernity, has been nothing but decadence. By engaging philosophy from the darker side of modernity, More presents philosophy's scandal—antiblackness.

The rhetoric of modernity (what it says) and its actions (what it did and does) is what is the concern for Mignolo. That, in the name of progress, redemption, and civilization, shows totally different experiences. The rhetoric and actions of modernity to More become important sites of philosophical engagement. The lived experience of the black, who are at the darker side of modernity, is the philosophical expression that has to do with the black situation—dehumanization. That becomes the departing point through which philosophical statements that have to do with identity and liberation are the ones which are not entrapped in the rhetoric of modernity but rather its actions. The philosophers who More confronts as propagators of racism are engaged through, as Mignolo argues, on "what they did, not so much what they said."[104] This is, indeed, the protocol of shifting the geography of reason. It is having to contend with the reality as it is and not as it is told by the forces that continue to deny that reality to the black.

Since modernity has been paraded around in the name of philosophy, it is with irony that the dehumanizing effects are still receiving scant philosophical attention. What is needed, argues Maldonado-Torres, is "opening philosophy to multiple languages and stripping modernity of its colonizing elements."[105] This is an effort that can be realized through the shifting of the geography of reason. But it cannot be expected for things to be otherwise in this sense as all there is to it is that modernity has been a racist project. Therefore, philosophy that is in the name of modernity will, as it has been done without irony, deflect the attention of having to look at itself. It is not the task of the black to expect anything from disciplinary management and disciplinary decadence of philosophy.

The shift of the geography of reason signifies a drift. It is a locomotion of that which is pushed and driven by More who, in putting philosophy to work, will not allow anything to brake this drift. Things are on the move because the drift is made in the face of what demands things to be in a halt. Things are on the move and the direction this drift takes cannot be contained by decadence. Decadence is against any move made by the black. This drift is a detour, the other path, a way to elsewhere. It is the moving of things to where the black wants. Here is a drift contra dread. No dead end in this path. Every limit is a possibility.

In shifting the geography of reason, Walsh argues for "a collective mode of thinking that is produced and thought from difference, towards liberation."[106] It is here where, as Gordon argues "the highest of collective aspirations are thoroughly understood by everyone implicated."[107] It is the collective insurgency that shifts the geography of reason, and revitalization comes into being as the collective project that gives birth to other collective projects. Coming from different existential lineages, those who are shifting the geography of reason are doing what Gordon calls "purposeful projects." Nothing is accidental. What is done is intentioned and deliberate. The purposeful nature truly means the mobilization of the body, mind, and soul of the collective. This is a movement of reality—shifting the geography of reason—for other realities. This is a movement against the movement that has claimed to be universal. The latter is the movement that More's philosophical project has been in constant battle with throughout. "This movement, negotiated through conquest, disputations, enslavement, brought to the fore reflections of 'man' on 'man,' with constant anxiety over the stability of such a category."[108] The discursive opposition to this movement is what comes from More who states that philosophy is "remains the most untransformed discipline" but continues to move in decadence.[109] Decadence is colonization and its colonizing move in the name of method leads Gordon to say: "Colonization involves the elimination of discursive opposition between the dominant group and the subordinated group."[110] This move is deemed rational. And, by justification, objectivity is mobilized. This is a decadent mobilization that is paraded in the name of truth. Everything is absolute, and reality is without its complexities. Objectivity, the maiden name for disciplinary decadence, is what is insistent upon. As Gordon correctly notes, "objectivity is always directed against the colonized."[111] The insistence of the colonial move continues to endure. "It is no accident that instead of the end of colonization, new forms of colonization emerge."[112] What is demanded, as discursive opposition, is to do philosophy differently. More, in doing philosophy in black, is engaged in this discursive opposition.[113] What these demands, argues Gordon, is the "willingness to go beyond philosophy, paradoxically, for the sake of philosophy."[114]

The disposition of this willingness, this leads to "the improvisational attitude necessary to capture the multidimensionality of human lived experience."[115] Since disciplinary decadence has no regard with the insistence of evolution and revolution, there is no way that what is deemed method can be put in the service of the human project. Since method is in the name of reliability and validity, with replication as the production of the same, what becomes different is dismissed as the methodological error.

By shifting the geography of reason, the question of method becomes an important one. Philosophy, as it positions itself as a rigorous discipline is found at the limits, if not wanting when it comes to putting itself into question. The valorization of method in the name of the purity of the discipline, concerns and practices being unleashed in the service of the status quo, is what will mean the destruction of the discipline itself. For, it will be alien to the lived experiences of those who are putting it to work. There are no short cuts here. Going in full force, Gordon argues that methods should be in service of human study and this means "degrading decadence," and thus they must be innovated in line with the complex nature of the human condition. This marks the insurrection of the human against the despotic affair of dehumanization. The reign of disciplinary decadence is put into question. The question of the human study punctuates the fact that method is put to use and this becomes "a more fundamental path toward degrading decadence."[116] This is made possible through putting philosophy to work and where method does not despotically reigned but it is put to use or suspended if not needed.

This allows "methodological innovation" to be a practice that is foregrounded in More's project of putting philosophy to work. Here, the method does not serve the legitimizing purpose. That is why it can be put into suspension and that suspension, itself, is a paradoxically a methodological one, in that it generates ways of doing philosophy otherwise. This, for Gordon, is "doing philosophy instead of simply studying it."[117]

By bringing different modes of understanding philosophy, More is for the tradition that makes philosophy of existence to be the testament of the existential struggle. This is the struggle of the everyday life where methods are engaged in complex ways to generate modes of survival and thus creating different life-worlds whose actualization and emergence is still violently denied. By surging on with the existential struggle, what happens is the very act of putting methods themselves in question. Nothing is left to decompose in this act of re-composition. By keeping the existential struggle alive, there is no stopping in shifting the geography of reason. Forging ahead is knowing that this existential struggle is the going on that will always get tough. By not wanting to gain audience in philosophy that has been remaining deaf to the plight of the black, More's philosophy in black becomes a way of unraveling disciplinary decadence through ways that alter reality as seeing things differently is what always emerges in shifting the geography of reason.

In putting philosophy to work, Mignolo insists on "the anchors that support the shift in the geography of reasoning."[118] These anchors, in amplifying Gordon, the "suspension of method" which is the radical effort that embodies the anti-colonial critique.[119] This is methodological decolonization (dissolve and obliteration) that comes in a form of what Mignolo deploys as "border thinking" and "border epistemology." The apparent geographical element of the two stand foregrounded in More's philosophical disposition. This is the radical refusal to be caught in modernity. It is to be outside modernity, its darker side, in order to see its darker side (what modernity does) and not be blinded by its rhetoric (what modernity says). The rhetoric and reality of modernity is what the shifting of the geography of reason is concerned with.

By engaging philosophy from the darker side of modernity, More is engaged in the geopolitics of knowledge which, to Mignolo, do not take modernity as the liberatory project. The darker side of modernity makes it necessary to confront the dissimulation of dehumanization and to see things for what they really are.

Since disciplinary decadence is what plagues philosophy as More engages it, Gordon states the problem as "the ontologizing or a reification of a discipline."[120] It is as if philosophy is singular and absolute and it will never change or there will be no other form of philosophy. What Gordon highlights is that philosophy is been made decadent in ways that it is a work of epistemic closure. "Such work militates against thinking."[121] The ontologizing and reification of philosophy stems from the spirit of modernity that claims purity and those who are regarded as modern are the only ones who can stand to be counted at the exclusion of anybody else. That is the attitude of decadence and it has even made the purity of philosophy to be fidelity to canonization. It means, as a discipline, it is as it is and it should remain as it were. That is why this canonization has even perpetuated the notion of "philosopher proper." This, according to Mignolo, is "disciplinary management" where there is no living thought but the solidification of what has been there.[122] Here is the protection of the modernity against any form of contamination. If there is anything that is called philosophy, it should only be philosophy if it is within modernity. This is, indeed, disciplinary decadence.

> The result of disciplinary decadence, which involves the closing off of epistemological possibilities of disciplinary work. This form of decadence is particularly acute at the level of method, where a methodology does not surface since such questions are closed. In effect, the discipline and its method become 'complete.' Life returns to disciplinary practices, however, through being willing to transcend the disciplines, which, as we have seen, is a teleological suspension of disciplinarity. What this means is that the thinker concludes that there are issues so important to pursue that method and disciplinary commitment must fall by the wayside if they inhabit exploration of those issues. In the case of philosophy, its disciplinary suspension—that is, the decision to go beyond philosophy—enables the cultivation of a new philosophy.[123]

Truly, disciplinary decadence in the name of philosophy is not philosophy as it claims to be "philosophy proper" but the hampering of the generative capacity of philosophy. It is, in paradox, the defense of philosophy that is against philosophy—own goal. It is the denial of philosophy to go through an evolution and revolution. The disciplinary management of philosophy is its decadence. As More notes, philosophy often resides in places that are not deemed philosophy proper.[124] But because disciplinary decadence is a firm hold and stranglehold, there is nothing worthy to be done except to maintain the status quo and the geography of reason will always remain Euro-North American-centric. Even if there are debates, they should be within this geographic and epistemic enclosure. The extent of decadence is heightened, so is the militancy against thinking. The room for what Gordon call "discursive oppositions" is closed and partially opened if philosophical matters are within the limited geography that is Euro-North American-centric which even has the audacity to declare itself universal. The irony here is that this limited geography claims to speak for the whole universe, whereas it is its small fraction. This is decadence and other philosophies that are not known are deemed to be the exteriority, unknown, and non-existent. The only frame that is deemed worthy and only philosophical is the Euro-North American-centric frame. Its aim, under the pretense of the universal, is to replicate other frames that are colonial. Walsh writes: "Of course, the problem is not with the existence of such frames but rather with the ways they have historically worked to subordinate and negate 'other' frames, 'other' knowledge, and 'other' subjects and thinkers."[125]

Disciplinary management as the constitutive part of modernity and that is what philosophy will remain addicted to disciplinary decadent in the name of method, and making sure that purism will be shouted while remaining silent on the contamination that philosophy does through dehumanization. Philosophy still stands in the name of "truth" while it is the ontological and epistemological fabrication of the black in the name of modernity.

By not allowing any form of discursive opposition, and claiming to be enclosed, disciplinary decadence border on epistemic arrogance that is laced with racism. The latter applies because of the shutting out and crowding out whatever that is deemed to be outside modernity. According to this warped logic, whatever that is outside modernity is not philosophical. Therefore, there cannot be any form of a philosophical discourse with what is not philosophical. The spelling out of the lived experience of the black is ridiculed, scolded, censured, and even dismissed out of hand as non-philosophical without having to attend to the modes of philosophizing that the black is engaged with.

What rules philosophy as still the same epistemic structures and the rule is that they must stay as they are. The sense of one's being-in-the-world should be about abstractions that are imposed on the black who do philosophy to adopt. In this sense, there is one script—the colonial script in the mask of the universal. The black are supposed to be in line with it in order to do philosophy. Even if the black become naïve to follow that script of the universal mode of philosophizing and being detached to their lived reality, they do not become philosophers but the phenomena with an adjective (black philosophers). As More states, this adjective is still a denial of one's own being as a philosopher. So, whether the black is in support of the colonial script or not, the outcome of being denied is still the same. The black, no matter what philosophical stance, is subjected to the decadent salvo of philosophy.

According to More, the disciplinary decadence of philosophy stems from the impassioned stance of not wanting to deal with the problem of human existence.[126] The existence of the black is what philosophy will bother itself with. The foundation of philosophy and its canonical formations are rested in the dehumanization of the black. The black, in the annals of philosophy, is a scandal.

By shifting the geography of reason, the black presents the scandal and does what has to be done in the name of philosophy without apology. By putting philosophy to work, Gordon obliterates what he calls "methodological colonialism," and this radical act allows philosophy to work in ways that stand against its disciplinary decadence.[127] By putting philosophy to work, the effort is to "fight against deeper, misanthropic forces."[128] The shift from colonization to decolonization is a decisive move that even delinks from modernity.[129] In calling for delinking, and thus dwelling in the darker side of modernity, Mignolo states that modes of operations should not be those drawn and mapped by colonial ways of thinking, knowing, and doing. What is called for by Mignolo is to read modernity from the silences and exteriorities it produces. By dwelling on the darker side of modernity is to see what modernity is—that is, not what it says but what it does. That, in point of fact, is the shifting of the geography of reason.

To conclude, More did what is necessary in putting philosophy for work. This, by shifting the geography of reason, demands the body, mind, and soul to be put in the service of the existential struggle. In the name of philosophy, it is very evidentiary without having to prove that shifting the geography is a living embodiment of More. This is the spirit that embodies him, and his philosophical drift. This is what has been animating him before he found home in the Caribbean Philosophical Association and Philosophy Born of Struggle. The sense of restlessness is what made More's spirit not to be at home in the place that dislocates him. By not begging to be assimilated and then opening his humanity to be assaulted, More's critique of philosophy in South African is the ethico-politico task, and it is one of the reasons of his dislocation. By exposing it, and more especially its racist mechanics and machinations, More did what a philosopher has to do in the face of dehumanization.

The existential struggle against More is not a matter of an arbitrary or luxurious choice. It is, in fact, a matter of necessity. This is the struggle that, in an antiblack world, is waged by those who will not allow their humanity to be degraded. It is a struggle that More saw it worthy to pursue away from The Philosophical Society of South African because of the association's racist history, its complicity, and its continued attachment to philosophy that turns a blind eye in the location it is in—racist South Africa. By leaving for good and vowing not to return to the philosophical community that dehumanized him, More's philosophical home in Caribbean Philosophical Association and Philosophy Born of Struggle re-energize his philosophical anthropology.

By being in the existential struggle, doing philosophy in black in the midst of other existential lineages, More's practice of freedom comes out of the necessity to shift the geography of reason. It is in the milieu of these existential conversations that the disciplinary decadence of philosophy is put into question by both philosophy and method in ways that make the shift of the geography of reason to be meaningful and profound. By doing philosophy as the project of life, it means that this is a necessity and this philosophy should be in service of what will make philosophy alive by freeing it from decadence. Shifting the geography of reason is making sure that what negates decadence is its production like other reactionary tendencies that claim to be revolutionary, whereas they become reactionary. Since philosophy cannot have the last word in its decadent spirit, the ways of putting it to work is what gives it another meaning—a liberatory project.

NOTES

1. Mabogo P. More, *Looking through Philosophy in Black: Memoirs* (Lanham: Rowman and Littlefield International, 2019). With its Euro-North-American-centric outlook, and claiming to be of nowhere, but universal, philosophy in South Africa, like many disciplines in the South African academy, disavows the question of race in its reality as it concerns South Africa's antiblackness. The philosophical anthropology of More is rooted in Azania, but it has the reach that is not reducible to the centrism that claims to be nationalistically pure. Shifting the geography of reason is not reducible to More's philosophical motto of the Caribbean Philosophical Association, but what is accented is him being a member of those who value each other and who love being valued as Gordon would always say. For a detailed explanation of More belonging to both Caribbean Philosophical Association and Philosophy Born of Struggle, and his philosophical contribution, see *Looking Through Philosophy in Black*.

2. Mabogo P. More, *Sartre and the Problem of Racism*. Unpublished PhD Thesis (Pretoria: University of South Africa, 2005), 4.

3. Ibid.

4. Ibid.

5. Mabogo P. More, "Complicity, Neutrality or Advocacy? Philosophy in South Africa. Ronald Aronson's *Stay Out of Politics*," *Theoria* 87 (June 1996): 124–135. Cited in 132.

6. Ibid., 124.

7. Ibid., 125.

8. Ibid., 126.

9. Ibid.

10. Ibid., 127–128.

11. Ibid., 128.

12. Ibid.

13. Ibid., 129. There is no way that philosophy, in a politically charged environment, can claim not to be political. It is a philosophy that cannot avoid to look at the maladies of the black condition. But, then, philosophy still continues to ignore this reality.

14. Ibid.

15. Mogobe B. Ramose, "On the Contested Meaning of Philosophy," *South African Journal of Philosophy* 24, no. 4 (2015): 551–558.

16. Ibid., 552.

17. Ibid.

18. More, *Looking through Philosophy in Black.*

19. Ramose, "On the Contested Meaning of Philosophy," 557.

20. More, "Complicity, Neutrality or Advocacy?
21. More, *Looking through Philosophy in Black*, 17.
22. Ibid.
23. Ramose, "On the Contested Meaning of Philosophy."
24. Ibid., 553.
25. More, *Looking through Philosophy in Black*, 155.
26. Mabogo P. More, "Philosophy in South Africa under and after Apartheid," in *Philosophy and an African Culture*, edited by Kwasi Wiredu, 149–160 (Cambridge: Cambridge Scholar, 2004), 152.
27. Ibid., 151.
28. Ibid., 153.
29. Ibid.
30. Ibid., 154.
31. Ibid., 159.
32. More, *Looking through Philosophy in Black*, 17.
33. Ibid., 20.
34. Ibid., 68.
35. Ibid.
36. Mabogo P. More, "Isn't Identity Informed by Experience?" *Mail and Guardian*, February 24 to March 2 (2017): 25. Cited in 25.
37. More, *Looking through Philosophy in Black*, 68.
38. Ibid., 69.
39. Ibid. In upholding his honor, and not to legitimize the antiblack reality he had to face, More stood for the principle and that would mean that he will not be part of the philosophical community that dehumanizes him. This is the affirmative stance which is also in line with the philosophy of Black Consciousness.
40. More, "Isn't Identity Informed by Experience?" 25.
41. More, *Looking through Philosophy in Black*, 193. These are the demands which have a long history. They are disavowed because white philosophers and blacks who are their allies see nothing wrong with the perennial problem of racism that still persists. In the name of philosophy, the pretense has always been business as usual.
42. Leonard Harris, "'Believe It or Not' or the Ku Klux Klan and American Philosophy Exposed," *Proceedings and Addresses of the American Philosophical Association* 68, no. 5 (1995): 369–380. Cited in 133.
43. Mabogo P. More, "Gordon and Biko: Africana Existential Conversation," *Philosophia Africana* 13, no. 2 (2010/2011): 71–88. Cited in 76.
44. It is worth noting that the Caribbean Philosophical Association and Philosophy Born of Struggle are fundamentally different. The former is global in scope and reach while the latter is North American. I want to thank Lewis Gordon in bringing this matter to my attention. It must be stated, however, that Philosophy Born of Struggle has the South African contingency.
45. More, *Looking through Philosophy in Black*, 129.
46. Ibid.
47. Ibid., 130.

48. Ibid., 130–131.
49. Ibid., 131; emphasis in the original.
50. Ibid., 132.
51. Ibid., 133.
52. Ibid., 121.
53. Ibid., 122.
54. Ibid.
55. Ibid., 127.
56. Leonard Harris, "Introduction," in *Philosophy Born of Struggle: Anthology of Afro-American Philosophy from 1917*, edited by Leonard Harris, xi–xxv (Dubuque: Kendal/Hunt, 1983), xxiii.
57. Lucius Outlaw, "Africana Philosophy," *The Journal of Ethics* 1 (1997): 265–290.
58. Ibid., 276.
59. More, "Gordon and Biko."
60. Lucious Outlaw, "African, African American, Africana Philosophy," *Philosophical Forum* 23, nos. 2–3 (1992): 63–93. Cited in 82.
61. Jane A. Gordon, *Creolizing Political Theory: Reading Rousseau through Fanon* (New York: Fordham University Press, 2014), xii.
62. Walter Mignolo, "Epistemic Disobedience, Independent Thought and De-Colonial Freedom," *Theory, Culture, and Society* 26, nos. 7–8 (2009): 1–23.
63. Ibid.
64. Ibid., 2.
65. Ibid.
66. Ibid., 3.
67. More, "Gordon and Biko."
68. Mignolo, "Epistemic Disobedience, Independent Thought and De-Colonial Freedom."
69. More, *Looking through Philosophy in Black.*
70. Nelson Maldonado-Torres, "Thinking through the Decolonial Turn: Post-continental Interventions in Theory, Philosophy and Critique—An Introduction," *Transmodernity* 1, no. 2 (2011): 1–15. Cited in 3.
71. Ibid.
72. Ibid., 3.
73. Ibid., 4.
74. Ibid., 8.
75. More, "Gordon and Biko," 76.
76. Ibid.
77. Mignolo, "Epistemic Disobedience, Independent Thought and De-Colonial Freedom," 13.
78. Ibid., 14.
79. Paula M. L. Moya, "Who We Are and from Where We Speak," *Transmodernity* 1, no. 2 (2011): 79–94.
80. Mignolo, "Epistemic Disobedience, Independent Thought and De-Colonial Freedom."

81. Moya, "Who We Are and from Where We Speak." The impression that is created and perpetuated is that there cannot be any form of knowledge production from the black. The black should just be seen as the site of extraction and also projections.

82. Ibid., 84.

83. More, *Biko.*

84. Moya, "Who We Are and from Where We Speak," 85.

85. More, *Looking through Philosophy in Black*, 173.

86. Ibid., 174.

87. Ibid.

88. Ibid., 177.

89. Ibid.

90. Ibid., 17.

91. Ibid. This is a question without a definitive answer. It is, in fact, a philosophical question. It will, for a long time to come, remain unsettled.

92. More, *Biko*, 58.

93. Lewis R. Gordon, *Disciplinary Decadence: Living Thought in Trying Times* (Boulder and London: Paradigm Publishers, 2006).

94. More, *Looking through Philosophy in Black*, 16.

95. Ibid.

96. More, *Biko*, 58.

97. More, *Looking through Philosophy in Black*, 16.

98. Mabogo P. More, *Sartre and the Problem of Racism.* Unpublished PhD Thesis (Pretoria: University of South Africa, 2005).

99. More, *Biko*, 5.

100. More, *Biko*, 33.

101. Walter D. Mignolo, *The Darker Side of Western Modernity: Global Futures, Decolonial Options* (Durham and London: Duke University Press, 2011), 114.

102. More, *Biko*, 35.

103. Ibid., 100.

104. Mignolo, *The Darker Side of Western Modernity*, 133.

105. Maldonado-Torres, "Thinking through the Decolonial Turn," 7.

106. Catherine Walsh, "Shifting the Geopolitics of Critical Knowledge: Decolonial Thought and Cultural Studies 'Other' in the Andes," *Cultural Studies* 21, nos. 2–3 (2007): 224–239. Cited in 232.

107. Gordon, *Creolizing Political Theory*, 155.

108. Lewis R. Gordon, "Shifting the Geography of Reason in an Age of Disciplinary Decadence,"

Transmodernity 1, no. 2 (2011): 95–103. Cited in 96.

109. More, *Looking through Philosophy in Black*, 124.

110. Gordon, "Shifting the Geography of Reason in an Age of Disciplinary Decadence," 99.

111. Gordon, *Creolizing Political Theory*, 80.

112. Gordon, "Shifting the Geography of Reason in an Age of Disciplinary Decadence," 101.

113. More, *Looking through Philosophy in Black.*

114. Lewis R. Gordon, *An Introduction to Africana Philosophy* (Cambridge: Cambridge University Press, 2008), 183.

115. Gordon, *Creolizing Political Theory*, 73.

116. Ibid., 24.

117. Gordon, *An Introduction to Africana Philosophy*, 74.

118. Mignolo, *The Darker Side of Western Modernity*, 208.

119. Gordon, "Shifting the Geography of Reason in an Age of Disciplinary Decadence."

120. Gordon, *Disciplinary Decadence*, 4.

121. Ibid., 5.

122. Gordon, "Shifting the Geography of Reason in an Age of Disciplinary Decadence."

123. Gordon, *An Introduction to Africana Philosophy*, 183.

124. Mabogo P. More, "Fanon, Apartheid, and Black Consciousness," in *Shifting the Geography of Reason: Gender, Science, and Religion*, edited by Marina P. Banchetti-Robino and Clevis R. Headley, 241–254 (New Castle: Cambridge Scholars Press, 2006).

125. Walsh. "Shifting the Geopolitics of Critical Knowledge," 224.

126. More, *Biko.*

127. Gordon, *Disciplinary Decadence.*

128. Ibid., 126.

129. Mignolo, *The Darker Side of Western Modernity.*

Chapter 4

The Figure of the Rebel

The rebel is the figure that fights for a cause. All there is for the rebel is advancing everything in the name of that cause. By not allowing the imposed order to rule against one's will and also demanding that the will yield something, the rebel is the one who wants what is fundamentally different—that is, the one who is against the status quo. The rebel does not rebel for the sake of rebelling. Or, crudely, the rebel is not one without a cause. To rebel is *to be against* and also *to be for*. This is the figure in standing and that actually means the existence of the one who stands against something and also for something. The effecting of change is the spirit of the rebel. It is this radical will that demands that there should be fundamental change. What is in the grammar of the rebel is the demand of what is deemed to be ethical and just. The fact of having being wronged is what the rebel demands as absolute alteration, restoration, and reparation in the terms that are dictated by the rebel.

Mabogo P. More is the figure of the rebel. He is, as a philosopher of existence, one who is in the forefront of the existential struggle. This is the spirit that confronts foreclosure and makes possible radical openings. This does not depend on victory; the rebel still fights even in the condition of defeat. The justification of the rebel is still that articulation and advocacy of radical demands and a different set of conditions. Even if foreclosure and impossibility can reign supreme, there is no way that the rebel can be stopped, except by being liquidated through death. The spirit of the rebel becomes rebellious not only in the condition of having to live but the radical insistence of life itself. This is the livable life which has to be different as it has to be lived freely. More, the rebel, is not cowed down by fear as s/he engages philosophical questions that have to do with matters of unpopularity.

By locating More as the rebel, this attests how his embodiment is one that transcends the bodily docility and it is the spirit of resistance that animates him and demands of him to stand up for life even in the face of consequences of his choices. The refusal of the rebel, More in this case, can be understood through the concept of rupture. In its animative force, rupture breaks whatever that holds the black in bondage and it the creation of freedom even in bondage.

In More's philosophical project, the rebel is the one who contends with what has been deemed sacred and what cannot be opposed. By being the one who does it anyway, the rebel is the figure who has to be free from fear. By confronting matters of his existence, More says "yes" to freedom and said "no" to unfreedom. He is the one who marshals these two conceptual opposites, brings them to operation, and then mobilizes and actualizes depending on the situation at hand. If the rebel is made to say no to freedom, the rebel will say yes, and the case applies on the opposite. In fact, More clearly shows that the rebel is all for freedom. What is it that necessitates the quest for freedom is how life must be and challenging the refusal of this possibility and necessity. So, yes and no, as the registers of the rebel are, in all situations, affirmative even in the face of death (its threat and fear). There is no ambivalence, and as it is clear from More, everything is the decisive fact of philosophy of existence.

FIRST AS PRINCIPALITY

What is all there is for the rebel is not the right to life but the necessity of life. The rebel is denied life by the very domain of rights, so what the rebel wants is life, as it is not contingent on any rights. The primacy of it all is life. Therefore, the life of the rebel does not have to be authorized; it is the rebel who authorizes such a life as it has to be lived. To be a rebel is to exist. Unfortunately, this existence is not a given. In this respect, it is one that is being fought for as it has been denied. To exist, as the rebel, is to be bound in the existential struggle for freedom. More fundamentally, it is worth punctuating the fact that the rebel is the being of freedom. This is the freedom that cannot be traded with anything and this is what the rebel stands for. To be the rebel is to be against the grain, to be on principle, to be what has to be just in the face of injustice. The rebel, according to Albert Camus, is the one who says yes and no, and this depends on the situation of freedom or unfreedom.[1] The rebel says yes to freedom and says no to unfreedom. More punctuates: "To be a rebel is to adamantly refuse to accept the oppressive situation in which one finds oneself."[2] This is principality. It is, in the annals of More's existential struggle and embodiment as the rebel, what can be termed, according to George Ciccariello-Maher, the "origin, source, or mandatory point of departure."[3]

The rebel insists to live the life of freedom. It is the free life that the rebel will be in the cause for. At the originary level, freedom means everything. There is everything in freedom to be lived for.

Standing for something means being bold and, as such, the one who rebels must be in good standing. It is standing for the good, even that might be soiled as unpopular and distasteful with regard to the reigning hegemonic sensibilities. The standing of the rebel is standing against what is familiar and popular. It is easier for the rebel to be discredited and not taken seriously. But the quest of the rebel is not to ingratiate oneself in these ontological foreclosures. Often, the rebel exposes what those in power have been hiding and meaning to hide all along. The rebel makes known what was not supposed to be known, and the cause of the rebel is always a different one.

This something that the rebel stands for is freedom. What is it, then, that makes More a rebel? Camus responds thus: "A man who says no: but whose refusal does not imply a renunciation. He is also a man who says yes as soon as he begins to think of himself."[4] More chooses to be different by making philosophy to face its own reality of antiblack racism.[5] He cannot be the philosopher of the popular script of South African philosophy. By taking the question of antiblack racism seriously, More refuses to disavow it. This good standing in the name of what is right and just in the country that refuses to deal with the lived experience of being black-in-an-antiblack-world, More's principality is the radical assertion of a "no." Departing from this disposition, he refuses that which denies his freedom. To say no is to say yes for what necessitates freedom. The life of unfreedom is what More will not live. By having to think of himself, More asserts what is of his freedom. He does not think of himself as the liberal bourgeoisie subject, but the being who must exist in freedom. More is always on the affirmative that he is his own freedom.[6] In an antiblack world, both his freedom is threatened. Since the two are entangled, he rebels for them to be intact. Even if this is ceaselessly violated through the imposition of unfreedom, there is the radical insistence of that freedom. It cannot be taken away, and this is fought for. For More, it is "no" to unfreedom and "yes" to freedom.

There is nothing insofar as what Hommi Bhabha will call ambivalence when it comes to the rebel.[7] If More's philosophy of existence is to be considered, it is the one that does not participate in the colonial discourse; thus, for its intended purposes and expression, it also has nothing to do with it being a performative gesture. All way through, it is clear where yes and no means, and there is nothing in between. The figure of the rebel will not, in all accounts, fit in Bhabha's schema.

The colonial discourse is not a totality of its own. It is the discourse that does not have the final say. As Bhabha states, the authority of this discourse is fixing its other for the purpose of its stability. It would want to impose colonial authority in ways that cannot be interrupted. Having the last say is what the colonial discourse is. It is, according to Bhabha, "a paradoxical mode of representation: it connotes rigidity and an unchanging order as well as disorder, degeneracy and daemonic repetition."[8] But, as Bhabha notes, the colonial discourse does not have the last say, and it is subjected to interruption. What has been fixated becomes instability, a counter-discourse to the colonial discourse in the name of what Bhabha calls ambivalence. Bhabha writes: "The analytic of ambivalence questions dogmatic and moralistic positions on the meaning of oppression and discrimination."[9] There is all there is to ambivalence, in that even the yes and no positions of the rebel will not be delineated in marked ways, but blurred together. In calling for a political space in between yes and no, Bhabha insists on what he calls articulation where yes and no deny, in their essence of being of "singularity" and the "original." Articulation will mean that ambivalence will give another validity. In a stultifying effort, Bhabha does not allow the yes and no to be what they are as absolutes. Their denotative character is blurred to be a connotative one. By way of articulation, there is no agreement on what yes and no mean. Articulation, by way of ambivalence, is what Bhabha calls the figure of doubling. If the yes and no are to be taken, each have their double, and they cease to be what they are known to be.

Bhabha's articulation of the colonial discourse is, indeed, in nature and character, couched to be verisimilitude. But this quality of being truth can be said to be, limitedly so, as the level of discourse as opposed to reality as lived. With verve, Bhabha writes: "If colonialism takes power in the name of history, it repeatedly exercises its authority through the figures of farce."[10] What gets produced are complex modes of representations. Ambivalence sets in, and with it comes what Bhabha terms mimicry. "Which is to say, that the discourse of mimicry is structured around an *ambivalence*; in order to be effective, mimicry must continually produce its slippage, its excess, its difference."[11] The double, at the level of discourse, means that Bhabha takes things to the performative level. They are the *it* who is not quite *like it*. Charging on, Bhabha insists: "Mimicry is, thus the sign of a double articulation; a complex strategy of reform, regulation and discipline, which 'appropriate' the Other as it visualizes power."[12] For Bhabha, this threatens and disturbs the colonial discourse. The excess and slippage that is produced is what makes things what they are not and for Bhabha, things become incomplete and virtual as the result of being partial. But what appears striking is Bhabha's admittance that this does not produce any form of rupture. What is settled for is the impurity of the colonial discourse.

What is striking in Bhabha can be stated in three questions: First, what is it at stake that makes the colonial discourse to stand erect without any form of obliteration but that which should be reformed? Second, why should it be at the expense of the colonized to engage in mimicry as opposed to being authentic and combative? Third and last, why is the colonial discourse the higher order that should have nothing to do with dehumanization? These three questions are cursory but they are however pointed when it comes to the figure of the rebel in the colonial condition. Since the symbolic order is one that is limitedly discursive rather than the ontological in Bhabha's frame, it is worth mentioning that the rebel has a different cause altogether. What Bhabha calls "colonial textuality" is not enough to confront the notion of origins. What Bhabha side/mis-steps is that colonial textuality is not reducible to the colonial discourse but the colonial infrastructure writ large. The rebel does not have to be concerned with the "interdictory desire" as the limit of this site is nothing but colonial textuality. The frame of colonial textuality to the total field of the everyday life is too much a point to emphasize. Also, what Bhabha calls *inter dicta* which is a discourse at crossroads might seem to have semblance with More's rebellious writing against the decadence of philosophy. But still, what looms large is what Bhabha valorizes as the desire of colonial mimicry which is nothing that has to do with the existential struggle for freedom.

The appendage of the colonized to colonial authority, whether through slippery or not, still means being dictated to by the strictures and edicts of the discourse of that authority. There is nothing in mimicry that can be said to be of value for the rebel even if Bhabha was to write: "Mimicry, as the metonym of presence is, indeed, such an erratic, eccentric strategy of authority in the colonial discourse."[13] There is nothing in mimicry because there is no principality of what the rebel will always deem authentic. What is the pulse of the rebel is being committed to the cause. This demands authenticity. There is nothing in the desire of the rebel to mimic what dehumanizes. The desire, however, on the contrary, yields what is authentic. Even at the level of discourse, the rebel will not deputize his articulation to be a double. Authenticity, in the philosophical impulse of the rebel, and More in this case, is one who, in good standing, will not be in an ambivalent position. In essence, all there is to the rebel is what that is not in Bhabha's articulation. Even if the contest is only at the level of the colonial discourse, there is nothing worthy for the rebel to mimic and thus compromise the authentic demands of its episteme. The structure of knowledge of the rebel is not the one that ingratiates itself to the colonial discourse. The good standing of the rebel is all there is—authenticity. This, then, shows that the rebel is free as opposed to Bhabha's amoebic subject who is formed and deformed by the colonial discourse. Arrested at the level of desire, fantasy, and play, this amoebic subject does not, even to the realm of the discourse only, stand out in its own name and claims. It is the one that is "strategic" in its disavowal of its own authenticity and demands this authenticity to be decimated in order to make the anticolonial struggle just a semantic play and minstrel show.

It appears as if everything is equal in the colonial discourse. The muting of epistemic violence that underwrites this edifice is what Bhabha wants to remain faithful not to see. The dimension of doubling that Bhabha evokes in order to give ambivalence currency is to make what marks identification in the colonial context to be what cannot be implicated insofar as dehumanization is concerned. The shifting of meaning which Bhabha locates in the slippages of the colonial discourse does not, in any way, show what are the stakes. According to Bhabha, it "is a strategy of ambivalence in the elliptical *in-between*, where the shadow of the other falls upon itself."[14] This strategy of ambivalence does not match with what is demanded in the pursuit of the existential struggle. The impression created here is that ambivalence is just a game of hide-and-seek. Since matters are too serious for the rebel, other modes of inscriptions are necessary. This means, the inscription of the rebel, just like in More's philosophical anthropology, the colonial discourse is rejected. What is mobilized, throughout the existential struggle, is the claims that affirm the being who is denied being. Indeed, Camus has been on the mark to suggest that the "rebellion is a constant illustration of this principle of positive claims."[15] This principality has meant the assertion of "yes" and "no."

All there is for the rebel is life of freedom. This is the life that has to be created. It is in this life where freedom can be fought for and defended, and the rebel can insist on its fidelity. The principality of freedom means the rebel must re-state the yes and no, which are any form of the double, but authentic codes that the rebel is informed and stands by. Camus is instructive here: "He means, for instance, that 'this has been going on too long,' 'so far but no farther,' 'you are going too far,' or again. 'There are certain limits beyond which you shall not go.' In other words, his 'no' affirms the existence of a border line."[16] The rebel is obviously a violated being who refuses to be bound by this violation. So, by marking and making a border line, this violation has to cease. It is only the rebel who can determine how things should be. This is the act of acting upon oneself as opposed to being acted upon. The rebel erupts and disrupts what has been, in More's case, the antiblackness that underwrites and structures the everyday life that is being denied the life of freedom. As the figure of the black, More's humanity is put into question. He is put in the conditions that are inhabitable insofar as the rightful life of freedom has to be lived. The life that More is subjected to is one that denies the very essence of life itself. It is the life that is not supposed to be the way it is.

For the life this is supposed to be lived, one that is worthy of being such, the rebel is, according to More, one who is justified by virtue of demanding such a life.[17] The principality of the rebel is the existential struggle and that, as mode of making reality actualized and livable, the existential conditions have to be just. The rebel is justified by the fact that things have to be just, and injustice must end. More rebels by saying no.

> He rebels because he categorically refuses to submit to conditions that he considers intolerable and also because he is confusedly convinced that his position is justified, or rather, because in his own mind he thinks that he "has the right to. . . ." Rebellion cannot exist without the feeling that somewhere, in some way, you are justified.[18]

To say no, by affirming one's being, is justification. That is why it is important, as Camus states, to assert and justify the limits that the rebel upholds insofar as making the borderline clear. The borderline is the territoriality that the rebel must preserve by all means and, if need be, enforce those limits. The self-preservation of the rebel is what Camus points as something that is forever present even though not apparent. It cannot be a paradox at all since the existential struggle is about freedom. Where freedom exists is in the domain of life, and this is the life that must be lived freely. The justification of the rebel is that of the life of freedom.

It is important to state the question as Camus frames it: "Why rebel if there is nothing worth preserving in oneself?"[19] The self that gives itself in the service of the existential struggle is not that of martyrdom, but the life of freedom. The rebel does not wage the struggle for the purposes of individualism. There is nothing bourgeoisie in being the rebel and as such, this is the struggle of those who embody the collective will. What oppresses More is what oppresses those who are in the black condition—being-black-in-an-antiblack-world. By justifying his existence, More is also affirmed by the collective justification of those who are rebelling in common. Camus punctuates to say the following: "He acts, therefore, in the name of certain values which still indeterminate but which he feels are common to himself and to all men [*sic*]."[20]

The black condition affects the collectivity of the black. The struggle that emerges from the black, which More partakes, is the one whose name is not for the individual. Antiblackness is the infrastructural condition that More confronts in the name of the reality of the everyday life of the black which is the life denied. To rebel, then, is the act of the collective will, in that More takes a stand and his modes of justifications are directed to a system that dehumanizes the black and this necessitates standing for the values of freedom. First of all, the rebel has to evoke a value of self-respect and that having to mean not allowing oneself to be complicit in the condition of one's own unfreedom. By not compromising, the rebel respects the self and it is on the basis of this self-respect that will make the rebel to stand for something. If the rebel does not stand for something, this means that the rebel will fall for anything. The rebel is informed by the value of oneself (self-respect) and standing for something (principle). It is the solidification of this that makes being justified to mean standing up for oneself and a worthy cause. This is what denotes a value—the conjoined nature of self-respect and principle. Camus is instructive here: "Not every value leads to rebellion, but every rebellion tacitly invokes a value."[21] By valuing oneself, More asserts: "I have always wondered what my existence in the world meant for me."[22] It is this wonder that continuously makes More to constantly solidify his justification and to continue to deepen the analytics of his existential struggle. It is this wonder that makes More to evoke value in his own being and also from the world that has been denied of value. The wonder that More wrestles with is the one of having been denied freedom. The collectivity of the black comes as the result of having a collective expression that calls for the value being something that is dispossessed from them. The cause that More is in is the black cause. So, he is the rebel with a cause, a black one at that. This is the cause of those who value freedom. The rebellion will be waged in the name of value. It is those who value their freedom. More is one of them and he values his being as that which he cannot trade in order to make gains that are fettered to their desires of antiblack. It is clear from this that the rebel is the one who cannot sell his or her soul for temporary gains that are at the expense of the collective will. There is everything there is to value that even transcends the imagination of the rebel or what might not even be known at the time of the rebellion.

The rebel is marked by value in the face of being devalued. Here, in More's case, value is what he accords and affords himself. In the world that dehumanizes him, More says "no" to this devaluing and says "yes" to his self-generated value. The value that will be accorded and afforded to him by antiblackness is not value, but devaluing in its blatant form. By having to engage the meaning of his existence, what came out of him is the eruptive force that is shaped by the choices he made in order to be free. This, on a different take, can result in the choice of questioning one's own humanity as the result of having one's humanity questioned. This will mean saying "yes" to dehumanization as opposed to saying "no." It is clear from here that the rebel is not the one who says "yes" because the rebel does not, in upholding one's own value, say yes to dehumanization. Since the rebel says "no," there can only be "yes" only in the conditions that affirm value—say, the rebel is saying "yes" to (re)humanization. It is this affirmative standing that makes the existential struggle to be the "yes" to everything that is for freedom. It is what the rebel will have been in identification with as value, the value of More as one which is of the being who is in struggle for his value and the value of the freedom of the collective will and that as the "yes" to the livable life as opposed to the black condition of dehumanization. There is a clear line that is drawn in terms of value. This is the value of freedom, and so its specificity in terms of Camusian differentiation of what value connotes.

What Gordon brings to the fore is the dimension of the lived reality of values, and this is key to position the centrality of black life as the axis of reflection.[23] It is this mode of articulation that makes reality to be a reflexive. What becomes the principal function of the rebel is to take a stance that "address the lived reality of values."[24] As if referring to More, Camus writes: "The rebel demands that these values should be clearly recognized as part of himself because he knows or suspects that, without them, crime and disorder would reign in the world."[25] This will mean, in insisting on different set of conditions of existence, the rebel will go on and all the way to stand justified in the face of injustice, to stand in the name of value and against all there is that is against this value. What is essential in Gordon is commitment, and it is the value that justifies the necessity of the struggle for freedom.[26] It is commitment that even fuels the existential struggle. The principality of value is, in the rebel's effort to create another world, the ethical question that emerges in the belly of antiblackness.

> For the black, in other words, the white *is* another human being, but the structure of antiblack racism is such that for the antiblack racist, the black is not another human being. The struggle against antiblack racism is such, then, that it involves an effort to achieve Otherness. It is a struggle to enter the realm, in other worlds, the ethical relations are forged.[27]

It is the rebel who forges this and it means that this is not the assimilationist and accommodationist affair as the scandal of antiblackness looms large in having the humanity of the black to be that which is in perpetual question. The ethical relations, as Gordon notes, needs to be unmasked both at the level structural and situational level. By this, he refers to the structural as ethical institutional relations and to the situational he means ethical relations between individuals. It is this total reconfiguration that sets in motion the tenants of the existential struggle as set out by the rebel who is ethically violated at the level of ontology. Antiblackness is the structural and situational ethical denial.

More, the rebel, is the one who is denied. The purpose is not for him to be permitted, it is what he brings to being that matters—rebellion. It is what he does because it has to be done. The value that More attaches to freedom is what he cannot prevent for it to be acted on and actualized. What is denied is what, by necessity, is value to be fought for, as it is worthy and just. There is all there is to value, everything.

When More is in good standing, him being of/in/with value in himself, that also means the rebels value what is being fought for. The existential struggle of the black means to be in defense of value. More stands for value, as the violation of value is the reality that he cannot accept. For him to be of no value is the condition that he overturns and overhauls; the overdetermination of this not being the last instance. What is value is what More authorizes from his philosophical project as the refusal of the abstraction of the black to be a thing of no value, a thing to be exposed and disposed to the domain of nothingness. In becoming something, by fighting for that something, what is value is the spirit that erupts from within that gives value to what has been abstracted from value to become a thing. A thing is what More cannot be. Seeing the ontological status of being-black-in-an-antiblack-world as a situation, this is what More rebels against and that there should be other terms of engagement. It is the rebel having embarked on the affirmation of value in order to obliterate the abstractions that renders the black to be a thing. The abstraction of the black is what is changed by the rebel to be a living embodiment.

The question of value is what has been made not to stand side-by-side with blackness. Denise Ferreira da Silva argues that the determination of value has been rare and obsolete insofar as that can be of substance, the very thing that can be said to be the "modern grammar," which is invested in the obliteration of the black, is everything that is the antithesis of value.[28] By calling for the activation of the disruptive force, this is what makes reality to be "exposed as the excess that justifies otherwise untenable racial violence."[29] What is absolute and determinate is what is shuttered, and in making this assertion, da Silva states that "blackness has the capacity to disclose another horizon of existence, with its attendant accounts of existence."[30] The way of fashioning existence otherwise, to be that kind of the different that is determined by the black and not the colonial different, nothing is deferred as the black construct itself in different modalities that necessitate the different modes of being-black-in-an-antiblack-world.

When it comes to all there is in terms of what is value, clearly the terms of conceptualization of this value are different. There is no way that the rebel can expect value from what negativizes. There is no value to be derived from what devalues by means of continued antiblackness. The insistent on the different, what devalues the black to be the different other, is what the rebel faces and it is in the name of what da Silva calls the "ethical indifferent"—the thing which, without irony, is so indifferent to ethics themselves. It is clear from da Silva that there is nothing ethical in this violation where all ontological formations to all things black are obliterated. The reality of the black is subjected to the different to solidify the determinate, to make it always a certainty. By throwing everything in the realm of abstraction, the operating logic is one of obliteration—the determination of value of the different—the devaluing of the black as what cannot be equated with anything of value. For, as da Silva states, "blackness occupies the place of negative life—that is, life that has negative value"—the different.[31] The different is imposed, in that the black assumes the negative, the very subtraction, and abstraction of value.

Being-black-in-an-antiblack-world is to be made to be subtracted from value. It is to be different as being-in-the-world. This situation, which More triggers being a rebel, is the "starting point human consciousness."[32] This is where value starts to be in its own terms. Those who are denied value come into consciousness to be in their own value and to value what makes their existence meaningful. It takes the rebel to authorize and uphold value. For, the rebel is, just like More, one who stands for something and is committed to the existential struggle to make reality to be radically different from what it was.

For More to be the rebel, it means that he must have a personal identity. That means, in this case, he is the one who is identified with freedom. It is not that he is freedom as if this is a given. It is the freedom that he, as a philosopher of existence, fights for in order to create a different set of conditions. As Camus argues, this "is the transition from 'this is how things should be' to 'this is how I want things to be,' and still more, perhaps, the conception of the submission of the individual to the common good."[33] It is clear from what manifest as value is not selling one's soul. More is the one who sees the principality of valuing oneself as what can necessitate clear ontological demands.

> The act of rebellion carries beyond the point he reached by simply refusing. He exceeds the bounds that he established for his antagonistic and demands that he should be now be treated as an equal. What was, originally, an obstinate resistance on the part of the rebel, becomes the rebel personified. He proceeds to put self-respect above everything else and proclaims that it is preferable to life itself.[34]

It is clear, insofar as the rebel is concerned, of how much valuable is value itself. It is this value that will make the rebellion to even be elevated to the realm of the sacred and anything to live for until such time conditions fundamentally change. Even beyond that, this value will be protected at all costs. It is not only having to know the sacrifices that are made in its own name but rather, more pointedly, it is something that is just. By valuing value, it is worthy to insist how the existential struggle cannot be delegated since this will mean its very abdication—devaluing. The rebel will not obey anything that comes at the expense of what is value. More writes:

> As black people, we speak because we dare to look in the mirror and see what we are not; we speak because blackness has come to represent negativity, nothingness; we speak because we seek to name ourselves, defines ourselves, re-invent ourselves—and we speak because we want to free ourselves.[35]

There is everything to value and value is everything.

Self-respect, which is the value of one's own being, also extends to the humanity that More identifies with as this is the fellow black-being-in-an-antiblack-world who have been devalued so much to the extent that they are made to accept their devaluing as a fate that cannot be challenged and changed as this is structurally deliberate. What More insists upon is the reawakening of the sense of value in being; "to fight for the integrity of one part of one's being"—to be one who is of value.[36]

The life of freedom is the one that cannot be compromised. To be complicit in what compromises freedom is the life that More refuses to lead and live. What is of value is what will be valued. The value of oneself is also the value of the very thing that one extends value to.

THE REPUBLIC OF SILENCE

The edifice of antiblackness makes itself that which is absolute, solid, invincible, mighty, and all things that are beyond any human possibility. The rebel is often warned, by way of discouraging, that nothing will change and there is nothing that the rebel can do. So, all there is to it is that the rebel must be silent.

The struggle to ultimate freedom, which is everything, to More, that is of value, is the refusal to be cowed down in silence.[37] As Edward Said notes, what is the animating force is "a desire for articulation as opposed to silence."[38] This desire is actualized seriously by More who, as the rebel, will speak anyway. What More takes seriously is not the right to speak but the necessity to do so. More speaks, necessarily so, in the name of freedom. He is speaking of/for what is denied of the black. He is speaking of what is both right and rightful. As a matter of fact, More the rebel is, in all accounts, one who is not only free but one who is freedom. Even in the conditions of his unfreedom, he should, all the time, be free to do so. What is denied of him is what he has to take. Being confined to silence is the mold that he must break.

The refusal to be silent is what the rebel is as this is the figure that speaks up/out. By being in good standing, the refusal to be silenced means saying "yes" to *saying it as it has to be said* and *telling it like it is*. It is the self that speaks in its own name and for what it stands for. It is the selfhood of freedom. This means More, the rebel, speaks of freedom from "a rebellious assertion of selfhood in a context bent on coercively suppressing that very self, a context bent on limiting the boundaries of possibility."[39] Reality is turned to be what the rebel wants it to be. The absolute rejection of the conditions that the rebel is in absolutely alters reality altogether in the sense that the rebel has a different outlook of reality. No more will it be a given, it is now exposed for what it is, and it is now in the eyes that look at it differently. In short, it is not what it is.

Truth is what the rebels stands for. As a philosopher of existence, More puts philosophy in the service of truth insofar as it is fundamental change and this, not being the cliché of the universal, truth here is the authenticity of waging the existential struggle in the name of the truth of being-black-in-an-antiblack-world without submitting to sensor and withdrawal.

The pursuit of truth is standing against false consciousness. It is to take sides and that means to be on the side of truth. The rebel always takes sides and that means taking responsibility. This is true consciousness and taking responsibility is being in the situation and acting in a manner that is always in the name of that truth. This, according to More, is "a decisiveness and resoluteness derived from an act of pure reflective consciousness."[40] Clearly, taking sides means, as More notes, "a search and a quest for authenticity."[41] It is this uncompromising take that means there is no neutrality that can be claimed. The authentic self does not suffer from false consciousness. The search for authenticity means standing for what is just in the face of what is unjust—dehumanization.

This is the truth that challenges what Jean-Paul Sartre calls The Republic of Silence.[42] It is in the oppressive conditions that those who rebel will, according to Sartre, find the deepest source of their freedom. It is here that rebellion will become manifest and this is the result of having to understand what are the stakes. Being high, and the status of being dehumanized, there comes the sources of being. It does not mean that Sartre valorizes the status of being dehumanized. It is realizing how deep should the rebel go to the source of being as the result of having been dehumanized. It is from the status of loss that will necessitate the rebel to insist on taking the stance if there is everything to lose and, on the other hand, there is everything to gain. This is not a contradiction, but these temporalities exist on the basis of the situation at hand. There is nothing to lose in fighting for freedom, and there is also everything to lose in fighting for freedom. What is made apparent here is that there cannot be any silence or enjoying life in the Republic of Silence.

Fidelity to truth means, for Sartre, carrying a message, and this meant taking risks. This is, in the sense of being the rebel, setting oneself freely, to Sartre, irredeemably so, "against the oppressor."[43] It is the oppressor who wants tongues to submit to silence and this is what is fiercely opposed by Sartre. Freedom comes with the responsibility of confronting its violation. To speak, which is the transgression in The Republic of Silence is the authentic duty that the rebel must undertake.

For More, to speak is to protect one's own freedom.[44] By not choosing silence and choosing to speak is freedom. It is to act in accordance to one's own will. To rebel is to act, freely at best.

The existential conditions of the rebel have been that of denial. The reign of silence is imposed. This means no one will speak against The Republic of Silence. But Sartre notes: "The more the omnipotent police tried to enforce our silence, the more each of our words became a precious declaration."[45] There is no way the rebel can be thwarted by the heightening power of oppression. All there is to it to fight to the end. This, as it is known, is the spirit of the level having reached the state of being enough, and reality cannot be ignored that the rebel must, at all costs, speak. To be the rebel means not pledging any form of allegiance to The Republic of Silence. By resisting and asserting the self of being, this is the being who speaks in the language of resistance to lies and standing side-by-side with truth. This is the truth of "black radicalism" wherein which, according to Cedric Robinson, "the total configuration of human experience requires other forms."[46] There is no way that More can accept an antiblack and dehumanizing infrastructure to be the absolute order and the last word that he must obey. Formidable opposition, which is the embodied spirit of the rebel, is what is brought into being, as Robinson notes, as a way of authorizing this total configuration. The dominant script cannot, at all, hold. There is no way that the rebel can consent to what should be formidably opposed. The other forms that the rebel brings into are those that have to do with fashioning a different conception of reality.

What is this reality, again, so to punctuate? It has always been the imposed reality. It has always been an antiblack reality. It has always been everything turned against the black. As to rebound, here is Robinson, stating fully thus: "The sum was the dehumanization of Blacks."[47] The distortion has been maintained in order to delegitimize any form of speech that the black will bring into being. It is this dehumanization that even went in perverted ways to still even deny any form of the black narrative to feature anywhere to what might even be termed the discourse. Indeed, in an antiblack world, the possibility of discourse is even eliminated.

The rebel, More in this case, will not allow the elimination of discourse to be what will prevail.[48] The modes of inscription that come into being then are the ones which do not seek to dialogue with the apartheid system, but rather against it. The apartheid discourse is The Republic of Silence and there is nothing worthy of it to be dialogued with because it will be comic to dialogue with what violently eliminates. More insists on asserting one's own being and speaking truth in the name of what one is. This mode of speaking otherwise means ontological totality, as Robinson articulates it, brings into being the politics of being as another attitude, and added to it, there is a break that insists on a breakthrough that is warranted by the existential struggle. Ontological totality, which More is in the fold of, is what has been existing, which in Robinsonian terms is black radicalism. There is everything to this black radicalism that locates More as the rebel who speaks against the Republic of Silence. There is, in More's philosophical project, both the foundational and collective expression.

Truth is pursued in the name of speaking against the conditions that the self is in. This truth is thorny to antiblackness as it would not want to be called out in the name of what it is. Being silent on reality and not raising a voice against it is what the rebel can stand for, but to, according to Said, engaging oneself in the act of speaking truth to power.[49] This means, according to Said, "being a witness to persecution and suffering, and supplying a dissenting voice in conflicts with authority."[50]

Robinson calls for the reanimation of myth and legend in order to break away from the imposed order of politicality.[51] The task is to expose what is imposed. The infrastructural change of how to live better is what the rebel is at. In the same breath with Robinson, More is concerned with a different set of conditions of creating life under duress. It is clear how politicality is what the rebel resists, and making sense of reality will mean having to think and actualize the reality of freedom. The rebel exposes what Robinson will articulate as "the contradictions resident in the political order."[52] By insisting that truth be upheld, the rebel is committed to "an active definition of the situation."[53] The rebel stands against what Robison identifies as maintaining of authority by agencies of power and this, in the name of order—the imposed "empirical matrix." The modes of speaking that are couched as proper ways is the legibility that is weaponized to impose silence to those who might be said to be speaking in obscene ways against politicality.

What is always important for the rebel is understanding the nature of the operations of power. More is of the belief that politicality has no interests of the people and they are subjected to the impositions that even interpellate them to consent. It is against this reality that there must be the emergence of collective will to engage in the practices of freedom by way of what Robin D. G. Kelley refers to as "freedom dreams" which, in all and potent ways, gives a powerful expression of the voice of the collective will.[54] Freedom dreams erupt from the conditions of being denied freedom and making this possible, they actualize life in the midst of denial. There vitality of freedom dreams is the confrontation with closures. For Kelley, the collective will, as articulated in freedom dreams, "opens new vistas for inquiry."[55] The way transformative assertions are actualized is, in all ways, puncturing the edifice of power, and thus unveiling its operations. It is in this spirit of black radicalism that the rebel knows what is it that is being targeted and why. The whole total field of existence is fundamentally changed because the rebel is not what was thought to be known. By doing what has not being expected—what is necessary to be done, though—it should be of no surprise that the black radicalism of the rebel, which Kelley locates in the realm of black radical imagination, will do what has not been anticipated.

By doing what is just, and for the collective will of the black, it is worth stating that having to operate from the locus of what Kelley calls "infrapolitics" by definition which is the collective expression of those who do not have avenues but create alternative one in the condition of antiblackness, other modes of existence are being insisted upon.[56] This is the spirit of rebellion and the politics of those who are being denied of being *homo politicos* comes to be authorized in their own name. The lived experience of being-black-in-an-antiblack-world necessitates infrapolitics to be intensified. It is in the collective will of blackness to be in common in the existential struggle. Even if there are various forms of struggles among the black, huge differences notwithstanding, it is not amiss to mention that antiblackness is a unified force against the black. To be black is to be at the receiving end of antiblackness and to engage in infrapolitics means contending with differences within the fold of blackness.

Kelley is correct to mention that infrapolitics is not about the fashioning of alternatives, but a way of gauging formations and relations of power. It is here that the apparent is not what is valorized, but what has, according to Kelley, "remained unacknowledged and unexamined."[57] The infrapolitics of the rebel have been relegated to the realm of disorder and nothing that is not worthy to have legitimacy extended to. But seldom is it asked, is it questioned how power is there, in its dominant mode, to write its own narrative and legitimate it. There is no quest for legibility on the part of the rebel, let alone the quest to be recognized in the terms of the imposed order. Since politicality is what is confronted, Robinson has consistently shown how politically engaged critique of power has been what is thought side-by-side with the everyday life of blackness.[58] It is these radical acts that life gets reconfigured by way of potentialities that continue to be articulated even in the face of impossibilities. Since freedom dreams actualize, there is this radical insistence that stays with the spirit of the rebel. The structure that organizes reality in its antibackness is the one that disorganizes the reality of the black. By rebelling, it is clear that More is organizing the reality of the black in the face of the disorganizing force. The disorganization that he faces is so petty and grand, in a sense that it dehumanizes. Infrapolitics is the reorganization of what has been subjected to disorganization. Since infrapolitics are driven by the rebellious spirit that Kelley calls the black radical imagination, this is cemented by the commitment that things will fundamentally change.[59] What is it that fuels the intrapolitics of the rebel, then? Kelley writes: "It is fundamentally a product of struggle, of victories and losses, crises and openings, and endless conversations circulating in a shared environment."[60] The rebel is caught with contradictions, and the emergence of the rebel is having to emerge out of them. What is clear is that at the foundation of the rebel is the standing for something, standing for what is right and just. It is in the annals of infrapolitics that the rebel will speak and will continue to speak without fear. There is everything there is that can make the rebel to recoil in silence, but this is not what the rebel will choose as the cause is even larger than the rebel. The very nature of the existential struggle does not demand any form of silence from the rebel. The radical imagination of the rebel should be translated to the everyday life of the existential struggle and that is why living with contradictions is the reality of the rebel. This is the reality of knowing that easy gains and settling for negotiations is not the way. What is a fact, as it is known, is that the radical imagination of the rebel always brings the impossible into being, it is the reality that becomes altered in the midst of what is not deemed real. What the rebel says and does is what is not supposed to be said and done. The Republic of Silence is supposed to be the last defining order and there is nothing that can be done about that. Having chosen otherwise, the rebel rejects the imposed order of The Republic of Silence. There is no way that this can be the order that the rebel will obey its command as it veers off from what is just and right.

There is no last saying of politicality. Even if it is presented as logical, stable, coherent, and just, these infrastructure of power and order serve as the empirical matrix that hides the everyday practices of dehumanization that the rebel is there to expose. Even in his philosophical insights, More shows that the rebel is the one who grows out of the system.[61] By refusing to be in perpetual servitude, the rebel is the one who, according to More, the system has to be spoken against and to grow out of it means getting out of The Republic of Silence. What the rebel does, as More notes, is having "refused to take the insults and restrictions in silence."[62] In The Republic of Silence, More states that there is no way that tongues will be in a halt, they will speak. More daringly declares: "As black people, we speak because we dare to look in the mirror and see what we are not; we speak because blackness has come to represent negativity, nothingness; we speak because we seek to name ourselves, define ourselves, re-invent ourselves—and we speak because we want to free ourselves."[63] It is clear that this is not a permission-seeking exercise. To speak is the prerogative of the rebel to do so.

For speaking against The Republic of Silence, the rebel knows that this comes with a price. As it is obvious, the rebel faces a backlash which is "much coarser and more instrumental processes whose goal is to mobilize consent, to eradicate dissent, to promote an almost literally blind loyalty."[64] But this will still make the rebel to be adamant. Having to say what has to be said is what the rebel stands for. To live free, according to More, is saying what has to be said without even having to ask for authorization.[65] Now, under the conditions of unfreedom, saying what has to be said is the value that More cannot part with. Not that saying something is the right (like the liberal and hypocritical notion of "free speech"), but saying the unsayable in the face of antiblackness. It is the saying of the one who does not possess the authorized speech. This, for obvious reasons, presents a scandal, in that The Republic of Silence fabricated reality to such an extent that dehumanization has made the black to internalize silence with the normal way of life. This is not the case and it shall never be for the rebel who, for the most part, all that has to be lived for has to be said in the name of freedom that was dispossessed. Therefore, the fight to speak in the name of freedom is not, for More, a flight of fancy. It is not only a serious matter, but a deadly one.

In the conditions of unfreedom, the rebel enchants by making silence speak, loudly so. This is the assertion that makes things to be what they have not been. It is saying the unsayable. It is making what has been unheard heart. In a sense, the foundations of The Republic of Silence become interrupted. Out of sheer determination to be free, the rebel confronts the Republic of Silence. To speak, then, is in the name of affirmation and as More rightfully notes, this is the opposite of negation.[66]

The rebel is situated, embodied, and in the concrete in The Republic of Silence underwritten by an antiblack world. It is in this reality that the rebel must speak. The self, as More insists, cannot be suppressed. The self has to declare itself liberated even in the clutches of unfreedom in order to wage the existential struggle. Truly, there is no existential struggle without speech. There is no existential struggle without the ontological inscription of rewriting the self into freedom. Since freedom is dispossessed, and dehumanization is imposed on the black, it is worth nothing that, again, the rebel is charged with the responsibility for freedom. There is no way that there will be freedom in silence. The Republic of Silence exists solely to make sure that there is no freedom. Since this is the rejected condition, the means of the existential struggle are justified. This justification is one that does not stem from claiming any form of legibility, but the truth that shapes the reality of being-black-in-an-antiblack-world. It means, by all means, the justification of black "infrapolitics" as per Kelley's concept which Tina Campt states is "practices of thinking, planning, writing, and imaginations new forms of freedom."[67] The rebel, in this fold of infrapolitics is nothing short of being rebellious. According to Campt, there is no legitimate authority in The Republic of Silence as the act of convening is also the corollary of conveying. What has to be said has to be said by all means.

In fidelity to truth, the rebel crafts a meaningful existence and what is conveyed is what is rooted in the spirit of not only being outspoken, but not submitting to silence. The truth about what must be said is always spelled out. Even if what is desired does not come into fruition, this does not make fidelity to truth to be abandoned. The existential struggle still surges through in the quest for truth, and in More's philosophical anthropology, what is always evident is the signification of the restless soul. How can the rebel settle when matters that are of life and death are unsettling the everyday life of the black?

The spirit of the rebel is that of critique, and according to Said, "critique is always restlessly self-clarifying in search of freedom, enlightenment, more agency, and certainly not their opposites."[68] From Said, it is clear that a position is taken and nothing is amoebic in character. In having to attest on what faces the rebel, Said attests: "None of this can be done easily."[69] The stance that More takes in his philosophical anthropology is having to ask thorny questions, and standing side-by-side with truth and not selling out. The spirit of critique from More is having to come from a principled position of the rebel's "yes" and "no." Critique makes it known where the rebel stands. The inseparability of the rebel from the critique is the very definitional task of the rebel. There is no way that the rebel can afford to be compromised by being complicit with what still dehumanizes the black. The radical altering of the total field of reality is what, according to Said, is the rejection of the fixed scheme. Against fixity, and against the assimilationist and accommodationist appellations it comes with, the rebel sets out a clear task of maintaining fidelity to truth. To be against fixity does not mean being flexible (if all there is to flexibility is having to be amoebic and not taking responsibility in the face of dehumanization). The principal purpose of one that the rebel will live by which is not being made to bend and also being bound. All the rebel is paying fidelity to is the truth that necessitates freedom.

Although, in a certain sense, the rebel is restless, this should not be mistaken as a luxurious choice. What is indissociably the making of the rebel is the conditions of unfreedom which will make the rebel not to rest, and there is no way that there can be a claim to rest when the everyday life of the black is structured in dehumanization. The absurdity of it all is expecting silence from the black. It will be a false claim that this is how things are supposed to be, reality as it has to be lived, and what the black should stand aside and maintain silence while everything is directed to the black. How possible is it to stand aside while reality directly confronts the black? It is rightful and justifiable for the black to act. What is the rebel's constant preoccupation is the question of freedom. The rebel cannot keep silent while being wronged.

That being said, More's existence depends on the will to be free, and it would thus be amiss to suggest that him taking a position he is exposing himself to the lethality of the racist state. Whether the black engages in rebellion or not, antiblackness will not stop to violate the black and still continue to cow the black in silence. What concretizes the freedom of the rebel is to fight for that freedom. So, More's freedom is contingent upon his existential struggle for freedom. He has, by all means, freedom to live for.

In The Republic of Silence, More is not its public, but rather, its counter-public. His radical reconceptualization of belonging is that of being categorically excluded, at best, ontologically eliminated. In a sense, he is not in the *polis* as he is not of it. If The Republic of Silence legitimates itself (illegitimately so, and doing so because it can) by means of vulgarity to the black, it cannot be expected that there will be allegiance from the black. How, then, can More accept, as the rebel, to be part of the polity that dehumanizes him? There is no way that More can be legitimated as the enunciating subject in this apparatus of exclusion. Not only does he not belong, he does not exist. Then, according to this logic, what is not there cannot speak. So, the black in The Republic of Silence is deemed not only mute, but at best, non-existent.

What is all the time radicalized is what the black is to the rebel and not what the black is as invented by The Republic of Silence. That is why the discursive order of The Republic of Silence remains unrecognized as reality. More, then, enunciates the expository speech. This speech, in a fundamental sense, signifies the oft-unspoken grammar—or, the unsayable whose articulation will always invite the wrath of The Republic of Silence. Since what Roman Grosfoguel terms "ontological extractivism" has been the logic of dehumanization, it has been expected that there will be no form of insurgency and insurrection from the black.[70] Ontological exractivism means the destruction of the lifeworld of the black rampant and continued dispossession—or worse, death. The ontological limit of the black, or what can be deemed its absolute qua excess is, in many ways, what can be deemed to be obliteration and obfuscation. Ontological extractivism, according to Grosfoguel, "is theft, pillage, and all plunder."[71] Clearly, nothing is expected to emerge from the black, even at the level of speech because all that is ontological is subjected to flatten out.

The discursive structure that rebel is—The Republic of Silence—is what Said calls the "force field" and being located in it means partaking in its rituals of discursive engagement. What, then, authorizes The Republic of Silence is what the rebel is not in service of and that to Said being that effort to "forestall deeper kinds of change or critiques of longstanding assumptions."[72] It is clear that the battle of the rebel is uphill, always. The rebel stands up and says enough is enough. The language of the rebel which is ethico-political stands to be interdicted, discredited, and pathologized just like the ontology of the rebel itself. This is because of not bowing to the liberal script. It is worth noting that the ontological erasure of the rebel is structured in ways that make any form of articulation mute in order to observe the absurd protocols of The Republic of Silence. The rebel is claimed to be the one who is tied to disorder. This is done in deliberate and systematic ways in order to make silence reign in the condition that it is not supposed to. Despite this, the trajectory that the rebel pursues is that of persisting to speak. Speaking from the condition of black suffering does not warrant any permission to be sought. It is this ethico-political stance that the rebel must assume and insist on throughout the existential struggle. Certainly, it is forever constantly costly for the rebel to stand for something. Obviously, to be a rebel is to stand besieged by the liberal script which accompanies dehumanization, hence its unforgiving condemnation when standing up for what is right is seen wrong if it is not the way that is palatable to the liberal sensibilities which, in form and character, are antiblack.

The voice of the rebel is the one which, most at times, and it is costly nature, mean the end of life. To speak of one's own freedom to die. The rebel speaks from having to experience—in the everyday life—the besiegement of wanton ontological violence and its murderous excess.

Why would it, then, be a taboo for the rebel to speak? Well, the rebel exposes the private desires of the liberal script's antiblackness and wanting nothing that has to do with the freedom of the black. Nothing, to the rebel, will remain unspoken as what has to be said has to be said—for, it is right to say something, even in the condition of unsayability.

The liberal script's architectonics are invested in the reformist-narrative-circuit whose articulations, agendas, and gestures have nothing to say and to do, with the freedom of the black in an antiblack world. All there is, and not surprisingly so, is the maintenance of the status quo, to be good and quite in The Republic of Silence. The reformist-narrative-circuit is not where the rebel, as More notes, finds "existential expression."[73] What the rebel stands for and articulates is what is not running counter to the trajectory of the existential struggle but what deepens it and surges it through even in the state of impossibility. The reformist-narrative-circuit stands as the structure and impediment of More's existential expression of the rebel which stands for freedom and thus, qua Camusian's disposition, the "All or Nothing." The reformist-narrative-circuit is a paradigm that violates the existence of the rebel. What is of interest is only to interdict and interrupt the rebel, and also to demobilize and demolish whatever the rebel stands for. The reformist-narrative-circuit is feted for having been antiblack in standing and character. This means there is no compatibility between the rebel and this paradigm.

The radical insistence of the rebel to speak comes from the spirit of saying it. It is being in service of the existential struggle, and that is why More rightfully calls this the existential expression which cannot be any form of deputized speech. For, there is nothing worthy of expression in the case of the latter, but silence that authorizes the standing of The Republic of Silence. That is why the reformist-narrative-circuit will not stand up/out and say anything in The Republic of Silence except only to be complicit in antiblackness.

There is nothing to be called existential expression in the reformist-narrative-circuit as there is no existential struggle to speak of in that paradigm. The reformist-narrative-circuit is all about respectability politics and this is where there is nothing of any sort that comes closer to More's existential expression. In pushing for respectability politics, the rope will be forever behaving to police the rebel and to arrogantly dictate to the rebel that it is important to "tone down" and to not "rock the boat." The principles of the rebel which want "All or Nothing" are always deemed downright immoral and irresponsible. The pathologizing trope is weaponized by the reformist-narrative-circuit to make respectability politics to be all there in having to effect change. There is nothing that the reformist-narrative-circuit can show in having to effecting change except being acted upon and also leaving the infrastructure of antiblackness untouched, and also tons of failures that are the resultant part of being complicit. No matter how passionately argued respectability politics are, they could not ward off the weight of disrespect that they fear to confront and having to choose silence as a refuge. The reformist-narrative-circuit is antiblack by virtue of its complicity. It has always been the abdication of responsibility. It has been deputized to such an extent that it serves as the tool used to wage a frontal attack on the rebel. It is paradigmatically positioned to be a silent partner in The Republic of Silence. It can even be said further that the reformist-narrative-circuit is The Republic of Silence. It is the closed circuit that wants nothing but silence. All there is to the reformist-narrative-circuit is narcissism and its corollary feel-good factor. It is in the reformist-narrative-circuit where the aspirations of the black will be frustrated as they are sanitized, distorted, censured, and rendered mute. This is nothing but depoliticization, at best, impotence. Since respectability politics are all about ingratiating into antiblackness and wanting everything to do with cosmetic changes as opposed to fundamental change, there is a lot of resentment and impassioned hate that is then directed to the rebel because the latter exposes the ethico-political degeneracy of the reformist-narrative-circuit which, in the final analysis, bears nothing that is worthy of being deemed "respectable" and "political." So, respectability politics are nothing but hot air.

The reformist-narrative-circuit and its proponents, as More asserts, are contaminated as "the system has used them for its benefits."[74] Cleary, More blows up the reformist-narrative-circuit as it is a paradigm that perpetuates black suffering. The blowing of this circuit through the existential expression is putting a stop to the strictures and obstacles the black faces. The form of ethico-political enunciations and formations are not that of liberal allyship. It is made known by the rebel that the reformist-narrative-circuit is not recognized. The principle stems from what is at stake. More's disposition is Camusian right through and through, and this is a matter that has to do with freedom and this cannot be asserted from the tamed spirit of respectability politics which, in its fixity into the reformist-narrative-circuit, is everything that is fundamentally antiblack. The rebel cannot act in self-destructing ways by relinquishing the responsibility of freedom to antiblackness. The freedom of the black is against antiblackness and there is nothing that can yield freedom from antiblackness. But why is it that the reformist-narrative-circuit insists the rebel to wage the existential struggle within its enclosures? This is more puzzling and the reformist-narrative-circuit cannot come to terms in having to answer this flat question. Another interesting thing is that the reformist-narrative-circuit wants change without change. Inside its grammar, respectability politics are passionately argued for even in their dead-end. Inside the grammar of the reformist-narrative-circuit are things like being "measured," "responsible," "credible," "lawful," and "playing by the rules," and all things that are nothing but evasive when it comes to having to face reality as it is. The naivety of all this is having to surrender to the assimilationist and accommodationist traps of The Republic of Silence, where it is falsely claimed (and that being a tiring cliché) that change will happen "inside the system."

While the rebel wants freedom in its absolutes, it is not clear as to what is a state for the reactionary elements in the reformist-narrative-circuit, the latter who happen to claim allyship while they are sworn enemies of whoever is the rebel. There is nothing for the black in this circuit, even blacks who are at its "commanding heights." All there is to it is nothing but antiblackness. Too, it is naïve to expect anything substantial coming from the reformist-narrative-circuit as it is ontologically corrupt and has nothing to do not only with the existential demands of the black but with the existence of the black *writ large*. This is, in all ways, dehumanization proper. It is having no regard for the black or whatever things, whatsoever, that has to do with the black. But as More states, taking away anything and everything that has to do with the livelihood of the black is what the rebel radically refuses.[75] The rebel is the one who refuses to be a lifeless life-form.

THE THREAT AND FEAR OF DEATH

The act of threatening is meant to illicit fear. Going against the grain, the rebel does not give up and even in death. There is nothing equivalent with death. The rebel does not suffer from what W. E. B. Du Bois would call "double consciousness."[76] The rebel is the one contesting death by the way it is instrumentalized to maintain dehumanization. The rebel is not martyr, but as More states, one who is in pursuit of the existential struggle. The rebel, in this instance, carries a duty of doing what has to be done.

What the rebel stands by is the principle that what has to be said has to be said and what has to be done has to be done. It is not only matter of saying or doing something or just anything, but what the rebel deems right and just, since the cause of the rebel is believed to be justified. Since the rebel lives by the word and deed, it is always expected for the rebel not to be in fear. In short, More as the rebel is the one who does not live in fear. It is the absence of fear that makes the rebel not to succumb to the fear of death. The rebel stands against the impediment and, obviously, the existence of the rebel is a precarious one, being in a predicament forever.

What is it, primarily, that the rebel wants? It has been made clear that the rebel wants *to be free*. What the rebel wants is what cannot be bought, sold, and exchanged. It is what must be created. As the responsibility of the rebel, freedom cannot, also, be a gift to the rebel. It is expected for the rebel to act on the change that must be necessitated. Nothing is for free. The cost of freedom is one that the rebel has to determine and examine. It is what the rebel wants that counts anyway. All this is in the face of imminent death. As More concurs, the determination to be free is one's willingness to encounter death and this is what fashions one to become the rebel.[77] In order to affirm oneself in the face of imminent death is to risk one's life, and this will, most possibly, lead to death. More takes note of the fact that to be the rebel is to risk one's own existence. It is to exist knowing that to live is to risk the very idea of living. Death is the surround; it is the totality that puts the ontology of the rebel in the hold and the stranglehold. Restrained and refusing, the rebel faces death but not submitting the self as the object to be sacrificed; here is a fighting being, one who stands against death through the affirmation of the life of freedom. The rebel faces death in order to be against it. This attitudinal impulse makes the fear of death not to be a determining factor whose last word and deed will send the rebel to fear of not taking the risk which, in the conviction of the rebel, is always worthy.

There is no going around the responsibility that faces the rebel, the responsibility which the rebel takes, one which the rebel is even prepared to die for. Here, it is clear that death is the last resort, since all there is to the rebel is not giving in to submission and complicity. What the rebel stands for, all which is in the name of freedom, is necessity. It is the necessity of what must happen, for it must happen. This, for sure, cannot be avoided. The rebel is responsible for what must happen. The waging of the existential struggle is necessary. The rebel exists because of necessity. All that the rebel wants is what will be fought for.

The rebel is the one who is willing to go into a battle. This is justified as the existence of the rebel in an antiblack world where war is declared on the black. The one who fights for what is just and right without giving in. The one who is willing to fight through and through until what is fought for is gained. What the rebel does is a continuation of history. The rebel has been confronted with death.

More, the rebel, is in the cause that can be said to be the insurrection of the oppressed. He comes from that reality and it is the reality that he still lives in. It is where death is refused to have the last say. The force of insurrection is the interruption to the status quo. There is no way that the infrastructure of antiblackness, in its modalities of the threat of death, as Abdul JanMohammed states, can reign as the sovereign power.[78] More cannot accept the threat of death, which JanMohammed deems to be extra-judicial, to be what will make the rebel not to take the responsibility to act in the name of freedom. The threat of death, which, in the condition of antiblackness becomes mundane, as a disciplinary practice, is what even goes to the extent of having death actualized. Within the protection of the antiblackness, what is done to the black, within the extra-judicial means, is what is sanctified. It is this spirit, which claims to be pious, and thus dwelling in the excess of immunity, that make the last say of the racist state to be, in all its perversities, to be exempted. Whatever that is done to the black goes unpunished. It is not only right, but it is sanctity itself. The threat of death to the black is articulated and expressed with no regard, it is the act that, according to JanMohammed, "is the *occasion* that is designed to produce the terror of death."[79] The implications of what negatively befalls the black are what justified antiblackness. And that, having been an extra-judicial affair, is even supported by what is deemed legal. So, there is nothing that can be said to be, in the infrastructure of antiblackness, legal or not. There is no difference because the threat or death, and its actualization is the very ideology of the racist state.

To be black is to be outside the juridical protection of whatever that can be deemed to be the legibility of rights that can be extended to the subject. The rebel, far outside of being the subject with rights, exposed and vulnerable to the wanton violence of death, its threat and actualization, is left with no other means but to act. What is worth noting is that whether the black acts or not, death will always maintain its operation. An antiblack world makes sense of itself by making the black to be, according to JanMohammed, "policed by the threat of death."[80] It is this instrument that makes the insurrection of the oppressed impossible, let alone the emergence of the rebel. By imposing this regime of policing, the threat of death is there to impose fear, and there will be no acting in the face of wanton violence against black existence. The threat of death is meant to solidify the might of the racist state, and when antiblackness is practiced and operates with excess and license, nothing should be done by the black. The practices and operations of antiblackness are foregrounded in the threat of death. The threat of death should, as to show the might of the racist state, actualize death. That is done to make the threat of death real. This is done in systematic, systemic, and continual ways. What this creates, according to JanMohammed, is the death-bound-subject "who is formed, from infancy on, by the imminent and ubiquitous threat of death."[81]

Such is the reality of being-black-in-an-antiblack-world which More is in and one that is the justified by the formation of him being the rebel. The threat of death is, as JanMohammed notes, one that can be said to lead to More's ontological formation. This is the formation that would, then, in its commitment to freedom, confront the fear of death.

More rightfully notes that the fear of death is heavily imposed and that becomes the mode of paralysis setting the black in apathy, inaction, and complicity. The black is made to be "a being who acceded to a servile relationship."[82] But it is clear that there is no relation of any form as the black is not even with relation to the self. This is a clear condition of being distant to what can be freedom itself. For, defeat reigns as being death-bound is what is imprinted in the consciousness of the black. This obliteration of consciousness makes the fear of death to become a way of life. This, indeed, is what is not a life at all.

Being bound by death is what More will not accept as the rebel as what reigns is "a natural instinct of self-preservation, a biological desire to live."[83] This is the spirit that stands to wrestle with the condition of being submissive and submerged in the threat of death. The rebel is what one is and also what one wants to become. In a sense, the existential struggle is waged from the reality of what is authentic. The authenticity of the rebel is not what will be realized by having gained freedom. Authentic existence, More argues, is "the search for a meaningful and dignified existence in the here and now."[84] It is in the condition of unfreedom that authenticity is heighted as value and that is intensified and sustained right through the very end of the existence of the rebel. To be authentic is to stand against the threat of death.

The absolute rejection of unfreedom, as the radical standing of the rebel, necessitates the existential struggle not to be assimilationist and accommodationist as these are tenants of having submitted to the threat of death. What JanMohammed importantly highlights is understanding "the threat of death as a mode of coercion."[85] This is made to coerce the black to be in the state of perpetual fear. It is to coerce the black not to act. As the mode of coercion, the threat of death does not anticipate being faced with the insurrection and insurgence that informs the authenticity of the rebel. It is in this authenticity that the rebel reveals what the threat of death dissimulates—its impotency. In as much as the threat of death that is backed up by what can be said to be the totality of the world and also its reason, the rebel still insist to bracket fear and also transcend it; and by launching the existential struggle, the cause is the one that will install the modes of articulation and narrations that, in their rejection of unfreedom, will stand at nothing to be assimilated and accommodated by the fear of death. The reality of the fear of death is the reality that the rebel is privy to, approximate to, and thus structured by it, but that which is authentic in the spirit of the rebel is the indomitable will to unsettle the solidity and oddity of what claims to be reality, hence setting forth another reality.

What is this another reality in this impending threat of death? Indeed, More does not accept to live under what JanMohammed marks as "a conditionally commuted death sentence."[86] Having stated that this can be withdrawn quickly, and the black being subjected to death, it is clear that the commuted death sentence is everything against the black. The black does not exist as being in the commuted sentence. In the commuted death sentence, there is nothing worthy of freedom, however conditional. The threat of death qua commuted death sentence means antiblackness. The perversity of deadly has nothing to do with the existence of the black.

> It is the imminent possibility of death that impels the one consciousness in the struggle to choose life as a slave rather than death. To a slavish consciousness, life under whatever oppressive and unbearable conditions is preferable to no life at all. It is this absolute fear of death that brings about slavery. But slavery is itself similar to being dead alive, for although one exists, one does not exist for oneself but for another. But since the slave is alive as a slave, his servile condition which is the overcoming of death is in fact death itself. As a dialectical transcendence of death, slavery in effect become the preservation of death in life. Having become a slave, the fear of death continues and is incarnated in the person of the master. The master becomes death itself to be absolutely feared and avoided. The master and slave relation is characterized by the bestial relation that is grounded upon brutality. Through this constant and perennial brutality, the slave is forced to internalized the fear and the terror that keeps him/her in a constant enslaved condition. The fear of death is inversely the fear of freedom.[87]

There are no relations in an antiblack world but the structure of subjection where the black is supposed to submit to dehumanization. According to More, assimilation and accommodation reify this structure that forces the black to accept dehumanization. This is supposed to be obliterated. In this obliteration means, according to More, the black must not be impotent in waging the existential struggle for freedom. There is all there is to freedom that demands, of the black, to be the rebel (one who is of the cause in the authentic pursuit of the existential struggle to live freely even at the cost of death).

It is unjustified for the black to live in dehumanization. The emphasis to overcome the threat and fear of death is, according to More, important in order not to perpetuate the oppressive conditions.[88] By choosing to act differently, by the black not acting in the way that antiblackness wants, More states that fear can be overcome, and when that happens, the logics of death become meaningless. What is referable, More states, is the raising of consciousness where fear is not the determining factor that there should be the stern refusal to be broken.

The rebel refuses to be clutched in the "paradoxical binding through death."[89] The submission to death is not what the rebel wants. There is everything to freedom that the rebel wants, and this makes the rebels to take a decisive step in advancing what the rebel wants. Things do not happen automatically, the rebel takes charge to effect change. Being death-bound is the deadly state, one which the rebel will not internalize. The fear of death, as More states, is instilled early by the act of the threat of death or its actualization to discourage the would-be rebels.[90] The conditions are made to be impossible, but the rebel's insurgent spirit makes them to be possible even if they do not yield the desired result. The rebel, according to More, "not only asserted his freedom but also simultaneously transcended the fear of death."[91] The rebel cannot be a mere thing that is death-bound. To live under the fear of death, whose threat is constant in the everyday life, the rebel's insurgent spirit writes the unpopular script: "no death shall bind." It is this spirit that makes life to be lived in the manner that it is deserved—its rightfulness, its livability. What is this if not the life of freedom? The death-bound subject does not live in the life of freedom. More states that "the oppressed participate in their own oppression by consenting to live under oppressive conditions."[92] To be under the spell of being death-bound is to be rendered impotent and worthless as being. In order to be being, the idea of worth living is fundamental and this is what cannot be a given, but what must erupt from the consciousness of the rebel and to make being to be what it is all for the life of freedom. Also, to be being in the terms that are set forth by the rebel. It is the freedom of the rebel that is threated and this is what the rebel must stand for. More locates everything that has to do with freedom squarely at the hands of the rebel. To fight for the life of freedom is to fight for the very idea of life itself, and this is the responsibility that the rebel must carry through and through. The life that the rebel wants is, having not to be in the subjection of being death-bound, one such that, at all times, should be asserted in ways that stand up against the threat of death and the fear of death.

It is to be expected that the threat and fear of death will continue to be intensified in order to put the black "in its own place." It means that the black must be in a stasis. But it is clear from More that the rebel disenchants stasis. What emerges, by way of the insurgent spirit, is More's ontological inscription of being-black-in-an-antiblack-world, and the discursive grammar of that positionality is anti-stasis thesis. It is in this thesis that the threat and fear of death remain challenged, combated, and challenged. This makes the center of antiblackness not to hold. Even there are no victories but defeats for the rebel, the existential struggle surges through in formidable ways in which, as it were, every start is a new start. The insurgent spirit is ever-charged to authorize the ontological inscription where the terms of being are that of the rebel and they are always that mode of continued self-definition and self-making. The anti-stasis thesis, then, is a radical refusal. The reign of the threat and fear of death are put in interdiction.

What matters is what the rebel wants. So, it is key to ask: What is it, exactly, that the rebel wants? Before answering this question, it is important to state that the rebel will not want what the rebel does not want in the first place. Whatever that is against the rebel is what the rebel will refuse. Stasis, by way of owning, controlling, and determining—that as the insistence of whatever that is against the rebel, makes it clear that the term of the freedom of the rebel cannot be engaged within the rubric of this stasis. The anti-stasis thesis makes possible what the rebel wants. Now, to the answer, the rebel wants fundamental change. To be exact, this is not cosmetic change. Therefore, the rebel wants fundamental change and does not want cosmetic change.

The rebel has a radical attitude. It is clear. What the rebel wants is clear. This radical attitude is captured well by Camus who states that it means "All or Nothing."[93] For there to the anti-stasis thesis, it is precisely because fundamental change is necessary for the life of freedom, the livable life that has to be otherwise, the otherwise determined by what the rebel wants. The radical attitude, therefore, in "All or Nothing" is decisive. This state of affairs is captured by Camus when he asserts: "Knowledge is born and conscience awakened."[94] There has been the submission of stasis; this is no longer. There has been the internalization of being death-bound; this is no longer. There has been the threat and fear of death that cowed the black into submission; this is no longer. The birth and the awakening of consciousness is the foundationality of the anti-stasis thesis. Things cannot be the way they were, they are subjected to radical ways of being-in-the-world where the black adopts the attitude of "All or Nothing." Here is the apt exposition:

> But it is obvious that the knowledge he gains in of an "All" that is still rather obscure and of a "Nothing" that proclaims the possibility of sacrificing the rebel to this "All." The rebel himself want to be "All"—to identify himself completely with the blessing of which has suddenly become aware and of which he wishes to be recognized and proclaimed as the incarnation—or "Nothing" which means to be destroyed by the power that governs him. As a last resort he is willing to accept the final defeat, which is death, rather than be deprived of the last sacrament which he would call, for example, freedom.[95]

The anti-stasis thesis is clear. It is "All or Nothing." Since everything in this existential struggle is in the name of freedom, it has to be fundamental. The threat and fear of death having been eliminated by this radical attitude of the birth of knowledge and awakening of freedom is, in pointed ways, the sacrament of the rebel. It is a place that the rebel will choose to dwell rather than trade it for anything. The soul of the rebel, being informed by this radical attitude, clearly means things are not what they used to be. Camus writes: "Previous to his insurrection, the slave accepted all the demands made upon him."[96] It is in stasis that this is the case. Now that the stasis is no longer there as the absolute, but what is fiercely contested, the anti-stasis thesis is the radical refusal that Camus captures thus:

> But with loss of patience—with impatience—begins a reaction which can extend to everything that he accepted up to this moment, and which is almost always retroactive. Immediately the slave refuses to obey the humiliating orders of his master, he rejects the condition of slavery. The act of rebellion carries him beyond the point he reached by simply refusing.[97]

The rebel dictates the terms of being-in-the-world. No longer will this be the terms that are imposed so that the condition of dehumanization by means of being death-bound will prevail. The ontological inscription of the anti-stasis thesis is "All or Nothing" and this clarity is what can be called being a literalist. In word and deed, More is a literalist as he calls for melting away what is solid, absolute, and stable in making the terms of fundamental change necessary for freedom. The literal way that freedom is demanded is what cannot be subjected to figuration. It is clear what the rebel wants, and it is laid out bare. Literality is deployed in the manner that is not troubled. It is an infusion to the question of what the rebel wants. In the face of death, where the threat and fear are literal, there is no figurative way the rebel will emerge in asserted the anti-stasis thesis and its attendant "All or Nothing."

In the struggle for freedom, according to More, "everything solid and stable has been shaken to its foundation."[98] The radical attitude and the radical refusal of the rebel is, in literality, stating clearly that the anti-stasis thesis, means there should be the end of the threat and fear of death.

There is, at the base of the anti-stasis thesis, the double movement of rupture and suture. Both are enjoined. The work of re-joining their split, or even to break each of them within, is what the anti-stasis thesis reconfigures all the time. It is the word and deed of the rebel to un/make the world. The reality has to be otherwise, in that the terms of death—its threat and resultant fear—do not, anymore, hold. The anti-stasis thesis is there to reveal and unravel. The thorny purpose of the rebel is what literality is. That is why the dispossession that the black has been subjected to is now in the mode of the reparatory grammar. There is nothing that the rebel hides as what is forever clear is that the conditions of freedom are forever denied. That will make the existential struggle to be always intractable. It is in the interests of the rebel to radically refuse subjection and radically insist on freedom. The threat and fear of death are subjected to ontological rebellion by those who, in the first place, were supposed to be dehumanized. The reparative grammar, being given birth by the anti-stasis thesis, ruptures what has been enclosed and it is the moment of the opening that new ontological formations of the black will come into being in ways that the black so desires. It means that this can only come into being if the rebel wages the existential struggle which, by its very nature, is offensive. As Julia Suárez-Krabbe accentuates: "The offensive struggles require rupture, not transition."[99] Rupture means, in fact, "All or Nothing." It is the total overhaul, the unmaking that brings another reality into being.

Rupture is necessary as what has been pervasive has been what mutes the reparative grammar of the black. The reparative grammar, as a mode of the literal inscription, does not hide what is it that the rebel wants. Having made this clear above, it is worth stating that what the rebel will face is death itself. Since the threat and fear of death have been challenged, death will be imposed to subject the rebel to subjection, to further heighten the might of ontological destruction, to discourage the rebel not to see the worthy of the cause. But the indomitable will of the rebel, the "All or Nothing" stance, will make the rebel to stay on cause. What the rebel wants is "All" that is freedom and "Nothing" that is unfreedom. It is the literal inscription that makes the cause to be necessitated, justified, and intensified. There is no compromise or retreat. The condition of the threat and fear of death cannot be obeyed. What is not obeyed is what Said points out as a situation where "one voice becomes the whole history," a stasis that the reparative grammar of the subjects to endless criticism.[100] There is always, in the spirit of the rebel, what Said points out as a new struggle to begin. The generative force that embodies the rebel is the one that, according to Said, is "oppositional to the overall national and official performance."[101] The reparative grammar's literality is the stance of the rebel that is not susceptible and skeptical to assimilation and accommodation as this means the forever muting that will make "All or Nothing" to be non-existent. That is why, in all cases, the rebel is dismissed as pessimistic and unreasonable by virtue of refusing to be in "dialogue" with what does not recognize the rebel is one with speech in the first place. The reparative grammar goes its own way, the way of the rebel, the way off—that is, veering off from whatever that is deemed to be stasis.

The rebel works, reworks, and works out the infrastructure of the threat and fear of death. Nothing can be obscure, as this operation of the rebels is everything literal. The rebel, in the face of death, does not mute and fabricate any ontological demands. These are made clear and they are not actualized by having to be considered by the infrastructure of antiblackess. They are erupting from the self-affirmative stance of the rebel. Since there is no dialogue to be held, there is the existential struggle to engage. The ontological demands are made clear through literality in the sense that death—the impediment of all sorts—is rendered irrelevant. Without any fear of death, the rebel is liberated. Literality, then, does not liberate speech, but it intensifies the existential struggle and authorizes freedom in the terms that are in line with what the rebel wants. What underwrites stasis does not hold because the anti-stasis thesis is what, according to Said, the radical to unmask configurations of power and foreground the authentic experience of the rebel.

To conclude, the rebel cannot stand side-by-side with antiblackness. More, whose philosophical anthropology is deeply excavating antiblackness, does not relent in having to concede to the exceptions of antiblackness as that which is changing or "not too bad" like before or rather claiming that the world is changing and so is this antiblack world. By stating clearly that the world is antiblack, More still holds on the fate of the rebel as always being the precarious one, and there is nothing for the rebel if there is no freedom. The "yes" and "no" of the rebel is the very fate of freedom. It is by all means that it has to be fought for and it cannot be given. The livable life of the rebel is one that the rebel will determine as opposed for it to be dished on a silver platter. There is all there is in freedom, thus its costly nature, its necessity notwithstanding.

The soul of the rebel is one that puts value on principle. It is not the commodified soul that is made to be sold, bought, and exchanged. If that is the reality, then, there is nothing of the rebel to speak of. The rebel is the one who is commodified and thus being made to be a thing that can be used, misused, and abused. In putting the self as that which is standing, principle is re-elaborated on the basis of the cause that the rebel stands for. The rebel, in short, does not sell out. That is why the soul of the rebel is not for sale. By demanding absolute change, the rebel sets forth what is fundamental and what cannot be compromised. The stakes are high, so is the nature of change. The being of the rebel is all there is having to demand and effect change and that must be upheld in all manners consistent with the nature of change that is anchored in the existential struggle. The demands that are made in the existential struggle are clear, so is the clarity of the principle and the character of the rebel.

More, the rebel, is a philosopher of fundamental change. Thus, he cannot pay allegiance to The Republic of Silence which is there to mute any form of expression insofar as the freedom of the black is concerned. There is nothing that The Republic of Silence has for the black except dehumanization. The battle lines should be clearly drawn on where is the rebel standing in relation to dehumanization. There has to be a form of antagonism, and black speech is its foremost form of expression. Indeed, black speech comes as at the cost of life, of everything that there is to the black. But because of being the rebel, More insists that there should be no fear of freedom and it should be pursued through authentic means so as to maintain authentic existence. The threat of death and its by-product—the fear of death—should not be treated as absolutes, no matter how mightily they are enforced. The rebel is the one who, by standing against the threat of death, should also overcome the fear of death. The rebel exists by way of overcoming death, and will rather choose death than servitude. The latter, as it is known, for More, is the worst form of death as it means being dead while being alive.

NOTES

1. Albert Camus, *The Rebel* (New York: Penguin, 1971). The rebel is forever clear. The word of the rebel is wedded to the deed. The rebel stands for freedom and he or she will always be clear on the demands that actualize that freedom. By having a clear stance, and forever being on the side of freedom, the rebel does not assume the position of a compromise. For the rebel, there is no way that the life of unfreedom will be tolerated. The rebel exists in struggle and what the rebel wants is what is being lived for.

2. Mabogo P. More, *Biko: Philosophy, Identity, and Liberation* (Cape Town: HSRC Press, 2017), 9.

3. George Ciccariello-Maher, *Decolonizing Dialectics* (Durham and London: Duke University Press, 2017), 153.

4. Camus, *The Rebel*, 19.

5. Mabogo P. More, *Sartre and the Problem of Racism*. Unpublished PhD Thesis (Pretoria: University of South Africa, 2005).

6. Mabogo P. More, *Looking through Philosophy in Black: Memoirs* (Lanham: Rowman and Littlefield International, 2019).

7. Hommi K. Bhabha, *The Location of Culture* (London: Routledge, 1994). For Bhabha, there is this position of being neither here or there. This is not the stance and the reality of the rebel. There are no grey areas, things are real, as they are, and not the other way. The struggle for the rebel is real, and not, at all, confined to the discursive level.

8. Ibid., 94.

9. Ibid., 95.

10. Ibid., 122.

11. Ibid. Emphasis in the original.

12. Ibid.

13. Ibid., 129.

14. Ibid., 85.

15. Camus, *The Rebel*, 19. The positive claims are the stance of the rebel and this has to do with fighting for what is just and right—that, in a way, as what is denied to the rebel. It is the positive charge to what must merge out of the rebel and it is freedom.

16. Ibid., 19.

17. More, *Biko*.

18. Camus, *The Rebel*, 19.

19. Ibid., 22.

20. Ibid., 22.

21. Ibid., 20.

22. More, *Looking through Philosophy in Black*, 3.

23. Lewis R. Gordon, *Existentia Africana: Understanding Africana Existential Thought* (New York and London: Routledge, 2000).

24. Ibid., 4.

25. Camus, *The Rebel*, 29.

26. Gordon, *Existentia Africana.*

27. Ibid., 85.

28. Denise Ferreira da Silva, "1 (Life) ÷÷ 0 (Blackness) = & - & or &: On Matter beyond the Equation of Value," *E-Flux Journal* 79 (2017): 1–11.

29. Ibid., 1.

30. Ibid., 2.

31. Ibid, 9.

32. More, *Biko*, 35.

33. Camus, *The Rebel*, 21.

34. Ibid.

35. More, *Biko*, 11.

36. Ibid., 9.

37. Ibid.

38. Edward W. Said, *Humanism and Democratic Criticism* (New York: Columbia University Press, 2004), 134.

39. More, *Biko*, 10.

40. Ibid., 15.

41. Ibid.

42. Jean-Paul Sartre, "Paris Alive: The Republic of Silence," *The Atlantic Monthly*, December (1944): 39–40.

43. Ibid., 40.

44. Mabogo P. More, "Biko and Douglass: Existential Conception of Death and Freedom," *Philosophia Africana* 17, no. 2 (2015/2016): 101–118.

45. Sartre, "Paris Alive," 39.

46. Cedric J. Robinson, *Black Marxism: The Making of the Black Radical Tradition* (Chapel Hill: The University of North Carolina Press, 2000), 167. This, in case of the rebel, will mean to dissent against the status quo. It is this dissent that will create a different set of conditions.

47. Ibid., 175.

48. More, *Biko.*

49. Edward W. Said, *The Representation of the Intellectual* (New York: Vintage, 1993).

50. Said, *Humanism and Democratic Criticism*, 127.

51. Cedric J. Robinson, *The Terms of Order: Political Science and the Myth of Leadership* (Chapel Hill: The University of North Carolina Press, 1980).

52. Robinson, *The Terms of Order*, 4.

53. Ibid., 8.

54. Robin D. G. Kelley, *Freedom Dreams: The Black Radical Imagination* (Boston: Beacon Press, 2002).

55. Ibid., 15.
56. Ibid.
57. Ibid., 230.
58. Robinson, *The Terms of Order.*
59. Kelley, *Freedom Dreams.*
60. Ibid., 150.
61. More, *Biko.*
62. More, *Biko*, 11.
63. Ibid.
64. Edward W. Said, *Culture and Imperialism* (New York: Vintage, 1994), 375.
65. More, "Biko and Douglass."
66. More, *Biko.*
67. Tina M. Campt, "The Loophole of Retreat—An Invitation," *E-Flux Journal* 105 (December 2019): 1–3. Cited in 2.
68. Said, *Humanism and Democratic Criticism*, 73.
69. Ibid.
70. Ramon Grosfoguel, "Epistemic Extractivism: A Dialogue with Alberto Acosta, Leanne Betasamosake, and Silvia Rivera Cusicanqui," in *Knowledges Born in the Struggle: Constructing the Epistemologies of the Global South*, edited by Boaventura de Sousa Santos and Maria Paula Meneses, 203–218 (London: Routledge, 2012).
71. Grosfoguel, "Epistemic Extractivism," 213.
72. Said, *Humanism and Democratic Criticism*, 125.
73. More, "Biko and Douglass."
74. More, *Biko*, 245.
75. Ibid.
76. W. E. B. Du Bois, *The Souls of Black Folk* (New Haven and London: Yale University Press, [1903] 2015).
77. More, "Biko and Douglass."
78. Abdul R. JanMohammed, *The Death-Bound-Subject: Richard Wright's Archaeology of Death* (Durham and London: Duke University Press, 2015).
79. Ibid., 6.
80. Ibid., 7.
81. Ibid., 2.
82. More, "Biko and Douglass," 105.
83. Ibid., 102.
84. Ibid., 107.
85. JanMohammed, *The Death-Bound-Subject*, 3.
86. Ibid., 19.
87. More, "Biko and Douglass," 102–103.
88. Ibid.
89. JanMohammed, *The Death-Bound-Subject*, 149.
90. More, "Biko and Douglass, 105.
91. Ibid.
92. Ibid., 106.

93. Camus, *The Rebel.*
94. Ibid., 20.
95. Ibid., 20–21.
96. Ibid., 20.
97. Ibid.
98. More, "Biko and Douglass," 108.
99. Julia Suárez-Krabbe, *Race, Rights and Rebels: Alternatives to Human Rights and Development from the Global South* (Lanham: Rowman and Littlefield International, 2016), 152.
100. Edward W. Said, *Orientalism* (New York: Vintage, 1978), 243.
101. Edward W. Said, *Culture and Imperialism* (New York: Vintage, 1994), 347.

Chapter 5

Authorship, Text, and Death

In philosophy, the question of death is meditated and authored to such an extent that it is no longer a strange affair. It is not even strange to find philosophical texts that investigate, profess, declare, reflect, mourn, resist, and affirm the question of death. Of interest is the question of the affirmation of death; it as facticity, a fate to be accepted, and a fact of life, as there is nothing that can be done about it. The affirmation of death is authored to a point of declaring the death of philosophy itself. The affirmation of death is a question that has haunted philosophy and even philosophers. Undeniably, the affirmed death of philosophy has proven to be exhausted, and thus a passé. Philosophy has proven, for obvious reasons, to outlive mortal beings, as it still continues in its classical and contemporary mutations. Philosophy declared dead by philosophers outlives its authors of death even to what can be deemed infinity, but as to when it will die it is not known. But the fact is that philosophy continues to exist! Here is a fact facing philosophers: they are born, they philosophize, and they die.

Mabogo P. More is a living philosopher who confronts death. It is what he regards as facticity and as such, it cannot be avoided. He is a philosopher who does not obsess with death, he frees himself from it by unmasking the unconscious and structures of censor by bringing death to where it belongs—the realm of the living. When death becomes a facticity, it is not subjected to closure, but it becomes an opening, it becomes the philosophical grammar—that is to say, the philosophy of existence comes to grips with the facticity of death. This becomes the liberatory force since death is part and parcel of existence. There is no philosophy of existence without death. Life and death are entwined. What lives dies, and there is no bracketing off that should take place because this will be a useless effort anyway—the fact of death remains.

More departs from the affirmative stance that death is for the living. It is this facticity that is worth examining, and this is not a matter of contesting death, but having to be attuned to its modalities and it as the reality that has to be understood. More, in this gesture, fundamentally opposes the dissimulation of death and finding comfort in the illusion of immortality. If death is for the living, it is the end of the living. Undeniably, the living are always confronted by the facticity of death.

The inscription of death texts, which is the authorship that attests to the end of writing of the dead, and the continuity of writing by the living, who will ultimately die, clearly shows that the living are responsible for the dead. Also, the dead are vulnerable to the living. For, they cannot engage in the act of the living. It is the living who will write about the dead and also bury them. More wrote a death text in a form of an obituary of Aimé Césaire, and this form of inscription is only to be read and thus became known among the living. In the obituary, it is the living who have the last word over the dead, and this authorship does not allow any interlocutory possibility—it is linear.

Other than an obituary, another death text that is worth examining is the Will. This is the one authored by More in the meditation of his death. The Will as a death text is one that is written in life and it will come into its functionality in death. More writes the Will and his position is that the Will is a futile exercise of immortality where the dead want to control the living from the tomb. One death text, which is not sitting comfortably with the living, is one writing about one's own death—the auto-obituary. More authored his auto-obituary, and in this meditation, taken from the black existential point of view, he wrote death as his own, and such a death is the one that he, himself, will have to come face-to-face with. In this intervention, it becomes clear that death cannot be delegated; one must die his or her own death.

THE FACTICITY DEATH

More declares: "Death is the perennial phenomenon that we live with."[1] To live is to die. For one to live, one must not bracket off death. Even if this bracketing is insisted, still, death is inevitable. The facticity of death is having to recognize its presence as the fact of existence. Martin Heidegger is concerned with the existential conception of death.[2] According to Heidegger, death is the "utter loss of Being-in-the-world" and it is "Being that is liquidated."[3] The being who is no longer alive is the one who is not in the world. Death as the loss of being means the end of existence. Death, for Heidegger, means no-longer-Being-there. The being who is in the world is no longer there. This being is dead. This means no longer being present. Also, not being present is not being there, in short, not living.

Heidegger points to one common phenomenon which is the experiencing of the death of others. It is the death that would mark a loss among the living.

> Death does indeed reveal itself as a loss, but a loss such as experienced by those who remain. In suffering this loss, however, we have no way of access to the loss-of-Being as such which the dying man 'suffers.' The dying of others is not something which we experience in a genuine sense; at most we are always just 'there alongside.'[4]

The living are the ones who suffer loss, and they mourn that loss. It is the death of their beloved one that makes them suffer. It is not the loss of their own lives as lived, because they are still alive. They lost the deceased, and the latter who does not suffer any loss. The deceased, in that moment of death and its aftermath, do not suffer. They have lost their lives already. The one who is dead is dead *tout court*! Those who are alive are not dead. They are there, while the deceased is no longer there. The one who was present is absent. The body of the deceased is the "corporeal Thing" and also as Heidegger states, "a *lifeless* material Thing."[5] This thing—the *it*—cannot do whatever the living are doing. It is there and cannot do anything—a corpse lying there. It is outside the realm of the living. "In it we encounter something *unalive*, which has lost its life."[6] This is the being who is no longer alive, and there is no capacity for the being to even be in the same state of mind. It is the living who are grieving the deceased, and they are the ones who are left with the responsibility to give funeral rites right until entombment. The dead are not alive and cannot bury themselves. It is the responsibility of the living to deal with dead.

Heidegger declares: "Death, in the widest sense, is a phenomenon of life."[7] It is a phenomenon of life, in the sense of it being its every ending. It is part of life. To live is the facticity of death. Death, according to Heidegger, "is the possibility of no-longer being-able-to-be-there."[8] Contra Heidegger, death is not the possibility. It is a given fact of life. There is no such thing as the possibility of death, as if this would mean there will be the end of life or not. Death certainly means the end of life. This end is death.

The conception of life and death is of interest if two positions can be put forth. First, life and death mean something different to the living. Second, life and death to the dead means nothing at all. The tragedy, event, and accident of death mean pain to the living. Life and death belong to the living. This is driven by forces that are structured by fear. The love of life, which is abundance, is related to death. Achille Mbembe attests: "But the relationship between the principles of life and death is fundamentally unstable."[9] But what is worth noting is that life and death, in their entangled form, bring the human experience in imbalance. But there is a clear separation, nothing in between life and death.

Those who are alive are not dead. "*Death is something that stands before us—something impending*."[10] It is the death that is always there, and when the time comes for the living to die, they are going to die. As to when it is that time, it is not known. But it is the time that is impending. Death, in short, is real.

It is the living who are affected by death. They have to deal with death. The responsibility of entombing the dead rests squarely on their shoulders. According to Heidegger, "death thus belongs to Being-in-the-world."[11] As More accentuates, "death is for the living."[12] Those who live are the ones who are in the world. "The deceased has abandoned our '*our*' world and left it behind."[13] The presence of the deceased with the living after the entombment is nothing. The dead will not ever be seen again. That is to say, the living presence of the dead will never be experienced. For being seen as dead, there is no possibility of seeing them alive.

The dead cannot do anything. "'One *is*' what one does."[14] What was their life is what has passed. To talk about the dead, even in the present tense is still to refer to the past tense. Insofar as existence is concerned, the dead are the past as they are not present in the present. Death is the end of "Being-with-one-another in the world."[15] The dead are no longer with the living. The living are no longer with the dead. In this radical separation, it is the living who must, in fulfilling the valedictory of the dead, do the work of burying or cremating the dead. It is the responsibility of the living, as Mbembe states, to carry the remains of the dead even if it is not them who brought them to dead.[16] It is the responsibility of the living to dispose the dead. This radical difference speaks clearly on the Heideggerian nothing of being-in-the-world where the living are there and the dead are not there. For the dead, the condition is "Being-no-longer-in-the-world"—the absence of the dead in the realm of existence. The absence of the dead is forever permanent, in that it is the condition that will never change.

The living do not know what is *there in* death. They have not died and cannot experience death. There is no ambivalence between being alive and being dead. The living only know what is happening in the condition of being-in-the-world. Other than that, there is nothing they know that has to do with death.

> The way in which everyday Being-towards-death understands the certainty which is thus grounded, betrays itself when it tries to "think" about death, even when it does so with critical foresight—that is to say, in an appropriate manner. So far as one knows, all men "die." Death is probable in the highest degree for every man, yet it is not "unconditionally" certain. Taken strictly, a certain which is "only" *empirical* may be attributed to death. Such certainty necessarily falls short of the highest certainty, the apodictic, which we reach in certain domains of theoretical knowledge.[17]

The absence of possibility clearly means that there is no one who is alive who will survive death. To think about death is also to think about that which is out of grasp. The idea of living is the one that keep the anxiety of death lingering. This anxiety is unhelpful, in that death is not some figment of imagination. It is the reality. This is because the fear of death creates anguish and this leads to the denial of freedom. This is "bad faith" in the sense of Sartre, where the being disavows her/his freedom.[18]

To live life is to be in the shadow of death. The shadow is wherever the body is (it is even present in darkness) and it is part of the body. Death is the constitutive element of life. Death is the fact of life.

To die is not, according to Heidegger, no-longer-to-be-present-at-end. Death is an end but it is still denied. The denial of death stems from fear. Derrida puts it thus: "We are afraid of the fear, we anguish over the anguish, and we tremble."[19] It is this fear that makes death to be pushed to others. It is this fear that, for Heidegger, creates "a sombre was of fleeing from the world."[20] This means it is a way of hiding oneself from the fact of death. It is to flee from the facticity of death by eluding oneself by externalizing and distancing oneself from it. This, then, creates what Heidegger would call "the *they*" which is the anxiety that does not want to deal with the oncoming death. More writes: "My father, mother, brother and a bunch of other family members died and I buried them without any thought that I myself might have to die some day."[21] Heidegger shows how, in this act, death is deferred to something that must occur later, and this becomes a sort of an authorized *doxa*.

> *In evading its death*, even everyday Being-towards-the-end is indeed certain of its death in another way than it might itself like to have on purely theoretical considerations. This "other way" is what everydayness for the most part veils from itself. Everydayness does not dare let itself become transparent in such a manner.[22]

This anxiety is also intensified into fear. This, then, invites a condition where the evasion of death becomes paramount. "By its very meaning, this evasive concealment in the face of death can *not* be *authentically* 'certain' of death, and yet it *is* certain of it."[23] Derrida explicates two forms of dissimulation along the line of authenticity and inauthenticity.

> Inauthentic dissimulation, that of the masked role, bores to the extent that it claims to unveil, show, expose, exhibit, and excite curiosity. By unveiling everything it hides that whose essence resides in its remaining hidden, namely, the authentic mystery of the person. Authentic mystery must *remain* mysterious, and we should approach it only by letting it be what it is in truth—veiled,

> withdrawal, dissimulated. Authentic dissimulation is inauthentically dissimulated by the violence of unveiling.[24]

Dissimulation stands because the existential conception of death has not been elaborated to the state of having to face death and not being evasive. There cannot be "authentic Being-towards-death *not* to be."[25] Death is the fact of being, and the authentic being cannot evade death. It is this being that will not engage in dissimulation of any sort but to unveiled.

More even scandalizes the notion of externalizing death which makes it as if it is just a pure accident. Death is there and it stands in its own name. Most at times, it comes unexpected. It comes in its own time. It is not known whether death knows its time. But what has been experienced by the living who come to be the witness of the dead is that the time of death is unpredictable. It snatches newborns, infants, children, teenagers, adults, and the old age at any time of the stage of life. It is, in point of fact, non-discriminatory. It happens any other time and everywhere (safe or unsafe places, conditions). Death does not even care whether people are good or evil, they die. Even those who kill others die, too. That is death. But, then, what about one's own death?

The sense of belief, which is a claim of "not believing in death," this pervasive banality, so to say, is the mobilization of belief against belief. Put simply, the refusal to believe in death (as if there is such a belief) is, in point of fact, a form of a belief. It is this "non-reflective consciousness," as Sartre calls it, which in structuring belief, and being interpellated in it, "performs the act of faith."[26] This act of faith is hiding from the fact that death is immanent and imminent. The act of faith, it disavowing what is not only in front of it, but what is the fact of life, is mobilized in the service of bad faith. No matter how much this faith gets addicted to "not believing in death," those who act in this faith will die. Death does not care whether they believe or not. In fact, those who express this overly exhausted cliché know, deeper in their consciousness which cuts throw the veil of their belief that they will die. In the act of bad faith, they deny this truth and continue to lie to themselves that death is not theirs. Under the layer of this bad faith, there lies something—fear. The suppression of "reflective consciousness" in favor of activating "non-reflective consciousness" is indeed bad faith. The belief of not believing in death—the impassioned belief that is, is not only meaningless but also nonsensical. But this absurdity becomes impassioned, in that when death occurs (by way of affecting others close to those who believe that they do not believe in death) they still fear. Why do they fear something that they do not believe in?

> The separation which separates belief from itself can only be grasped or even conceived in isolation. If we seek to reveal it, it vanishes. We find belief once

> more as pure immanence. But if, on the other hand, we wish to apprehend belief as such, then the fissure is there, appearing when we do not want to see it, disappearing as soon as we seek to contemplate it. This fissure then is pure negative. Distance, lapse of time, psychological difference can be apprehended in themselves and include as such elements of positivity; they have a simple negative *function*. But the fissure within consciousness is a nothing except for the fact that it denies and that it can have being only as we do not want to see it.[27]

Belief is not itself-for-itself; it is the value that being acts toward and the fissure that Sartre refers to can be linked to belief in the exercise of bad faith. It is to be in the condition of deprivation of life. This manifests through the fear of death where the refusal "not believing in death" is actually a belief—the fear of death. To fear death is to be subjected in its clutches. It is to resign one's self from freedom by way of wallowing in "non-reflective" consciousness. It is to die too many times before the actual death. It is to refuse to live life before its finality—death. It is to be in bondage of bad faith. Bad faith is a lie before life and untruth toward death. For, death cannot be lied to; it is facticity. Thus, being is being-towards-death. There is no any other path; all paths lead to their final destination—death.

In the exercise or excess of belief, where consciousness still lurks in its reflective mode (believed or not), as the passion is more toward "non-reflective consciousness," death does not care. Death is absolute, the last word was a speech act. Death does not care it is believed or not, feared or not, avoided or not, deferred or not, suspended or not.

The soul is set free when it is in preparation with death. Derrida claims: "By means of the passage to death the soul attains its own freedom."[28] Even though there is freedom in this, but it is not known what is that freedom to the dead. What can be stated with certainty is that they do not have to be with the living to deal with the burden of existence. Heidegger would call this "anticipation" and it is a mode of not evading death and it is opposite to unauthentic Being-towards-death.[29] For Heidegger, this anticipation is the self freeing itself from fear of death and to accept the fact that death is the end of existence. With this, Heidegger points something important.

More is right to state that death is individuated.[30] It is the death of the one who dies. To die, in this sense, is to own one's death. No one can die for another.

> Death is very much that which nobody else can undergo or confront in my place. My irreplaceability is therefore conferred and delivered, "given," one can say, by death. . . . It is from my site of death as the place of my irreplaceability, that is, of my singularity, that I feel called responsibility. In this sense only a mortal can be responsible.[31]

Death cannot be delegated. It is one's own. More recounts:

> The reality of death hit me when my late brother's son was diagnosed with osteosarcoma (cancer of the bone) and we had to try all sort of medical options to prevent it from spreading to his lungs. Death became a reality a perennial feature of my existence which I had to live moment after moment of his young life; right in my face as facticity. We had amputed one of his affected legs in a bid to halt the spread of this cancer, and in a way to halt reality of death. Each day became a lived experience agony with the immanence of death itself. Unfortunately, all our endeavours to save his life failed and he ultimately succumbed to the finality of death.[32]

More gives another account:

> My second encounter with the stark reality of the death came when I had a close near miss with death myself. I had an attack of *brain aneurysm* and had to undergo surgery where a coil (clip) was inserted in my brain to block the ruptured artery from bleeding into my brain. Brain aneurysm is an instant killer not easy to survive. My doctor even calls me "miracle man." The point here is that the possibility of re-bleeding exists such that I am constantly living with death as the outmost possibility of all my possibilities. It can happen anytime and anywhere. The problem with this thinking about my aneurysm condition is that death has always been a possibility the moment I was born, way back before aneurysm; but I had, just like most of us, relegated the possibility of death to the realm of death of the Other.[33]

One owns and is owned by death. It is a matter that, in terms of responsibility, one is responsible for one's death. To be bound by such responsibility is a reality to be lived with. Death is a responsibility. The one who dies carries that responsibility. As Derrida emphasizes, "death is the place of one's irreplaceability."[34]

> In order to put oneself to death, to give oneself death in the sense that every relation to death is an interpretive apprehension and a representative approach to death, death must be taken upon oneself. One has to *give it to oneself by taking it upon oneself*, for it can only be mine alone, irreplaceable. That is so even if, as we just said, *death can neither be taken or given*. But the idea of being neither taken nor given relates *from* or *to* the other, and that is indeed why one can give it *to oneself* only by taking it *upon oneself*.[35]

Even those who claim to be protected or safe from death under the illusion of some sort of immortality and expecting those who guard them or who "prolong" their existence to die for them, this is forever impossible. They will have to come face-to-face with their own death. Even if this death can be the name of another, Derrida states the impossibility of this, in that this death will be of the one who is dying and no one else. This is the logic of sacrifice, and it has nothing with dying being a form of an extension of oneself, to claim to have died while others died.

> I can give my whole life for another, I can offer my death to the other, but in doing this I will only be replacing or saying something partial in a particular situation (there will be a nonexhaustive exchange or sacrifice, an economy of sacrifice). I know on absolute grounds and in an absolutely certain manner that I will never deliver the other from his death, from the death that affects the whole being.[36]

Derrida clearly states that it is impossible to die for the other. One cannot give one's life to another. This is what More says about his beloved nephew, Moeketsi More:

> What was special about this particular death is that I had in the process developed this absolutely close and cherished relationship with him to an extent that he was practically my son. I really loved him and I assume he also loved my brother and I as fathers. My love for him was such that I would have been willing to trade places with him, to assume his immanent death as my own in order for him to live. Then it dawned on me that death is fundamentally one's own.[37]

More is with Heidegger, Sartre, and Derrida that death cannot be delegated. "Unfortunately, there can be no such substitution for death."[38] The one who lives is not dead and the one who is dead is dead. No one can live for the other and no one can die for the other. If that is insisted upon, it will just be symbolic and sentimental. It is not reality as it is. It is reality as imagined. Thus, there is nothing that can be actualized in terms of living for the other and dying for the other.

THE OBITUARY AND THE END OF WRITING

The obituary often addressed the dead as if they are alive. The reality that has been created is that the dead must be remembered fondly. The dead are even absolved from their earthly deeds. They are given a sacred status. Hence, the dictum "do not speak ill of the dead." But seldom is this dictum interdicting what is popular and banal—lies. They are telling lies about the dead, pretending to love them and being pained by their loss, while that is not truth, is something that is not even questioned the textual practices of the obituary writing. The living can lie about the dead, and the dead will not even refute that. The dead are given clemency. They are said to be beyond what they have lived for. They are elevated to the state of grace. All is forgiven. Clean slate.

What is emphasized about the dead is that they must be addressed with sympathy, hope, and warmth, and that is even directed to the living who must mourn in peace. If there is anything that is scandalous about the dead, it should, for the moment of mourning, be interdicted. There is no time of setting the record straight, settling accounts, point scoring, holding to account, or whatever form of scandalization. All what the living should do, as mourners, is to pay their last respect for the dead.

The grammar of interdiction is what reigns among the living about the one who is dead. It is not a matter of upholding the truth. Lies will rather be paddled for the sake of respecting the dead. The dead are even addressed as if they agree with what is said. Mourners are told what they want to hear, as if they do hear.

Those who author death, of others and not of themselves would, most at times, include themselves in this death text called the obituary. The obituary is memory work. It is the re-inscription of remembering. As the death text, it aims, by its citational practices, evokes the dead by repeating their words, lifting passages from their utterances and texts, and sharing a joke, sometimes. This is all done to make the dead present, to do memory work as if the dead are present. The obituary is, at the level of citation, semi-autobiographical. This is the *memorium* inscription. It is this text that gets to be written and read in memorial services, sermons, mass, and funerals. In the strictest sense of the textual production, it comes to be read as the ode, dedication, eulogy, and the like. The obituary is one death text that gets to be read. In its semi-biographical form, it cites and highlights the relation of the living and the dead, and it emphasizes memory. It is the lamentation of loss, one that the living self will claim incompleteness without the dead. The obituary is not only the stating of the name of the dead, but the deed (all good most of the time) and the aim being to make the name and deed one. The citational practices by the one who writes the obituary is having to state, in the semi-autobiographical form, the sad loss that has been experienced and the difficulty of having to live with it. Those who mourn the loss of their beloved do so under the collective of "we are all going to die, someday" or "death is for all of others." Even in that gesture, they still separate themselves from the dead. They often write about death as if it is not their own death, it is the death of others. They do engage in self-writing about the matter of death; but, why not their own death?

For having suffered a loss, the obituary as the work of memory, makes mourning possible by remembering the life and times of the dead. Writing the obituary in the event of mourning can be a difficult task, more especially if the obituarist has a relationship with the dead. Also, it has to be stated, as indicated above, that the obituary can be written in a pretentious way. It can be laced with hypocrisy where the dead will be "respected" and "honored" in the condition of their death and not while they were still alive. Those who will pretend to having loved the dead in their lifetime will even have the chutzpah to say the dead will be missed forever, and they will even summon everyone to remember them fondly. But it is well known that this is a staged act, and it having to enjoy the protected privilege of the funerary grammatical interdiction; no one is allowed to hold the lying obituarist to account. The lying obituarist will even go to the extent of saying the dead loved them, and they loved the dead. It is even possible for the enemy and murderer of the dead to come to the memorial service or funeral to give a moving tribute in front of unsuspecting mourners while this is nothing but a stack of lies. The dead will not even be able to defend themselves by dismissing all these lies. Comforting and consoling words will be said, and gestures of mourning will be pulled to the last end, crocodile tears will be shed nonetheless. No mourner is allowed to contradict this scripted act. Promises and guarantees will be made, but that is only for the show in the event of the memorial service or funeral, after that there is nothing that will be fulfilled in the light of heightened expectations. It is also known that mourning can be choreographed and orchestrated in deceptive terms. There are some who will be happy that the dead is no more—good riddance!

The obituary, in its serious sense of fidelity to truth (ideally so), should be written from the heart. The obituary should be written by those who are genuine both in their word and deed. This is an uncontested fact to More's obituary on Césaire as his subsequent works following the obituary still hold him in high regard.[39] What More meant in that obituary is evidentiated by his work. It must be stated that More does not write about himself as an individual in Césaire's obituary.[40] There is no semi-autobiographical posture. What prevails, in fact, is the intellectual mantle of Césaire and his formidable influence and monumental legacy. More writes the obituary not in the testamentary fashion that Derrida does.[41] Both More and Derrida are obituarists; their obituaries are about the living thought of thinkers. They write these death texts to give more insight on the dead by way of telling a tale of the dead and narrate their being *which was* as it is *no more*. More having delivered a *memorium* to Césaire, Derrida has a number of his contemporaries. One thing that stands out is that Derrida writes an obituary in a semi-autobiographical fashion; this, as earlier noted, is not the approach that More follows. The reasons for this can be that More never met Césaire at the level of personal encounter, and Roland Barthes, Paul de Man, Michel Foucault, Max Loreaux, Jean-Marie Benoist, Louis Althusser, Edmond Jabés, Joseph Riddel, Michel Serviére, Louis Marin, Sarah Kofman, Gilles Deleuze, Emmanuel Levinas, and Jean-François Lyotard are those that Derrida knew and were known to each other as friends, colleagues, and interlocutors. But this difference does not mean that anything much in this regard. But it is worth highlighting that the obituaries of More and Derrida are different.

Derrida delivered the assemblage, the systematic and innovative *oeuvre* of death texts of his contemporaries.[42] It is Derrida writing his word and delivering his testimony on the dead. It is him mourning the loss of his fellow interlocutors. The facticity of death is what Derrida is confronted with and it is what he confronts. This leads him to be responsible for the dead, to write a word about them, to testify for them. In his semi-autobiography, the *topos* of death in the familiarity of the obituary, the task is taken further, and here it is worthy of examining the first and the last obituary in Derrida's corpus. The two obituaries will be examined in terms of haunting statements that Derrida is dealing with. The obituary of Barthes and that of Lyotard will be engaged in terms of the statements that each said to Derrida. It is these two statements that challenge the *topos* of death, and which, through More's existential meditations on death, will be criticized.

In the obituary of Barthes, Derrida recounts meeting the impossible utterance "I am dead." This is the statement that even made Derrida to devise the title of his obituary as "The Deaths of Roland Barthes." It is in this plurality that Derrida even went further to state that death can be understood as a form of a composition and also the counterpoint. In having to state the dead, and them being related to the name, it is worth noting that the dead can no longer answer to their own name. As Derrida notes, "Roland Barthes is the name of someone who can no longer hear and bear it."[43] Coming to terms with the facticity of death, Derrida is haunted by the figure who once declared, in his lifetime, that he is dead.

> And he will receive nothing of what I say here of him, for him, to him, beyond the name but still within it, as I pronounce his name that is no longer his. This living attention here comes to tear itself toward that which, or the one who, can no longer receive it; it rushes towards the impossible. But if his name is no longer his, was it ever? I mean simply, uniquely?[44]

The death of Barthes means that he is no longer appellative to his name. Yet, what Barthes said to Derrida is a rhetorical statement insofar as his declaration of his death is possible. It is not even possible to utter a statement of fact in relation to the death of oneself. The one who is dead cannot say anything. It is only the living who will say that the one who dies is dead. "I am dead" is what cannot be uttered. However, as a rhetorical device, it can be figuratively said so. The utterance "I am dead" as articulated by Barthes, is the statement of the unsaid. But Derrida asks: "Would the impossible utterance 'I am dead' really never have taken place?"[45] Derrida goes to the rhetorical detour to pursue this utterance. He poses more questions. By evoking the notion of utopia as per the manner that Barthes deploys it, Derrida still in the rhetorical mode, locates this utterance in the realm of possibility and impossibility. It is here that he argues that time and imminence are at place, and in the content of realism, where death is facticity, Derrida still puts death in as the interruptive force, and locates "I am dead" in "'emanation,' 'ecstasis,' 'madness,' 'magic,'"[46] "I am dead" is a punctual statement insofar as it is rhetorical. It is saying something figuratively, and on the living, it is the interruptive utterance. Even though this utterance will be known not as true by the living, they will still be unsettled by it. This, according to Derrida, is the contrapuntal statement, and the obituary of Barthes as the plurality of his death is the contrapuntal inscription. There is an important question that Derrida poses: "How to believe in the contemporary?"[47] The obituary of Barthes, as the rhetorical inscription, is one which, in its haunting utterance, what is linked to the last obituary of Lyotard.

Encountering another impossible utterance, and this time by his close friend, Lyotard, Derrida is haunted by "There shall be no mourning." Derrida writes: "There shall be no mourning was thus like a drifting aphorism, a phrase given over, abandoned, exposed body and soul to absolute dispersion."[48] The one who died commanded this impossible utterance. Mourning is for the living. They will mourn the loss, by their natural act is denied. Having to reinscribe this command, Derrida writes: "As for mourning, there shall be none. There shall be *none of* it."[49] Still, even if Lyotard can deliver this command, those who are pained by his death cannot follow it, they will mourn.

> And of course the "no mourning" left to itself, can mean the perpetual impossibility of mourning, an inconsolability or irreparability that no work of mourning shall ever come to mend.
>
> But the "no mourning" can also, by the same token, oppose testimony, attestation, protestation, or contestation, to the very idea of a testament, to the hypothesis of a mourning that always has, unfortunately, as we know, a negative side, at once laborious, guilt ridden and narcissistic, reactive and turned toward melancholy, if not envy. And when it borders on celebration, or *wake*, one risks the worst.[50]

The mourning is for the living who must not let themselves fall in the command of the one who uttered the statement that denies mourning. The wishes of the dead in this regard will be suspended, in that mourning is not the feeling that the living chose, it is what they experience as they are dealing with the pain of death. It is the pain that only affects them. "There shall be no mourning" is an impossible utterance.

Derrida's two obituaries are burdened by rhetorical inscriptions that are contrapuntal in nature and they are ones which prove impossibility in the realm of the living. Even in their rhetorical gesture, the utterances of Barthes and Lyotard have not been made a reality. Derrida wrote the obituary of Barthes in the event of his death. Derrida wrote the obituary of Lyotard to mourn the death of his friend. So, the impossible utterance of Barthes and Lyotard was rendered impossible. The matter of life and death is a clear one. There is no in-between. Barthes and Lyotard wanted to blur this distinction in uttering the impossible. For the fact that this utterance is made possible, that is only so in the rhetorical realm. It could even be said that both Barthes and Lyotard made narcissistic statements. These are the statements that will obviously shock the living and the reality of having to live with such statements, impossible as they are, will destabilize their way life is and how it is lived. The thing is that these statements are, on another level, one's way of confronting death in the sense of making it to be in the domain of speech. It is in this domain that it is also denied. For, to speak about one's own death is considered to be an omen. By Barthes declaring his death and Lyotard denied the living to mourn, Derrida shows how death was in the living thought of these philosophers. Nothing can be done with what Barthes and Lyotard said. More writes: "After all, that person is dead anyway."[51] Both Barthes and Lyotard are dead. Derrida's obituary is about the dead.

Derrida, in his semi-autobiographical mode and also through his assemblage of obituaries, seldom does he confront his own death. This is because he authored the death of others and not his. Obituaries were written on Derrida as he died on October 9, 2004. The death of Derrida brought a shock to the world, just like the death of philosophers he gave odes to through his obituaries.

More writes the obituary of Césaire and locates him in the realm of interlocution (living and embodied thought).[52] More's obituary of Césaire, who died on April 17, 2008, is a moving tribute to one of the founding figures of Negritude. More announcingly opens the obituary of Césaire thus:

> We the living shoulder the historical responsibility of ensuring that the deeds and words of the dead should not fade into oblivion unnoticed. Since the dead (ancestors) will always be there, confronting us directly or far off on the horizons of our being, our duty requires that we accept this responsibility with a clear consciousness. The death of Aimé Césaire—the last Martiniquean poet, politician and revolutionary—last week calls on us to carry out the responsibility that we owe the dead.[53]

It is here that mourning is made clear and the pain of More's loss is narrated, even though not in elaborate and narcissistic terms. By detaining the thought, work, and praxis of Césaire, More locates the legacy of Césaire in connection with Azania. The work of Césaire is, according to More, of relevancy and what should be continued with.

In his obituary, More here offers, through the death text, the death of another as everything that has to do with the necessity of continuing to life. Indeed, it is the text of the one who died and not those who are living. The latter are only left with carrying out of the responsibility of the dead. More, in the autobiographical way, writes about one who touched and continues to touch his life. Césaire, for More, is one of the founding figures of Black Consciousness. That is why More writes the obituary for Césaire on the basis of the influence of Negritude on Black Consciousness. According to More, "Césaire articulates a philosophy whose origins and content reads as if it were a narrative about the origins of the South African Student Organisation (SASO) and Black Consciousness in South Africa three to four decades later."[54] More even punctuates that Leopold Senghor, Leon Contras Damas, and Césaire "were probably the founding of Black Consciousness philosophy and ideology of our country and elsewhere."[55] It is not a missive to find More having to write the obituary of Césaire.

Negritude, according to More, is foundational to the historicity of Black Consciousness.[56] With qualification, More says the following: "Negritude, therefore, was a preoccupation with questions of identity and liberation through self-consciousness and self-definition."[57] Here is Césaire:

> I would rediscover the secret of great communications and great combustions. I would say storm. I would say river. I would say tornado. I would say leaf. I would say leaf. I would say tree. I would be drenched by all rains, moistened by all dews. I would roll like frenetic blood on the slow current of the eye of words turned into mad horses into fresh children into clots into curfew into vestige of temples into precious stones remote enough to discourage miners. Whoever would not understand me would not understand the roaring of a tiger.[58]

It is obvious from Césaire that he is making it clear what Negritude is all about. Césaire, in coining Negritude, associates it with Haiti, where the slave revolt and the first black republic were founded. As the philosophy of existence, Negritude takes the liberation of blacks seriously. This is the philosophical stance that More takes and him paying tribute to Césaire is the very articulation of the philosophy of existence. Césaire goes on, in the name of Negritude, to criticize dehumanization.[59] By giving a damning account of dehumanization, Césaire declares: "The dossier is indeed overwhelming."[60] It is this dossier that makes More to feel responsibility to Césaire and this is what he has to state, as one of the ways of carrying the responsibility for the dead.

> While Senghor's Negritude was Africa-centered and much more oriented towards cultural consciousness and a metaphysical element that concentrated on the ontology of the being of the African, Césaire's Negritude was, by contrast much more existentialist and thus focused on the consciousness of black people in the context of colonial and racist situations. For him, Negritude was more of a mode of being-black-in-the-word, a consciousness of colour, race and history. In other words, Césaire posed the question of black existence through the lens of Negritude.[61]

It is the existential affinity that compelled More to write the obituary. It is him writing a text that is not only a tribute but shouldering the responsibility of the existential struggle which must continue in the event of Césaire's death. Clarifying Negritude, More writes:

> Negritude, in his definition, was "a concrete rather than an abstract coming to consciousness" of black people who lived in an atmosphere of rejection and developed not only an inferiority complex but were also ashamed of their blackness. This coming into concrete consciousness in an antiblack world generated one of the most persistent questions among black people: "Who am I."[62]

More's philosophical project is informed by the definitional account of Negritude, and his existential breath, in various registers, is still animated by the existential question—"Who am I?" The one who dies pursuing this question is engaging in the works of freedom. For, that is the aspiration of the existential struggle. Negritude is the existential struggle. Negritude here, the Césairean variant, one that More locates in black existentialism, becomes the animating force that confronts dehumanization. The Negritude that is often ridiculed, dismissed, and declared dead, one which reams of obituaries have been inked, is one which, to More, is a living testament. Césaire's death, according to More, is not even Negritude's death. The Negritude that is declared dead is, contrary to the popular belief, a tour-de-force. Cheikh Thiam affirms: "No, Negritude is not dead. It is more relevant now than ever."[63] This relevance is marked by the fact of being-black-in-an-antiblack-world. Also, Thiam states, "Negritude is still relevant today because race still matters."[64] Negritude is revitalized and rescued from all forms of enclosures that declared it dead.

> We the followers of Césaire in this country are grieving over this man "worthy of respect" who was, so to speak, the unshakable affirmation of black personhood. Someone just dead remains alive. I believe that Césaire still is because it is difficult to say he was. He retains, at the beginning of his absence, a towering presence. The ambiguity of presence in an absence characterizes the death of people who have made an indelible mark in their lives of others.[65]

The fact that hits More is that Césaire is dead and it is his memory that will be converted into presence that will animate the spirit of his existence. Césaire as a physical being is one who should be subjected to memory works. In mourning Césaire, More evokes the living spirit. The existential struggle that Césaire has been involved in throughout his life is what commanded his towering presence and what cannot be thrown in to oblivion and obscurity.

The dead cannot write anything. Writing is a past tense—say, the dead wrote. What is in the realm of the living is the trace of the dead. They are no longer present to write again. The dead will be written about. Even if there will be the publication of their posthumous works, this is still the textual production of the dead by the authorship that happened in their lifetime. One form of authorship that is of interest is the obituary. It is the text of the dead about the dead. It is written by the living about the dead. Whether what is in the obituary is true or false is immaterial. The thing is that the obituary is the text that the dead will never get to read, refer, refute, reply. It is the writing that re-elaborates the inscription on the tomb. Since this is the marking of the grave, the obituary is the inscription of memory.

The obituary is the writing of death of the other. It is the exterior text. Even if the author can refer to him or herself, this is the death of the other. To write the obituary is to give a testimony of the dead, and not the self. It is only in the citational moments where the obituarist will refer to the self and the dead. But all this citation and narration is the landscape of the past. Everything that is written is memory work, mourning, celebration, and all-affective registers that can be devised to evoke the presence of *what was* and not *what is*. Everything is in the past tense and the future tense can be evoked in sentimental expressions like "till we meet again," but this is actualizing nothing insofar as the presence and present are concerned. The dead can no longer be with the living—no severance.

THE WILL AND THE ONTOLOGY OF THE SIGNATURE

Only the living can author death texts. These are texts that deal with death, and they are semi-autobiographical. The Will is the death text that is authored by the living, and when they are dead they cannot author anything. It is worth stating, speculatory so, that More has a Will—that is, *The Last Will and Testament of Mabogo Percy More*. This is the text that is authored by More to protect the living while he is dead and for him to be protected from the living while he is dead if the living will be predators of his estate. By writing a Will, death is made to be a forefront matter. The modes of writing a Will means confronting one's own death. The Will serves its "protective" role only in death, and it can be written only in the event of life. So, More writes his Will as the living author and the Will, then, comes into being as what is read by the executioner as the word of the dead author.

The Will, according to More, is the desire of the living, when they are dead, to have control of the living when they are dead.[66] More opines:

> The realization that at death the chips are down, one cannot control what happens to one through the mediation of one's property and belongings after one's death, and because the desire for justification of one's existence and for one's Being in the face of contingency, one the draws a Will which will guarantee and justify not only his/her perpetual and perennial one's absence. The Will is a classical expression of the paradoxical desire to be both a presence and absence at the same time, the desire to be present in one's absence.[67]

The root of this desire is based on having their estate intact. The Will is by the testator with the full knowledge that it will affect the living (whether positively or negatively depending on how the testator feels or may so wish). The testator authors the Will by means of exercising the individual right to do so. To have full control of her or his estate, even from the tomb. According to More, the Will and also human reality, there lies the desire for finitude. To control from the tomb, the Will as such a tool, More states that this is based on the idea of immortality.

What More points out as well is that the living write the Will so that in the event of their death they are protected against the predatory tendencies of the living who will devour the estate that they did not work for and which they do not own and thus not entitled to inherit. The dead will not be able to protect themselves because they are not alive. The dead are, according to More, the "prey for the living."[68] So, the Will is what is necessary for them to have control on the living.

The Will is authored, in that the dead, as Kirsten Smolensky argues, want to have rights when they are dead.[69] The dead, who are no longer with the living, states More, still want to exercise control and by writing the Will, the living will live according to the dictates of the dead.[70] The Will is based on the interests of the dead. The dead have no rights like the living. "Often, the dead cannot marry, divorce, or vote."[71] There are many rights of the living which cannot be extended to the dead. However, the dead can be legal holders of rights and this is only possible if they left a legally valid Will. "When these interests are protected by legal rules, the dead are granted de facto legal rights that can be enforced against the living."[72] But it is known that the dead are not juridical persons. They are dead and rights do not apply to them. But then, the Will is what Smolensky refers to as "posthumous rights" can be rights that are exercised from the tomb. "While it is true that only a subset of interests may survive death, and even a smaller subset receives legal protection, death does not necessarily cut off all interests, and consequently, it does not end all legal rights."[73] The interest based on these rights stems from the value of respecting and honoring the dead. But the Will Act of 1953 does not make those interests arbitrary. Even if these rights, in fulfilling the interests of the dead, they should have, in the case of the Will that does not have a firm legal standing, should not the interests of the living.

> On the other hand, various legal institutions have spent considerable time trying to protect the rights of the dead. As a result, most testamentary distributions, burial requests, and organ donation designation are held to be valid even if they contradict the preferences of the living. Certain destructions of property requested in the wills are honored even though they may have a negative impact on the living.[74]

According to More, the Will is a standing document.[75] It is the document of the dead on the living. The Will must be prepared by the living, as they will not be able to author it when they are dead. What remains the wishes of More is what should be actualized in his lifetime. He has to author the Will. It is the text of the event of his death. It is the event that is going to occur anyway. More is going to die and that is why he authors the Will. It is the facticity of his being as the mortal that necessitates the authoring of the Will. In this case, it means that he has a statement and testament that comes into being as his word, which then becomes a written formulation. Then, a textual folding of the Will needs to be sealed in order to have the authentic status. In a sense, More's Will should be a legal document. It is the document that is about the event of his death and his wishes are stated clearly in the Will.

Initially, the Will is one's preparation for death. It is in the event of death, the Will serves its purpose. It should be valid and it means that it must bear the power of the signature. As a valid document, one which has a legal standing, it must fulfill the wishes of the deceased. Of course, the Will cannot turn out as initially planned. More's Will is valid insofar as it is signed. It is valid insofar as he did it in accordance with the Wills Act of 1953. His Will only applies to the South African jurisdiction. This is the country where his estate is. This is where his heirs are. In that regard, his dissolving of the estate in the event of his death will make the Will to come into effect.

His Will is also subjected to "conventional procedures" as Alexander Düttmann states, those which are prescribed law and which will make the Will legible and legal.[76]

The Will is depended on the discretion of the testator who then determines who gets what, when, how, and to what portion, scale, degree, size and so on.

As a clearly stipulated text, the Will should always be framed in unambiguous terms. It is the clarity that will make even the unforeseen disputation and family feuds to be lessened. It is clear terms that will make the Will, if valid, to be a text that speaks in itself. The word and deed of the dead doing the talking and it is only in the condition of being legible and authentic that this capacity to speak can come into being. If the Will has no legal standing, it can be left to the state to decide in line with the Will Act of 1953, and it is here that the wishes of the deceased will be fulfilled or not. The deceased has no last say anymore. The Will that the deceased left behind is not the one that will carry the wishes. The Will, as the authored text, should be authentic and authoritative so that it can have the last say and it can be absolute. More as the testator lays down clear instructions that are clearly stipulated in relation to the dissolving of asserts and how they should be distributed to his heir or heirs.

The Will is a death text. Jacques Rancière says something close to it thus: "This text tells us of a voice by which the orator would like to have been preceded, in which his voice could have been merged."[77] This is the text of the deceased, in the case of his death or the one who is living knowing something has to be said textually before death. It is here that the voice and text are one. It is what the Will says that will embody More's word, his deed, his wish. It is the Will that will stand for his voice in the event of his death.

The Will is the dissemination of clear intention, and this comes out in a transparent manner. This transparency is only in the content of the Will itself. However, this transparency is not clearly pronounced to the heirs in the event of the lifetime of the deceased. Transparency, which will come as a surprise to the heirs, and those who are excluded in the Will comes as something shady as the intention of the deceased only gets to be known in the event of death. So, transparency only emerges at the event of death. It is the Will itself that says what the testator says. According to Düttmann, it is "the transparency of the speaking agent's intentions."[78] This becomes clear in the Will. These are the intentions that could not be articulated during the testator's lifetime (in terms of making them known with the loved ones, as it could be imagined what this will do). So, transparency had to be compromised and secrecy maintained. The wishes of the testator will only be made known in the event of death. It is the living who will be affected by the testators wishes (negatively or positively; pleased or disappointed; guaranteed or betrayed, depending on how they feel, and that being their feeling as the testator is no longer here to account, but having fulfilled his or wish). The content of the Will is the last saying of the testator.

The Will is drafted by the testator and it is made to belong to the "contextual frame" which, for Düttmann, allows the operations that necessitate iterability and also its alterations. The Will must be authored in the manner that the testator deems fit, but this is a situation that is marked with making decisions. There is no Will in the state of indecisiveness. Iterability, according to Düttmann, is a matter of life and death. The Will, being such a document, is the concern with the death of the testator and the life of the heirs. The Will is, for Düttmann, the extension of iterability to life itself. The Will qua iterability is a discourse of life and death. The Will is the reaffirmation that the end-of-life Will be its continuity for the other. Düttmann pronounces: "The feeling of life is self-refection's shadow."[79] There is a tension that comes in iterability as life becomes a matter of "only-once" and "once-more," the aporetic inscription that Düttmann puts clear, and one which even remains a matter of the Will, and the idea of life and death itself. Life is "only-once" and "once-more" is the wish for death to be suspended. But this is impossible. Thus, it is a wishful fallacy. The Will, then, framed in the context of "only-once," is the wish for "once-more"—that is, the testator is prolonging his or her life through heirs. But this prolonging only means the estate, asserts and money being taken care of as the testator would have wished. It is clear here that "only-once" is a facticity that the testator has come to accept and the desire for "once-more," through the Will, is just a wish. The reality of death is "only-once" and not "once-more."

More as the testator, thus authoring in the formal sense, writes and signs the Will. He writes the Will according to his wishes, as he pleases. The heir(s) will inherit, trustees will be appointed, and this also includes guardians and executioners. The executioner is the one who will deal with More's asserts in terms of how they must be distributed and to which heir(s), and in what terms. The executioner will act in terms of More's instruction insofar as that is consistent with the Wills Act of 1953. The executioner will also deal with More's creditors, guardians, agents, and third parties, depending on what is relevant. It is clear in the Will who inherits or does not inherit. But the testator has limits. If children are involved, they cannot be discriminated in the absolute sense. This is where the notary must inform the testator about the juridical limits that are in place insofar as the Wills Act of 1953 stipulates.

If More argues that death is his facticity, his Will is written with the full knowledge and acknowledgment of this facticity. He is going to die and that is why the Will is important. His estate must be disposed. For signing and validating his Will, this makes it to stand as long as it is within the Wills Act of 1953. There must be the legal admissibility in terms of his dissolution of his asserts.

The Will is the Will insofar as it has the legal standing. If More were to write a Will in a form of an holographic inscription, it being handwritten, and thus it being done because there is no time to do a proper Will, this will not be a standing document and it is one that will lead to disputes as it has shaky legal grounds. Thus, its authenticity will be questionable even if the veracity of his handwriting can pass the verification test. This also includes his signature. Yet, there are legal grounds that the holographic Will was written in the times of an accident, danger, and desperation, such a Will does not have string groundings even if countersigning might be implemented as a form of inscription. The Wills Act of 1953 does not even recognize oral Will. The Will should be notarized so that it has a distinctive provenance. This is what provenance is all about as it is a way of legitimizing the historical record.

According to Michaela Fišerová, the signature is a civil sign, one that bears the juridical standing.[80] It is the authorial work that is individually styled. It is all about originality. The signature, which is a mark, is a signifier of this originality. Here is an important question Mark Dorrian poses: "How might we think about the relationship between image and trust today?"[81] This is the question that has to do with the signature of the sign of the signature as the very embodiment of the original. Fišerová asks more questions: "What is a handwritten signature? Is it a reliable and recognizable trace of civil identity? Is it an authentic and singular word of art?"[82] Indeed, the answers to these questions are on the affirmative "yes." It is this "yes" that Fišerová attest to, and thus adding that the signature is the mark of the author, and it is a mode of a personal trace, a mark of an individual identity.

This is akin to what Derrida notes thus: "A signifier is from the very beginning the possibility of its own repetition, of its own image or resemblance."[83] What is signified as original should withstand consistency and veracity in any condition of replication. Fišerová states that "the writing of the signature is often illegible: all letters of the writer's name are not clearly recognizable."[84] The signature should not only appear, it should stand out. It should be the frame of reality. In terms of the Will, it should be a mode of authorization. Brian Massumi writes: "Its reproduction provides an inductive for the serial emergence of subsequent events."[85] This is because, as Massumi states, the signature is a mode of "self-referentiality," in that it stands for the name of its own signatory and it stands with everything that, according to Massumi, has everything to do with reproduction. It is, argues Massumi, "the folding back of the event onto itself, towards its repetition."[86]

> Recognition makes an event typical. That is to say, boring. Its residue of uniqueness makes it "interesting" (an attractor, an inducting sensation) for a body positioned outside its space (with a perspective on it). The event dimension of self-referentiality is the inclusion in becoming (as a multiple-singular, a proliferation of uniqueness) and its perceptual concomitant (perspective). Self-referentiality, as a subdimension of the event, is the field of potential of transcendence-becoming-immanent. "Interest" is the sign of that inclusion.[87]

What must come in a recognizable form, what must make the Will to stand the legal test is the signature and countersignatures. It is this regime of signs that, in their representation which must be recognized, should be in terms of the name. The notarized signature is one that is authenticated. This is the legal standing of the signature. The one who signs, according to Alan Bass, does so in her or his own name.[88] Linking this with Massumi's self-referentiality, Bass submits that the signature is self-designation. Bass argues that "to sign one's name is to signify oneself in the insignificant—beyond the sense and the concept."[89]

The signature is the inscription of the name in its fundamentally distinct way. It is the writing that distinguishes the inscription of its author from anybody else. The signature is, according to Fišerová, individual and personal, in that it is both repeatable (for authentication) and unrepeatable (against forgery). Fišerová argues that the trace of the signature is maintained and that creates a form of what he calls "self-imitation" and the authorial style has to be maintained. "The signature must repeat itself *and* must be singular, different, other."[90] This is a form of signification. The identity of the signature is identifiable with its author. For, it is unique.

For Dorrian, signification is the embodiment of image and truth.[91] The signature is the form of writing that stands close to what is referred to as original. It is the unique form of writing that stands to supplement the name. It is More's signature, his own, that bears his writing. The Will is not a register of ambiguity which, to Susan Wolfson, is a "spectral antonym" because it is written by the living and it should be legible and very clear.[92] The signature is, as a matter of fact, an intentional sign. The signature, in standing for the name, means the signatory will, according to Wolfson, do as follows: "He'll stand with it by it, underwrite it and subscribe to it with his initials."[93]

The Will, as the last Will, signed and countersigned, should have a date which is usually next to the signature. This is to make it clearly known who signed and countersigned and when and where. If there are multiple Wills, the last one has a standing if it is signed and countersigned. Yes, the signature and date will tell. Time is made clear and it is what the date is. It will come to the knowledge of the living as parties concerned to know when the Will was finally sealed. According to Bass, the signature is "time and its rules."[94] An important question is thus posed and Bass asks: "What kind of name is time and how can it leave a signature?"[95] Without wanting to explore this, it is well fitting to state that the name of time and its signature is More's word, his testament and Will, his last word.

When More signs, he does so in his name, next to it, by it, for it, in it, and all this is from the name that is inseparable from his signature. More's signature can be termed to be what Derrida states as "meaning, origin, and function of the written."[96] The signature as the signifier is the pure identification of More. His writing is his own, his own being, the reality of his life. For, he is the author who is identifiable with any form of inscription. Derrida writes:

"The sign is always the supplement of the thing itself."[97] This signature, by all means, is More. He marks and remarks his existence through writing. In terms of the Will, which is sealed through his signature, he disseminates statements in a form of what comes to be a testament, his Will. It is his Will, written in his words, sealed in his own signature.

The word of the one who died, the written word more especially, remains permanent insofar as the document that is being written exists. It is the existence of the document and what is written on it that proves essential. Speech gets disseminated and evaporates. It is what was said. It is a heresy. It is the past tense. It is what gets heard by those who were with the one who spoke. Those who are not there will not get to hear it, and only those who were there will relay it to them. But it will not be pure as it was. Speech is subject to supplementation and manipulation. Originality is subject to being compromised. Speech can be believed or not. What is written has, at least, some level of authenticity because writing precedes immediacy. Writing even transcends the author of the text. What is said on the text has more durability than what is said. But still, writing itself can be subjected to the violations of speech itself. That is to say, writing is not immune from manipulation. The forged text is as old as writing itself.

The living, often worry about death, and this is a worry about something that will happen anyway. The idea of living makes worries to be constant or suppressed. One of these worries, one that is always perennial is about the livelihood of the living and how they will live if they have died. This worry comes not in death, but while the living are thinking about the death (which is the aftermath of life anyway). This worry, one that has to do with the loved ones, those who are better off in the living presence of the living one who is anxious about death, will bring the issue of securing the living. One such gesture has to do with making sure that there will be security for the living. This comes, in most instances, with authoring the Will. The writing of the Will is the writing about the matter of the afterlife, even after the event of death.

More wrote the Will and this has to do with his estate. It is his own secrecy of what is the content of his Will. It is the document that he has been having and he thus subjected it to revisions, which are matters not known to his heirs, for it is his notary and witness who must be involved. He drafted the Will with full knowledge of what he wants in terms of who should be the heir and who should not. He exercised this discretion and the Will creates the impression of wanting to rule the living while in the grave. But it should be seen as the preparation that is done while still alive. Obviously, the dead cannot prepare let alone do anything. The Will is the work of the living, their own preparation.

The Will is a document of the living about matters of the death of the testator. More's loved one's will get to know who is in the Will and who is not, who gets what and how much. More, as a testator, writes the Will knowing that it is the document that is in the realm of the living and the dead. The Will of More is drafted while he is alive and this very same Will then gets to be executed in the event of his death.

The Will starts to serve a function in the event of death. It is the inscription of the document of death. It is the estate plan. It is also the dissolving of the estate of the dead and for it to be distributed to the living. The Will is what should happen after death. This is the final word of the testator. It is the instruction of the living so that the final word can be actualized. It is not that the dead will see whether the Will has been executed in the manner that it was planned. The Will contains matter of probate. The Will is subjected to probate to establish its validity. Probate, as the most fundamental step, is what is undertaken to administer the death estate. This process under the Wills Act of 1953 is the court-supervised, and it is the determining and verifying instance. The Will has to be the last Will. This is the conclusion of all legal and financial matters of the deceased. According to John Gretchko, the Will should have clear contents and this is crucial for understanding the nature and worth of the estate.[98] This is crucial for the matters of probate. It is made clear who is the heir and what is it that is distributed and for what proportion and value. The dead are dead and they have no control with how the Will be taken by the heir. The heir, in the realm of the living, is not bound by the intention of the Will. They will carry out the estate according to their own discretion. Even if the Will can state clearly what the heir should do, the deceased is not present to hold the heir accountable.

The signature stands as a supplement of what is replaceable. It is the thing itself and also in-itself. It is what stands there. The signature, drawing from Rancière, can be "a resemblance that defines the relation of a being to its provenance and destination, one that rejects the mirror in favour of the immediate relationship between progenitor and engendered: direct vision, glorious body of the community, or stand of the thing itself."[99] It is the standing of the irreplaceable. The signature, for Peggy Kamuf, stands as form of singularity, it is, in the context of the Will, its own event but it is not absolute as it has limits.[100] The limit of the signature lies in it being double, being forged, being erased, and making what it is imprinted on to even disappear altogether. That is why the Will has to be stored in a safe place as it can be stolen and tempered—forgery. That is why it often lies in the possession of the executor. The Will must be stored away safely, just like a buried object, the Will should be entombed in the name of safety. Kamuf, in telling the limits of the signature, has this to say:

> A signature, that is, cannot determine the limits on its own validity, and there is, theoretically at least, no first and final occurrence of a signature. This is to

say that a signature never occurs as a pure event, without precedent and without copy. Its possibility only arises from this limitation on pure singularity.[101]

The limitations of the signature, what bears the name of the signatory, should produce the event in the sense of the signature standing as the authorial inscription, it standing to the iterability and intention of the document at hand. The Will, as the entombed document, stored away safely away from the hands of the living, can be said to be, in its own form, a dead document. It is a document that lies there buried. It only comes to be evoked in the event of death. It comes to be a living document when its testator is dead.

The signature here, according to Kamuf, should perform a "stable function." It should have a standing and withstand all forms of veracity. The signature must, as the work of writing, not only say something but also have a final say.

In the name of the original. In the name of the thing itself. In the name of the real. The sign, in this instance, is that of clear identification. The signature is the clear sign that is pointing directly to More and no one else. There is no tyranny of the sign and it being the resemblance of anything. If, the practice of identification is that of authorization, verification, authentication, the provenance of things means they must be what they are, and there is no room for fabrication. This, for Rancière, is "hyper-resemblance" which makes More's signature to be, in itself, the original.[102] The signature and More are one. According to Rancière, this hyper-resemblance, even if it were a replica, should be one that originates from More and it should not be forged. It is More's signature that demands its image to be original. Anything that is different from it in a form of a mark, trace, and inscription is not his. The reproduction of More's signature must be his act, and no one is permitted to do so. His signature still stands. "To tell the truth, however, it never disappears."[103]

There are terms in More's Will, and in its standing, it serves as what Rancière calls a "prescriptive statement."[104] More puts his signature to what he prescribes in his Will. These are the statements of his wishes in the event of his death. The prescriptive nature of the Will is More's word, his last word in the event of his death. And the Will that is in front of the executioner, one that he prescribed last, his last word, one that is signed last, is the last Will. It is, as an embodiment of the sign, what Rancière captures thus: "Visual and textual elements are in effect conceived together, interlaced with one another, in this concept."[105] This concept being More's Will is one that makes his prescriptive statements clear. The signature not only stands for something, it is also what Rancière calls a "communicative reason." This is what More says in his Will, and the words that are stated in clear terms in the Will are the power of this communicative reason. It is the power of the statement, its officialization. It is not just a mark or a trace; it is the inscriptive power "capable of combining everything with anything."[106]

The signature authorizes the *testimonium* and attestation clause. The signature authorizes the testator's instructions. For the Will to have any form of juridical standing, it should be prepared and signed. It must be a valid signed document. It is the document that is even co-signed by the notary and the witness or witnesses. One signature does not stand. It should be an original document. It should serve as the legal proof that it is notarized. If the Will is to be reviewed, it demands what Derrida refers to as "countersigning" which means the presence of the signature that can validate and/or invalidate signatures that are there.[107] But Derrida goes further to state the complexity of the signature in the realm of countersigning that it can be an authenticating act and also its opposite—forgery. It can be to validate the first signature or to even invalidate it. It is in countersignature that there should be the understanding of the signature not having the last word more so in a case where there are other signatures that are needed. If there is an authored document and for it to be in effect as something that needs signatures, the signature of the first signatory is not sufficient. In case of the Will, the signature of the testator is not sufficient. The Will must be signed, and the event of its signature is referred to as the signing ceremony. During the signing ceremony, there must be the notary, testator, and witness present. All must be in the same room.

There is a need for other signatures that are going to validate that initial signature. If these signatures are not there, no document will stand, as these signatures will be required in the form of authorization. More's signature in the Will needs to be countersigned by the notary and the witness. The notary, testator, and witness, even if they know each other, must be (re)introduced to each other. The dispositive intent of the Will does not have to be known by the witness, even if this is the person that the testator trusts. The testator must be there to countersign. Countersigning can mean the notary and witness agreeing to sign or not agreeing to sign. The double gesture of countersigning clearly shows that it can be both negative (unauthorizing) and positive (authorizing). As Derrida notes, the first signature is subjected to countersigning which can be a way of validating the truth or falsifying it. In case of the latter, Derrida notes clearly that countersigning can be the act of counterfeiting the truth.

The signing ceremony is the event of countersigning to validate the truth. The witness, who agrees to sign the Will, must be able to stand as a witness and testify in court, should the Will be disputed in the event of the testator's death. It is countersigning that validates the Will and those who signed it do so within the frame of the Will Act of 1953. The testamentary intents are stated clearly in line with the wishes of the testator, since this is the figure of who is the author of his or her own death. So, the agreement with death should be clear as possible.

There is no Will outside the regime of the signature. It is the inscription of the signature that makes the Will to be a living document. Without the signature, the Will is just a worthless paper. The words of the deceased that are written on it do not have any form of standing. Kamuf powerfully concludes:

> Repeatability, improperness, representation as exclusion, countersignature: all are traits or traces of an otherness that insists in the very place of identity's signature. If they do not form an as yet recognizable set of features, isn't that the way it has to be? For who can sign for the other?[108]

In whose name is the signature for? Still, the signature will be inscripted in that name. Even countersigning is in the name of that signature. The signature is specific, and since the Will has the contractual standing, it is, according to Kamuf, "a text in which the issue is the contract between a particularity and a more extensive generality."[109] It is in this frame that countersigning should take effect and that being the validation of the Will as the text to have a legal standing. Countersigning, to Kamuf, is a "signature surplus," the very thing that exceeds the signature itself. That is to say, the apparent nature of things that countersigning may validate and invalidate the initial signature, and also countersigning can also be countersigned. There are limits and constrains. There is, on the other hand, their obliteration. Countersigning is what Kamuf calls "unlimited extension"—that is, the very thing that "signature surplus" is. There is room for agreement and disagreements.

If More's signature is imprinted on the Will, it needs to be countersigned by way of it being authorized. But it can happen that the witness, who must countersign, refusing to sign. This will mean that the signing ceremony will not proceed unless there is a willing witness who will sign. The Will must bear the signature of More and the countersignatures of the notary and the witness. Signing and countersigning the Will bind signatories. By their authorship, and this being the status of reality, the Will means the testator, notary, and witness made their intentions clear and, as Kamuf states, are "represented by a signature."[110]

The scene of writing, as what has been a concern for Derrida, is fraught with the meaning of the signature in the condition of death.[111] Clearly, this signature is not one that stands on its own as it is supplemented by countersignatures which, to Derrida can be the opposite of this supplementation—"instead of authenticating a first signature, sets about imitating it, that is counterfeiting it."[112] How is it guaranteed that the Will of the testator will be carried out in/at its word, as the last testament? How is it, then, possible to know that the Will shall stand as the living testament in the event of death?

Derrida clearly shows that there can be testimony and betrayal and also testimony and signing. Clearly, this is the matter of the living. The testator will not be there anymore. Will not know and will never get to see whether the Will has been executed to the intentions of the last word. Derrida, in showing the other dimension of countersigning, illuminates clearly the very basis of having no absolute guarantee in terms of the Will in its signed and countersigned status. "The countersignature can thus betray itself in betraying what it countersigns."[113] It is here that authorization, which should stand for truth, Derrida shows how, to an extreme negative end, countersignature can be weaponized to betray the signature. Derrida gives a clear exposition of signing and countersigning.

> Clearly in countersignature, the word has the meaning of proximity and vis-a`-vis. It is what is facing us, beside us . . . . When it's a question of the indelible, irreducible anteriority of the signature, the proto-signature, in relation to the countersignature, authorized or authorizing, things immediately get complicated and are contaminated precisely by the betrayal of truth. In effect, a performative value determines every signature and every countersignature. The signature, like the countersignature, is a performative. When one signs, one doesn't merely write one's name, one affirms: "Yes, I am signing, and naturally I promise to confirm this yes." Or again: "Yes, it's I who's signing and naturally I can confirm that it's I who signs by countersigning if necessary." This performative value is already affected by an immediate iterability: as soon as I sign, I promise that I can do so again, that I can confirm that it was I who signed, etc. There is thus a repetition that, from the moment of the proto-signature, from the first act of the first signature, prohibits distinguishing a before and an after. The repetition of "Yes, I sign," "Yes, yes, I sign" is at work from the moment of the proto-signature. Rather than repetition, I would say repeatability or what I call iterability, the possibility or need to repeat. Iterability, to determine it, is already haunting the proto-signature, or archi-signature, which is therefore from the outset its own countersignature. Consequently all future countersignatures come to countersign what was originally a countersignature, an archi-countersignature.[114]

In this complex illumination of signing and countersigning, Derrida shows the modes of inscriptions and what is at stake with regard to the name and the sworn commitment that this name is taking. Putting the name on paper, and signing for it, is the authorial statement. One signs and countersigns in his or her own name. In terms of the Will, the form of authorship that takes place is one that signs and should be countersigned in the mode of testation. The testamentary nature of the Will should not undermine the authorship that the testator carried out. It is incumbent upon the testator to revisit the Will, to revise and update it, should the need arise, and the signing and countersigning should be undertaken by repeating the signing ceremony.

Having illuminated the contradictions of the countersignature, in terms of the Will, it is expected that the signature and the countersignature should have a legal standing. Derrida even shows that the word "counter" does not only mean opposition. It is even obvious in terms of this word being deployed to a signature. The countersignature is the validation of the first signature. What Derrida exposes are the leaks within the regimes of signatures, and the obvious one being forgery. Following the legitimacy and the legality of what things must be, the order, it as the ritualized aspect, the regime of the signature stands for whatever that is truthful, authentic, and original. Countersigning is there to strengthen the first signature.

> In principle, the signature precedes the countersignature. The signature is thus first, it preexists the countersignature. And apparently nothing can make this antecedence disappear. The definition of the countersignature says clearly that it is "a second signature destined to authenticate the main signature." The countersignature is thus a second signature which can "second" the first one to mark an agreement but which, in all cases, remains secondary. The one countersigning intervenes after the one signing.[115]

The signature is the validation of the Will, it is the mark of what Jane Gordon and Lewis Gordon term "chain of signs" whose significance is the fulfillment of what is required, this being the sign that corresponds neatly with countersigning.[116] The chain of signs, the link and bond of the signature of the testator and the countersignatures of the notary and the witness, is what is visible in the Will. As Derrida notes, this signifies "chains of differential marks."[117] This chain is what seals the Will. For, the signature is what seals the document but in the Will this is accompanied by the supplement, that emergence of the element of identification. The Will is known and identified as such not only at the level of its form and content but the sealing nature of the signature and countersignatures. This is the manner in which, according to Derrida, legibility will come in by the chains of signs being repeated in order to be noticeable at the level of their veracity. The Will is where "the legal *signature* emerges."[118] The Will, according to Derrida, should be understood not as a performative statement, but the constative statement. It is here that the substance of intention is what is emphasizing what is said in authority and what should have a legal standing. The signature and countersignatures are there even to supplement the statement. The statement, in the sense of the Will, becomes a testament. It is the sworn oath, the intentioned writing which opens in a declarative inscription "I, Mabogo Percy More." What is being signed and countersigned is the word of More, a living word insofar as the Will is being evoked and read aloud in the presence of the living who will get to know what More has decided with his estate.

The Will is the communicative inscription. It is the document that says something as a final word. It is the saying of the last decision. It is the speech of the dead. "In speech, a subject appears to the community as a valued perspective."[119] What is More saying in the Will, his writing becoming his voice, him no longer speaking but his voice being represented by the executor, his Will read aloud, this speech event commands listening to the voice of the dead. It is the dead speaking by way of a testamentary gesture, a command of some sort. The instructive nature of More's speech makes him appear in the community of the living. The writerly voice of the one who is no longer with the living but is living with them through the final word that has to do with his estate. What Gordon and Gordon call "unusual speech" is what can be the form and content of More's Will. It is the testamentary nature of this "unusual speech" that makes More's word, through the written medium and inscriptive codes, to become a valued perspective that Gordon and Gordon point out. Indeed, the Will is a speech and it is here where the dead say something after all has been said and done. In the memorial service and funeral, there are eulogies, tributes, prayers, libations, rituals, obituaries, and the like, where all is being said. All the things will be said about the deceased, but the deceased will also have the last word, through the Will. It is the word of the dead that will live to haunt the living.

The presence of More will be the one of the scriptor who is no longer there, but who will be there in word—a living testament. According to Derrida, the Will is a written communication and it is different from spoken communication.[120] The one who writes a Will is no longer there when the Will is resurrected from its entombment. As Derrida states, a written sign is what remains and the Will, as the living word of the dead, now stands to represent the dead who can no longer speak anymore.

The Will, as the constative statement is what is not a claim, but it is the word that is said, finally—the final word. More cannot say anything anymore, nor could he answer for what he has written in the Will. Even if he can be challenged, cursed, screamed at, and asked, he cannot say anything—he is dead. His word is the last in that sense, and he died with his word. He will account to no one.

In the context of the law, what is signed according to law is its last saying. This is the same with any other legal document. The signature is a non-elaborative form of authorship just like the form and content of the Will. It is a mark that authorizes and solidifies the Will. The signature, then, in terms of More, is apt in a sense that it is his death text. He signs and he is countersigned. Expectedly so, this should be the supplement by countersignatures. Clearly, signing and countersigning can only happen when More is alive and not dead. When More is dead, he cannot sign anything.

ON THE AUTO-OBITUARY

The authorship on the death of a philosopher has been ubiquitous, but seldom has it been the case that a philosopher writes about her/his death. The meditation on the auto-obituary, the opposite of the autobiography, is what is of interest. The text written by the author her/himself, one of life (autobiography) and one of death (auto-obituary) is of interest and more focus will be on the latter. The philosophical encounters of death, authored by a philosopher, demand serious attention and more so if it is the death of a black philosopher who survives in the machinations of dehumanization. Death is not some abstract notion whose romanticism will just lead it to conceptual fantasies. Here, death is approached in its material sense as not only being narrated by a philosopher in external terms (the death of others) but also internalized (her/his own death) and that being delivered in a textual medium hitherto referred to as the auto-obituary.

This is not to claim novelty on part of More who, still in his lifetime and at the one year apart with the publication of his autobiography, scripted his own death by means of an auto-obituary. This is not a suicide note as he is not taking his life or thinking about doing so (a fact only known to him as he knows what he is thinking), but him scripting what can be called an auto-obituary. This is not also a sentimental, romanticized, and experimental text; it is a philosophical statement and testament without any form of dissimulation as it is helpless to hide from death which will happen anyway without it being delegated to somebody else. More's auto-obituary is a form of vulnerable authorship whose bravery lies in the honesty that confronts the internalized bad faith of not wanting to bring death to the psyche and experience of oneself. The philosophical practice of More, in his auto-obituary, is openly existential—death thought from the facticity of being-toward-death.[121]

This unpublished text, which is of interest, but a taboo if it gets published as opposed to the reception of his life in his autobiography, the latter that is published, demands serious philosophical reflection. Writing one's own death is indeed a scandalous and scary affair. In bad faith, philosophers and human beings, in general, do avoid writing about their own death, and that being rigorously engaged as a matter of facticity. Rather, they will author the death of others and the phenomena they are meditating on as opposed to matters that have to do with themselves. To be freed from the fear of death is one of the freedom's gifts.

More's auto-obituary, from the Sartrean perspective, is authored from the "for-itself," the being who is free by way of exercising reflective consciousness. More's authorship is of a being who is not structured in the negation of his freedom. By not investing in "non-reflective consciousness," which means resigning from his situation as living freedom, he confronts death not by believing in it (which would mean the opposite of those who "do not believe in it"), but him being reflectively conscious of the facticity of death. This is different from belief, in that "the for-itself is free."[122] Being free as being-toward-death, to follow More, and thus being the opposite of resignation (the latter which can be twisted to be in bad faith by wallowing in belief qua non-reflective consciousness).[123] This makes More the author who is in good faith in terms of the auto-obituary.

By writing as the for-itself that is free, More does not author a sainthood sermon—"the last words" or the dying words of a philosopher. Rather, he is philosophizing about the matter that is not reducible to his individuation, but engages in the philosophy of existence. The question of death, which should be lived through this philosophy of existence, death as a way of life, life words death, life conscious of death, life that is supposed to be meaningfully lived knowing the limit that death is, makes More's authorship to be a living text that has nothing to do with any form of a sanctuary.

A damning account emerges from More against the conception of accidentalizing death, as if its occurrence was not supposed *to be* while in fact it is known that *it has to be* and *it will be*, no matter what.

More's auto-obituary is not about how he lived his life and how he came to die. He is writing about his death, what he will encounter at any point of his life. Not that he is making a preface or textual composition to it, but he gets in the realm of his consciousness, he wrestles freely with what refuses to be touched. The question of death as what is suspended, is what More, in the inscription of his own death, reactivates and brings in the open. This is not a temporary exercise, but a deliberate intention that bears the markings of freedom. More is concerned with the existential conception of death, and in writing his own death, he argues that he is living his own freedom.[124]

All is in the open, More's auto-obituary is not a secretive or sacred text. Death is an open question. The only thing is that he philosophized about the mystery of death in mysterious ways. In that act, he makes philosophy of existence to be open to itself. For, it should reach not only its limits, but what also transcends it.

It is clearly apparent that death, in More, is not an obsessional (pre)occupation. Rather, more than it being argued as facticity (which is a matter of fact), it is worth noting that, from a logical and relational point of view, that it is impossible to engage in philosophy of existence which is about all matters attaining to one free sense of the self and living in freedom without also considering one's death. Philosophy of existence is not a philosophy whose *telos* are death, but it emerges from the conditions that are structured by death. So, the facticity of death means being in its surround. Philosophy of existence, in knowing different set of conditions, necessitates life which will ultimately be the end, death. All there is in this philosophy, its principal task, is to make life meaningful.

More's aim is to bring death to life. That is to say, it is to make death to be in the consciousness of the living rather than it being hidden in the realm of the unconscious. It is to make it apparent as something that should be lived with. By narrating death as something of his own, this becomes a liberating exercise. It is to bring death to life, to make it apparent as it were. This does not mean that this will medicate pain. It will be there, and the shock, dread, anguish, and all the downs that come with it will be there. But what is different is the condition of not hiding from one's own death.

The substantiation of death, a fact that stands on its own, one which cannot be contested, needs the outlook which comes in a form of writing about one's own death. More argues that death cannot be opposed, and there should be no denial of death. Death confirms that the living do not have absolute control of their lives. In his auto-obituary, More does not, in any account, valorize death. He is putting its facticity out there. It is his own death that is of concern. It is what he, himself, should face. Facing death is not its actualization. Rather, it is coming to terms with it.

Whatever death is, whatever it means, More is not figuring it out as something exterior, but death is confronted as one's own. He is not dead, and it is only the dead who know what death is, and since they are not in contact with the living, the living cannot now tell what death is except it being the end of existence. That is why More's auto-obituary is not the revenant's inscription. More never died, and of course, his auto-obituary is not of the one who experienced death and who, then, returns to the living. There is nothing spectral about the auto-obituary. It is, in fact, the death text in the existential sense. It is the writing of the living about his or her individual death. More offers a pointed facticity, and in authoring his own auto-obituary, is facing his horizon, his factual end.

The auto-obituary is a meta-form. It is the stretching of form, its alteration, its obliteration. As the meta-form, the auto-obituary changes the whole understanding of the idea of living. Since the idea of living wants to suspend death, this is seen as the denial of life having been lived in its fullest sense. Yes, it is undesirable to think death. According to Slavoj Žižek, "death is the symbolic order itself, the structure which, as a parasite, colonizes the living entity."[125] The anxiety over death, as Žižek states, is based on the desire for immortality. It is the suspension of mortality (the very act of impossibility) that heightens the desire for immortality (the very act of impossibility). This double of impossibility, this denial of death, does not help matters as death occurs anyway. According to Hannah Arendt, the living want immortality while they know that they are mortal beings.[126] They want what Arendt calls "deathless life," the very idea of the double impossibility. In deploying what he calls "sickness unto death," Žižek states a situation where the notion of the immortality of the soul is believed, but there is still the fear of death.[127] By wanting to remain immortal, the desire is fueled even in its exhaustive failure. The refusal to face death is what reigns. Clearly, the aforementioned double of impossibility is the act of sheer desperation. It is the desire that is the fetish, the phantasmal, the unreal.

According to Arendt, human beings as the mortal, and distinct from animals, are able to produce work that can stand the test of time.[128] This is what Arendt calls the works of hands, the works which surpasses any age. This is the work that possesses durability. But Arendt warns:

> The durability of the human artifice is not absolute; the use we make of it, even though we do not consume it, uses it up. The life process which permeates our whole being invades it, too, and if we do no use things of the world, they also will eventually decay, return to the over-all natural process from which they were drawn and against which they were erected. If left to itself and discarded from the human world, the chair will again become wood, and the wood will decay and return to the soil from which the tree sprang before it was cut off to become the material upon which to work and with which to build. But though this may be the unavoidable end of all singe things in the world, the sign of their being products of a mortal maker, it is not so certainly the eventual fate of the human artifice itself, where all the single things can be constantly replaced with the change of generations which come and inhabit the man-made world and go away. Moreover, while usage is bound to use up these objects, this end is not their destiny in the same way as destruction is the inherent end of all things for consumption. What usage wears out is durability.[129]

Indeed, the work of hands creates what outmatches human mortality. But it depends whether care is taken for durability to be everlasting. As for humans, death is not dependent on the usage and care of what humans created. The human life is, according to Arendt, biological. It is birth, life, and death. Arendt attests: "This is mortality: to move along a rectilinear line in a universe where everything, if it moves at all, moves in a cyclical order."[130] The life of the mortal is that of the end.

By standing on the very end, More writes that text that goes back to the very essence of being and coming to consciousness with the fact that life comes to an end, and this should be thought in the individuated sense of consciousness. The auto-obituary, standing in one's own mortality, is scripted by More, is not of the one who waits for death as it cannot be waited for. More writes: "The problem with death is that one cannot wait for it."[131] Life has to be lived, and waiting for death is just an elusive exercise. It is the added fact of the double impossibility. There is no death to be expected, it comes at its own time, unexpected. Death, according to More, "is the end of all expectation."[132]

For More, to write his auto-obituary is coming to the fact that his own death is the end of his living. It is this end that means the end of him. He will no longer live and those who are going to be burdened by his death are the living.

> Death is event that is certain, indefinite, non-relational and cannot be outstripped, out-maneuvered or outfoxed, yet is uncertain and indefinite. It is paradoxically a possibility which rendered all my further possibilities impossible. Put differently, death is the immediate human contact with *non-being*, with nothingness.[133]

By confronting death in an honest way—taking it as facticity—More shows how the mortals are always vulnerable to death. One lives to die. It is this attitude toward death that will propel the idea of living. More writes: "Death is a phenomenon of existence which I have discovered in myself and towards which I must assume some kind of attitude."[134] This attitude does not mean living in the realm of the death wish, but of living a meaningful life that is opened for it having to come to an end. Thus, More's auto-obituary is the text that removes all the constraints that have to do with the constrained life. There is the life that is in the bondage of fear of death. The attitudinal stance that More adopts, that of opening oneself to the facticity of death, serves as the liberating tool. More's obituary, then, stands as the testament that contents taboos on death, and it is a seething critique to the desire for mortality.

More writes the auto-obituary knowing that death is what, in the words of Massumi, can be called an "ungraspable event."[135] It is the event that one cannot make sense of. Even if death is attempted to be grasped, it is the event that directly affects the dead and the living. There is a difference to be obviously stated: the living are not dead and the dead are dead. The manner in which death affects is therefore different. In this ungraspable event, it becoming the matter of concern, and as More avers: "Death is for the most part and fundamentally for the living."[136] This does not mean the living are dead, they are affected by death, and they must deal with it. It is the death that will also mean the living having to die their own death. What affects them is their own death and the living are, in their own death, going to become the dead who will in turn affect others, the living. By writing the auto-obituary, More is changing the whole scene of authorship. The auto-obituary is indeed a different form of writing which will not sit well with the living. In line with Massumi, it might shift the course of writing altogether.[137] It is strange and estranged, uncanny and unfamiliar. It is, according to Massumi, that writing that "tries not only to accept the risk of sprouting deviant, but also to invite it."[138] It has to be stated, however, that there is nothing deviant about the auto-obituary. It is just that death has been declared a taboo and what is interesting is that it is not only interdicted at the level of speech, but in thought too. It is declared wrong to think about death. But, there it is, nothing can wane or ward it off.

Death is that event of life, its end. "Death permeates the whole human existence (life), influences it and confers meaning to it."[139] But the meaning of death is one that the living will not want to be conscious with. "Because of this, death can thus be approached through heroic resignation or be considered in a cowardly manner."[140] By writing his own death, and coming to consciousness that it is indeed facticity, is something that has to be faced and it cannot be delegated or postposed. The necessity of More having to write about death and his own death is what is informed having courageously and affirming its facticity. This is important because avoiding it "can become a matter of utter anguish or indifference."[141] Having looked at death differently, More radically insists on saying the following:

> I shall die in order to demonstrate the impossibility of living and immortality. I am, however, attitudinally not afraid of death per se; I am simply afraid of not living. As a matter of fact, death does not concern me, because it is the moment of life which I never have to live.[142]

More powerfully concludes his auto-obituary by making a clear distinction on the fear of death and also the fear of the idea of not living. It is life that the living know, and it is death that the living do not know. What is feared is having to lose the known, and this translates to the fear of fearing what is not known. As a matter of concern, death is a feared phenomenon as it is the end of the very fact of living. The meaning that death has on the living being is that frightful thing, the thing that the living do not want to come into contact with.

As the grand gesture that promotes life, More's auto-obituary insists on the life of freedom. That is why, in terms of the *topos* of death, this auto-obituary is against formalism, sensibility, and sterility of the tone and tenor of death because it has only one purpose, to obliterate all the diktats and strictures that are found in death texts. The very idea of the death text which has nothing to do with one's own death is what the autobiography opposes. This text is not in the poetic register, but the existential one. It is the totality and fidelity to one's sense of being, to come to consciousness with the fact of death, and focusing on the meaningful life that will ultimately end. This writing of the one who faces death, and who obviously is going to die, is not any form of textual martyrdom or narcissistic musings, it is the one who is going to die just like other human beings. So, in its non-reverent nature, the auto-obituary is the text of the living.

It would be a grave mistake to see More's auto-obituary as resignation. He lives and insists to live but without hiding it from himself that his life will ultimately come to an end. The auto-obituary can be seen as a mysterious rather than a dialectic form of authorship. It is mysterious in the sense that no one knows what death is and no one who died came back to narrate what is it like to be dead. Those who live do not know what death is. Even if they will claim "Rest in Peace," it is not known whether there is peace in death. In short, no one knows death. Even those who survived tragic moments (terminal, fatal, and comatose) and were supposed to die do not know death. For, they did not die. Even the survivors of torture (who are masochistically and sadistically brought near death) did not die. This even goes to those Orlando Patterson declares as "socially dead" and the slavery (to this time that refuses its "postdate") did not die.[143] Humiliation, suffering, and tragedy that mark dehumanization is not death as the ultimate end.

To conclude, it is worth stating that death is not an easy matter to deal with. The conception of death in More is not carnivalization.[144] Death is real and it is not a word play. To write about death not as an abstract notion by the daily reality of the living is the testament of More's philosophical commitment. So, death is real and More is dealing with it in the real sense by bringing death to the realm of the living. It is in this sense that he creates ways of being free—free from the fear of death. In the most important sense, More confronts the fear of death. It is this fear that is the impediment of freedom. The life lived in fear of death is one of prohibition and perpetual bondage. It is the life that is lived in bad faith, the flight from responsibility and freedom. For one to be free, one must be responsible for confronting that fear—one must actualize freedom—by way of freeing oneself from the fear of death. More is not fascinated by death. In his eyes, and bodily lived experience, he is with death which can occur any time.

For More, it is clear that philosophy of existence as the project of freedom should not hide from dealing with the question of death. Death, as the fact of existence, does not depend on possibility. It is going to happen and all the living live toward death. It is this death that they cannot postpone and avoid. To live is to live with one's own death. Being-in-one's-own-death is the death that cannot be delegated to another. Put simply, the living own their death. Death is the absolute, and it has the last say.

To be obvious, it is right to say More lives through his body, and it is the death of this body that will mean the end of his life. By giving a damning account on the body, More states the body can drop dead at any time. This is what is the tragedy of death, it is not known. That is why it is also important to note the fact that More does not know his lifespan, even if he can be consciousness about death as the uncertainty of the living and it is happening anytime. It is that anytime that makes it impossible to determine the exactness of the event of death. It is his body that testifies that he is a living being, his presence. He is well—alive and well insofar as he is alive and not dead. He is well in his body and he is alive in this body. He is being-in-the-living-body. The facticity of death is not a mythical conception. In the event of death, there will be More's lifeless body where his being is not there. There is no possibility that can transcend this condition.

To write about death, in the generality of the death text, it is to write about what is unknown by the author. The death text as is authorial practice of the living. Only the living can be authors. Therefore, the death text is the writing of death by those who know nothing about death. There is no one who died and then producing a text thereafter. Authorship is the real of the living and death is the very end of writing itself.

More, in writing the obituary, the Will, and the auto-obituary did so as the living author. Whatever that bears his writing is the authorship of his lifetime. In the condition of his death, he will not be able to write anything. More's writing about death remains the practice of the living. To be an author is to be alive. It is death that prevents any form of authorship because it is the ultimate of anything. So, there is no writing from the tomb.

NOTES

1. Mabogo P. More, "Thoughts on Death," Unpublished Paper, 2018. The genre of this text can be called the auto-obituary as More is writing about his death. This is not death as an event, but what must be faced, the reality that More, in his Heideggerian move, calls it the end of all possibility. The end of life is what death is, and this is what cannot be evaded.
2. Martin Heidegger, *Being and Time* (New York: Harper and Row, 1962).
3. Ibid., 280.
4. Ibid., 282.
5. Ibid. Emphasis in the original.
6. Ibid.
7. Ibid., 290.
8. Ibid.
9. Achille Mbembe, *Critique of Black Reason* (Johannesburg: Wits University Press, 2017), 132.
10. Heidegger, *Being and Time*, 294; emphasis in the original. Death is there and there is nothing that can be done about it.
11. Ibid., 295.
12. More, "Thoughts on Death," 2. It is the living who have to deal with death, and they are responsible for the dead. The dead are vulnerable to the living. It is the living who have to experience the aftermath of death. They are the ones who experience grieve and mourning.

13. Heidegger, *Being and Time*, 282. Those who are dead are no longer living in this world. They are not in this world and it is the living who are in this world. In this case of death, the living are dealing with the absence of the dead in the world.

14. Ibid., 283.

15. Ibid.

16. Mbembe, *Critique of Black Reason.*

17. Heidegger, *Being and Time*, 301.

18. Jean-Paul Sartre, *Being and Nothingness: An Essay on Phenomenological Ontology.* Translated by Hazel E. Barnes (London: Methuen, 1957).

19. Jacques Derrida, *The Gift of Death.* Translated by David Wills (Chicago and London: The University of Chicago Press, 1995).

20. Heidegger, *Being and Time*, 282.

21. More, "Thoughts on Death," 1. Many of these deaths happened in the same year of 2016 and it was the time where More thought about the facticity of his own death.

22. Heidegger, *Being and Time*, 302; emphasis in the original.

23. Ibid. Emphasis in the original.

24. Derrida, *The Gift of Death*, 37.

25. Heidegger, *Being and Time*, 304.

26. Sartre, *Being and Nothingness*, 75.

27. Ibid., 78; emphasis in the original.

28. Derrida, *The Gift of Death*, 40.

29. Heidegger, *Being and Time.*

30. Fred Moten, *Stolen Life* (Durham and London: Duke University Press, 2018).

31. Derrida, *The Gift of Death*, 41.

32. More, "Thoughts on Death," 1.

33. Ibid.

34. Derrida, *The Gift of Death*, 41.

35. Ibid., 45.

36. Ibid., 43.

37. More, "Thoughts on Death," 1.

38. Ibid.

39. Mabogo P. More, "Aimé Césaire," *Hydrarchy*, 12 May 2008. http://hyrdracy.blogspot.com/2008/05/aim0csaire.html?=1 [O] accessed 22 February 2015.

40. More, "Aimé Césaire."

41. Jacques Derrida, *The Works of Mourning.* Edited by Pascale-Anne Brault and Michael Naas (Chicago and London: The University of Chicago Press, 2001).

42. Ibid.

43. Ibid., 45.

44. Ibid.

45. Ibid., 65.

46. Ibid., 66.

47. Ibid., 55.

48. Ibid., 217.

49. Ibid., 218; emphasis in the original.

50. Ibid., 221; emphasis in the original.

51. More, “Thoughts on Death,” 3.
52. More, “Aimé Césaire.”
53. Ibid., 1.
54. Mabogo P. More, “The Intellectual Foundations of Black Consciousness Movement,” in *Intellectual Traditions in South Africa: Ideas, Individuals and Institution*, edited by Peter Vale, Lawrence Hamilton, and Estelle H. Prinsloo, 173–195 (Scottsville: UKZN Press, 2014), 174.
55. More, “Aimé Césaire,” 1.
56. More, “The Intellectual Foundations of Black Consciousness Movement.”
57. Ibid., 175.
58. Aimé Césaire, *Notebook of a Return to the Native Land*. Translated and edited by Clayton Eshleman and Annete Smith (Connecticut: Wesleyan University Press, 2001), 12.
59. Aimé Césaire, *Discourse on Colonialism*. Translated by Joan Pinkham (New York: Monthly Review Press, 1972).
60. Ibid., 65. The colonial crimes are in a glare. By presenting a scandal, Césaire shows how irredeemable is the colonial violence.
61. More, “Aimé Césaire,” 2.
62. Ibid.
63. Cheikh Thiam, *Return to the Kingdom of Childhood: Re-envisioning the Legacy and Philosophical Relevance of Negritude* (Columbus: The Ohio State University Press, 2014), 121.
64. Ibid., 4.
65. More, “Aimé Césaire,” 4.
66. Mabogo P. More, “About the Will,” Unpublished Notes, 2020.
67. Ibid.
68. Ibid.
69. Kirsten R. Smolensky, “Rights of the Dead,” *Hofstra Law Review* 37 (2009): 763–803.
70. More, “About the Will.”
71. Smolensky, “Rights of the Dead,” 763.
72. Ibid., 764.
73. Ibid.
74. Ibid., 763.
75. More, “About the Will.”
76. Alexander Düttmann, “The Feeling of Life,” *Oxford Literary Review* 36, no. 1 (2014): 49–61.
77. Jacques Rancière, *The Future of the Image* (London and New York: Verso, 2007), 36.
78. Düttmann, “The Feeling of Life,” 55.
79. Ibid., 58.
80. Michaela Fišerová, “Pragmatical Paradox of Signature,” *Signata* 9 (December 2018): 485–504. The legitimacy of the document, its authenticity, or originality should bear the signature. The signature is not only a stroke of a pen, but a mode of authorization, the inscriptive force.

81. Mark Dorrian, "Transcoded Indexicality," *Log* 12 (Spring/Summer 2008): 105–115. Cited in 105.

82. Fišerová, "Pragmatical Paradox of Signature," 485.

83. Jacques Derrida, *Of Grammatology*. Translated by Gayatri C. Spivak (Baltimore: John Hopkins University Press, 1976), 91.

84. Fišerová, "Pragmatical Paradox of Signature," 486.

85. Brian Massumi, *Parables for the Virtual: Movement, Affect, Sensation* (Durham and London: Duke University Press, 2002), 83.

86. Ibid.

87. Ibid., 84.

88. Alan Bass, "The Signature of the Transcendental Imagination," *The Undecidable Unconscious* 1 (2014): 31–51.

89. Ibid., 33.

90. Ibid. Emphasis in the original.

91. Dorrian, "Transcoded Indexicality."

92. Susan J. Wolfson, "Will Plus Words Plus Worth: What's in a Name?" *ELH* 84, no. 3 (2017): 649–688.

93. Wolfson, "Will Plus Words Plus Worth," 652.

94. Bass, "The Signature of the Transcendental Imagination," 38.

95. Ibid.

96. Derrida, *Of Grammatology*, 119.

97. Ibid., 145.

98. John M. Gretchko, "The Will of Herman Melville," *Leviathan* 20, no. 2 (2018): 95–96.

99. Rancière, *The Future of the Image*, 9.

100. Peggy Kamuf, *Signature Pieces: On the Institution of Authorship* (Ithaca: Cornel University Press, 1988).

101. Ibid., 119.

102. Rancière, *The Future of the Image*.

103. Ibid., 9.

104. Ibid.

105. Ibid., 35.

106. Ibid., 43.

107. Jacques Derrida, "Countersignature," *Paragraph* 27, no. 2 (2004): 7–42.

108. Kamuf, *Signature Pieces*, 120.

109. Ibid., 147.

110. Ibid., 59.

111. Derrida, *Of Grammatology*.

112. Derrida, "Countersignature," 7.

113. Ibid., 8.

114. Ibid., 18.

115. Ibid., 17.

116. Jane A. Gordon and Lewis R. Gordon, *Divine Warning: Reading Disaster in the Modern Age* (Boulder and London: Paradigm Publishers, 2009).

117. Jacques Derrida, *Margins of Philosophy*. Translated by Alan Bass (Sussex: The Harvester Press, 1986), 318.
118. Ibid., 327.
119. Gordon and Gordon, *Divine Warning*, 79.
120. Derrida, *Margins of Philosophy*.
121. Moten, *Stolen Life*.
122. Sartre, *Being and Nothingness*, 484
123. Moten, *Stolen Life*.
124. More, "Thoughts on Death."
125. Slavoj Žižek, *The Plague of Fantasies* (London and New York: Verso, 1997), 89.
126. Hannah Arendt, *The Human Condition* (London and Chicago: The Chicago University Press, 1958).
127. Žižek, *The Plague of Fantasies*, 90.
128. Arendt, *The Human Condition*.
129. Ibid., 136–137.
130. Ibid., 19.
131. More, "Thoughts on Death," 2.
132. Ibid.
133. Ibid. Emphasis in the original.
134. Ibid.
135. Massumi, *Parables for the Virtual*.
136. More, "Thoughts on Death," 3.
137. Massumi, *Parables for the Virtual*.
138. Ibid., 18.
139. More, "Thoughts on Death," 3.
140. Ibid.
141. Ibid.
142. Ibid.
143. Orlando Patterson, *Slavery and Social Death: A Comparative Study* (Cambridge and London: Harvard University Press, 1982).
144. More, "Thoughts on Death."

Conclusion

By Way of Liberation

What is liberation if it is not that matter of necessity, and what is forever urgent?

The question of means and ends is not a deterministic finale, as well as having to consider that liberation is not, at all, the final adjudication. The existential struggle of the black has been intractable to radically insist on liberation, it being, of course, doing what must be done as that is necessary. So, it is right and just to wage the existential struggle for liberation.

Definitely, all there is to liberation is what has to do with the undertaking of the project of liberation itself. It is not about the outcome of liberation, but the very act of doing philosophical anthropology in Azania. There is no decoupling of Azania from liberation. The two are knotted. What Azania confronts is the racist-settler-colonial-segregationist-apartheid-nonracial-constitutionalist-apparatus which is the very idea of South Africa which, in its formation, has nothing to do with the black but everything against the black. South Africa, it has been forever clear, is antiblack.

More's tireless work has been working against the grain because what has been happening to the black is what has never stopped happening—antiblackness. The lived experience that is structured, calibrated, and elaborated by apartheid is what More draws his philosophical anthropology from. The reality he faces is one that he cannot avoid.

The philosophic grammar that deals with what cannot be avoided is the one that is committed in confronting reality, and also having the responsibility of creating different conditions of possibility. The grammar of More's philosophical anthropology is what illuminates the possibility of what must be done by the very act of doing it. The circle and circuit of his philosophical project is dealing with conditions that must be changed. Part of this change deals with putting a challenge that is restless and relentless as More does.

That is why More's disposition is critical in spirit and the reason for this is to take philosophical anthropology deeper and deeper into the abyss and to also emerge from that abyss—dehumanization. All there is with this indomitable will that is necessary for the existential struggle is being revelatory. It is this revelation that emerges as philosophy is put in the service of clarity as opposed to obscurity with regard to the matters of the black condition and the inner-workings of dehumanization. So, things are laid out bare.

In the light of this, there is everything that makes More's philosophical anthropology relevant as his evocation of Azania is a specter that haunts, the enigma, and the bane to the post-1994 South Africa; thus, the call has always been for ways where thought, knowledge, and action make philosophy to be in service of liberation. To say liberation—to think, to practice, and to actualize it—what wholly depends on the present is philosophy's radical task. That is why the struggle for liberation is an urgent task, and those who are dehumanized think, practice, and actualize it at the present time they are in to chart a path of what should be the possibility. If dehumanization reigns, surely it must be confronted by thought, practice, and actualization that necessitate liberation. That is why it has always been a pressing matter because dehumanization should be ended by the black. It has been a matter of historical record that the projects of liberation have been frustrated, derailed, sabotaged, corrupted, betrayed, suppressed, and absolutely crushed. But there is this spirit of radical continuity, and it is what never ceases. The existential struggle surges on as dehumanization has always been intensifying.

Truly, More is a philosopher who never compromises by being complicit in dehumanization of the black. His philosophical anthropology is the liberatory orchestration whose transformative power radically insists on the being of the black and knowingly from the lived reality of being-black-in-an-antiblack-world. It is this fact that will call for fundamental change and South Africa, which is resistant and vile to that change, is still confronted through the pressure point of Azania where philosophy is outside the script of the colonial and Westernized philosophy that reigns through the annals of South African academy. Since More's philosophical anthropology is the challenge to the decadence of this philosophy, his philosophical anthropology in Azania is existentially embedded. His script, contrary to the status quo, is the quotidian script, one that originates from the lived reality of blackness. It is not philosophy that gives in to any form of fatalism or nihilism, nor is it submitting itself to idealism and hope. Rather, it is the philosophy of necessity, of actionality. More's philosophical anthropology is the critical unfolding that is predicated on what must be done for change to be brought into being. That change is fundamental, thus necessary. In this critical unfolding, where fundamental change is charged, something must be done because actional beings make liberation to come into being. Liberation is indexed here as the phenomena that is identical with the naturality of having to act, of responding to the times that one is, of not having any choice other than to choose the exercising of that liberation. The condition of inhabiting the desire for liberation is liberation itself. It is not a matter of it being the outcome or it having to be realized. The creation of the conditions of possibility is what philosophy as liberation should cultivate, nurture, and defend throughout the contours of the existential struggle. Moreover, it is insufficient to leave liberation to its own devices. Liberation is not automatic. It has to be lived, through a radical praxis. This means, further, that it does not come into being by way of a miracle as post-1994 South Africa has been absurdly dubbed. The actional being, one that More is, makes philosophy to fulfill this task. He is such a being because he gathered himself and exercised his philosophical might (as he radically continues to do in consistent ways) to radically question the dehumanizing logics of antiblackness that radically question his very being. Clearly, the being whose humanity is radically questioned is the one who is in pursuit of liberation.

What is the matter; or put simply, what is it that matters and why does it matter? Well, everything matters insofar as it is dehumanization. Dehumanization matters as what has to be defied by the existential struggle for liberation. It matters that the black is dehumanized and all there is to it is the matter of how the black fights for liberation. It is important to note that the matter at hand is, for More, what matters.[1] What matters is what he has to deal with, and in so doing, knowing that this is a responsibility too costly to neglect, delegate, and defer. It is that matter of fact—liberation. Certainly, liberation come as a matter of focus for More because it is what has to be done and being in the milieu where there are different set of questions in relation to dehumanization, he has to take the path that will articulate these questions from his lived experience. It is the matter of liberation which, for More, is the way, and that not being the only way, but whose many paths lead to liberation. Yet, it should be taken into account this will depend on what More is dealing with and how the actualizations of that liberation are brought to the fore and advocated. Even in the face of failure and disappointment, the matter of liberation is engaged as the way of liberation because dehumanization is confronted. The singularity of the path leads to the dead-end. The rupture of enclosures, the radical insistence even in the face of impossibility, makes the matter at hand to be of those who are committed to the work that they know that it is the matter that matters. It is the work of those who matter and as such, the matter of liberation cannot be a small matter. It is, so to say, the meta-matter. It is what cannot be disavowed and what is lived with because of necessity. As such, the meta-matter comes to the fore in More's philosophical anthropology as liberations means everything to him.

Liberty, equality, and justice, as Frantz Fanon cautioned, do not matter to the black where the stakes are very high—for, these values are not extended to the black and their grammar cannot account for dehumanization.[2] For the fact that their origin, intent, and value stems from the colonial belly, there is no way that the matter of liberation can find content and expression in such an enclosure and totality. The matter of liberty, equality, and justice, as Fanon shows, embodies the master morality and still does not account for the dehumanization of the black. The ending of an antiblack world is not a matter of concern, but maintaining the status quo is what matters. So, the grammar of More's philosophical anthropology is the meta-matter of liberation which will come not as a result of the mask reform, but the radical obliteration of an antiblack world. It is this matter that does not find a place in the colonial/racist order of things, and it is this matter, by force and elevation of being meta-matter, that demands insurgent's urgency. There is no time to defer what matters to be a small matter. The grand scale of things, what More's philosophical anthropology has led things to be, is that radical insistence that has moved from *what is* to *what-ought-to-be*.

The stakes are high. What is of concern is what lies before the black. It is what the blacks must do in order for there to be *what ought to be* and that, as More shows, is a matter of responsibility.[3] Liberation is of the black and it should be by the black. Failure to abdicate this responsibility means, as Fanon's per warning, black will be acted upon. It is the responsibility of the black to act, and no one will act on behalf or for the black in order to attain liberation. It is the black who must do it, and for that matter, the life of the black depends on the very liberation that must be insisted upon. This is what is demanded of the black, and it is the black who must demand. By way of Fanon, it is because everything depends on the black.[4]

So, what kind, so to ask, is the form and content of this liberation? It is clear that this is the liberation from dehumanization by the black. It is not the liberation that is given to the black but what the black is taking. This meta-matter means that liberation is everything. It means the livable life of the black. There are no half-measures in this. An antiblack world should be brought to an absolute end as there is nothing that can be regarded as liberation under it.

What is the matter with the black? The answer to this question will border on the erroneous if, in its richly connotative manner it will be made to denote, for obvious reasons, as that which is dealing with the concern of the black, the concern which is questioning the black as if there is something wrong with the black. It is a question which will appear as if the black does not know what can be deemed to be the fact of the matter. By demanding liberation, this will be deemed as something that does not matter. In fact, this is the structure of legibility which deems all the act of the blacks illegible. By erupting from this condition of being refused legibility, More takes the matter of the black in light of the afore-posed questioned as that place of dwelling as it is not in the interests of the black in pursuit of liberation that wants to be legible. In point of fact, what is the matter with the black is the meta-matter of liberation and this is something that cannot be subjected to the dictates of the politics of legibility. It is clear, anyway, that there is nothing deemed legible for and by the black, and it is then logical not to ingratiate to the realm of the politics of legibility whose interests are to maintain antiblackness and to subject the black to dehumanization under the guise of liberty, equality, and justice. The latter three are not what is at stake, but what they actually dissimulate—dehumanization. What matters is liberation, that is why, at the level of seriousness it is understood as a meta-meta.

More's ways of thinking, knowing, and doing philosophy mobilize, formulate, and voice out the problematics that have to do with the bodily being of the black which is denied by dehumanization. No wonder it is fitting for More to engage in philosophical anthropology of Azania because he lives in the country that is antiblack, and also the world that is antiblack. It is this existential condition that warrants him to act, and philosophy as a conduit of liberation, it being grounded in the lived experience of the black, becomes fundamental. Undeniably, the question of being human, with regard to its specificity being a denied one, features highly as part of his philosophical anthropology. And the ways of thinking, knowing, and doing, More's ways, in particular, take philosophy as liberation. It is the evolution and devolution of duty to become being and to continue to struggle for the dignity of that being, however denied. For sure, it is philosophy of existence, more in particular, Africana existential phenomenology where the liberation of being is philosophy's primary matter. Then, it being fought for is a matter of necessity.

The way liberation is thought and practiced has to do with the question of existence and how that existence should fundamentally change. It is the existence that is not a given. It is not what it should or supposed to be. This change should be actualized by those who engage in the opening of radical thought and practice that stems from the existential struggle to become being. It is here that philosophy as liberation, More's primary tasks, radically alters even the practice of philosophy by imperiling it to the questions that have to do with the denied being of the black.

It shall remain forever so that there will be a radical pursuit of liberation. Nothing is brought to relief; everything is heighted. It is what is being made, what is brought into being in the present as opposed to deferring it to the future, or waiting for liberation to come, its necessity notwithstanding. It is all about the intentioned acts, deliberate efforts, tireless strivings, and audacious undertakings that clearly attest to the fact that liberation is not handed over; it is fought for and brought into being by those who want it.

There are three descriptive contours that do not bring any closure but the unfolding of radical possibilities—rupture. They are iterations whose eruptions and interruptions serve as an open thesis, a mark that calls everything that marks subjection, subjectification, and subjugation into question, including the diacritical and auto-critical stance against liberation itself, should it have limits or impediments for the actualization of conditions of possibility that infuse philosophy as liberation.

In his practice, More always puts philosophy in service of existence and the human question, in its specificity as being-black-in-an-antiblack world. An antiblack world does not want the black present in the world as the bodily being. It is not only the inscriptive force that informs his philosophy, but him being actional. Philosophy is that which is a living practice. As such, dehumanization is combated in ways that are life affirming. This is the life that is not lived in the deferral sense that there is a better future that lies out there but rather, the present which is informed by the past and the future, should be worked at in order to create a different set of conditions.

More is clear that there should be no dehumanization. This is not just the statement of call, but the rearticulating of critique that is necessitated by *what-ought-to-be*. There is no negotiation in this radical gesture by the insistence of that things cannot be the way they were. They are made to be different by the very spirit of putting philosophy to work. By this, it is meant, philosophy's task is out of the clutches of decadence as what is the meta-reflective task, as Gordon notes, is the human condition.[5] It is philosophy as lived, as opposed to philosophy being in the realm of pure abstraction. It is, so to say, philosophical anthropology as the quotidian practice. The genre of life cannot be a genre at all since this genre is in the realm of the living. The *poiesis* that result as the original work of the human, the very act of creating and making it possible and necessary to live is what More is not only concerned with, but what also drives him. The genre is in the realm of the living, so is *poiesis*. It is here that the past, present, and the future are, as Achille Mbembe notes, a sedimented epochs.[6] There is no concern with being contemporary or relevant.

There is all that is necessary. What is all to it in More's philosophical anthropology is the imagination and actualization of Azania. First of all, it must come to the consciousness of the black that oppression is what denies the being of the black in its totality. It is, therefore, necessary for the black to know that liberation has to be attained by having to know what the stakes are (them being high of course) in relation to the black condition. By giving it his all, there is no turning back for More. He is, according to Archie Mafeje, engaged in combative ontology as the mode of articulation and interlocution in the epistemological, as well as on the ontological field.[7] This filed which is the place where More's philosophical anthropology erupts, is actualization of giving oneself what has been dispossessed—liberation. For Mafeje, it is clear that the denial of humanity will justify the means and ends of those who resist in the name of their own humanity. The dishonor of the humanity of the black is what cannot be lived with. Combative ontology comes through the way of doing philosophy in ways that dwell on the necessity for liberation. It is, in a sense, going full force at it. It is the (re)affirmation of being by way of the politics of being. The combative ontology that erupts from being-black-in-an-antiblack-world is what was supposed to be the place of fatalism, complicity, apathy, and stupefaction. But, then, this is radically different as the quest for liberation is the questioning of the life that was not, in the first place, supposed to be. The combative ontology that underpins More's philosophical anthropology is having to claim and living liberation in the condition where it is denied.

There is the spirit of commitment that when evoked, there is no backing down, backing off or breaking down or breaking off; that which is Mafeje's combative ontology comes into being as the radical force of what is necessary, and right at that, it should be by all means necessary.

Liberation is what More lives for. It is those who live who will want to live by the fact of having been denied life. As one of the living, More is doing philosophy of existence. In this philosophy, everything that has to do with dehumanization has to be confronted through Mafeje's combative ontology. In his articulation of the politics of being, More avers that they are "the politics of Black being in an antiback world."[8] These politics take the question of existence not in its abstract terms, but what has to be the liberated existence. Since there is everything to it that has to do with liberation, it is necessary for the politics of being to be not a given, but what is actualized in the face of denial. It is, as More states, "the way to critically engage that human being through the so-called non-human beings' struggle for humanity."[9] To be liberated from dehumanization is what informs More's philosophical anthropology. The question of existence is the matter.

After all, it is all and everything. There are no concessions. There is nothing to lose except having to lose the spirit of being liberated. There is all to it when it comes to being liberated. The only way, for More, is being liberated. There is no way that antiblackness will allow the liberation of the black. The parasitic ontological structure of dehumanization is what can stand unshaken as long as there is no existential struggle waged by the black. So, the way of liberation can be a path that is only chart through by way of liberation. This liberation is not there in the future waiting to be attained. It must be lived through the existential struggle. In essence, this is the struggle of the now. Liberation has to be fought for in ways that will not allow failure, betrayal, disappointment, and all foreclosures not to have a final say.

By way of philosophizing, More states clearly that he has to engage it fearlessly and with the spirit of seriousness that will make philosophical commitment to be everything of value.[10] That, in a sense, makes the existential struggle necessary. Everything is made just in the eyes of those whom their lives have been made to be attacked and down-pressed by unjustness. Philosophy has to have a liberatory dimension. Therefore, it can be said that More's philosophical anthropology makes him to be, in the sense of Enrique Dussel, a philosopher of liberation.[11] It is a philosopher who, from the outset of engaging in philosophical work, who is doing the work of liberation. That is to say, liberation is already infused in the philosophical work. The philosophical anthropology of this kind is, by the black, one that does not make matters of black life secondary, but primary insofar as that primacy is everything to live and die for. As Nelson Maldonado-Torres states, this mode of philosophizing can be regarded as the first philosophy.[12] If, then, this is the case, as it is of course, philosophy of liberation not only takes upon different thematic preoccupations, questions, and orientations, but it is turned to be what More has sternly affirmed as *what-ought-to-be*.[13] That as being the matter of urgency, which then springs from the insurgent spirit and critical insights that are the matter of life (and even death), then, to defer will be to work against the necessity of *what-ought-to-be*. This insurgent spirit, this necessity, is everything there is to More for there to be liberation. As Gordon argues, this represents disruptions and rupture for there to be a different set of conditions.[14]

What has to be done by way of liberation has to be done by any means necessary and no any other way if that way, in case of the latter, is what will not necessitate liberation. The philosophy of liberation is tied to what Dussel coins as the ethics of liberation that is invested in a livable life as opposed to "the problem of nonfeasibility" which justices the colonial/racist order of things.[15] More's philosophical anthropology is what Dussel argues as putting the criticality of it there as the capacity to produce victims through dehumanization. This, to Maldonado-Torres, is the suspension of ethics.[16] What is then put forth by More is not the concern with ethics having to distinguish what is right or wrong. Rather, the issue is the ethics of those who are wronged. It is the ethics that do not have to do with the dissimulated order of things as ethics are chained to the structure of dissimulation.

If by any means necessary is all there is in philosophical anthropology as More couches it, the ground through which philosophy is done has to be inhabited as opposed to philosophy being pure abstraction and all things transcendental. The ethics of liberation qua philosophical of liberation are, as the constitutive elements of More's philosophical anthropology, what embodiment of the existential struggle as necessity. What More insists that philosophy has to be lived and as such, it is the reality of being black-in-an-antiblack-world.[17] This is a way of writing one's own being which to John Drabinski is "writing identity" and "writing memory" which is "not merely play or expression or decadent enjoyment."[18] The sight of struggle, its insights and citations, take philosophical anthropology to be on the quest for liberation as the two aforementioned modes of writing clearly shows that all there is in this writing is liberation. So, the two modes can even suggest that identity and memory can, through any means necessary, be reconfigured to be in the service of liberation. Their form and content are radically changed. Indeed, what is liberation in what should be for radical change.

In this way, South Africa is made to face upon itself, and there is no demand for any redemptive gesture just like the theatrics of the post-1994 Rainbow Nation to be performed. All that is clear in More's philosophical anthropology is that Azania should come into being and that would mean the end of South Africa. Azania is not only the installation of the name, but the reconfiguration of reality as a whole. Therefore, the upshot here, the radical departure point, is that More's philosophical anthropology in the conquered Azania is not only a just medium, but a holistic project which Cedric Robinson calls "ontological totality."[19] There is all there is for liberation, it is coming for everything. It is turning things upside down and inside out.

The absence of what there is that does not allow liberation will mean clarity has to be sought all the time even in murky situations. This does not mean that everything is at the level of precision. Since the quest for liberation is the existential struggle with uncertainties and pitfalls, the stance has to be taken even in the face of trial and error, as long as commitment to the cause if the fundamental principle. In other words, everything is based on political commitment. There are no ambiguities. The befalling of pitfalls will mean starting all over again, but it is with great fortune that this need not be the task as More's predecessor laid the foundation and his contemporaries are standing on it, even if the trajectories of the existential struggle differ. Of course, it is in these differences that lessons can be drawn and learned.

Fidelity to memory is everything that informs the reality that repeats the scared memories that cannot be buried in bad faith. The forgetting of black suffering and whitewashing of the brutalities of formations of conquest, and that being what South Africa is as it is littered in the triad of dispossession of land, labor, and humanity, this is a recent history too gory to forget. What has been the formation of the ontology, or whatever that has to do with the question of the subject is what has been absent to the black. There is nothing of the black when it comes to the reality that More's philosophical anthropology is concerned.

What is South Africa is a formation of dehumanization. What is Azania is a formation of being from the death-scape of being dehumanized. Liberation is the formation of other formations. It is the insurrection of those who are still yet to relive the pain they have been subjected to. There is no writing off that can make that pain disappear. This, according to Drabinsky, "bears the pain of history within itself and is unimaginable without that pain."[20] The pain of constant humiliation that, without fail, consistently runs through the racist-settler-colonial-segregationist-apartheid-nonracial-constitutionalist-apparatus is what cannot escape More's memory; thus, having being birthed and living through that pain. What informs the formation of South Africa is what More's philosophical anthropology in Azania negates. Liberation, by way of formations of restoration of the black bodily being and ontological integrity, is in the terms of that are set by the blacks as this is the task that cannot be given to anyone.

Liberation is fidelity to memory. Forgetting is the antithesis of this liberation. The formations that come from More have to do with philosophy as the lived praxis. It is the actualization capacity of philosophy that makes it possible to work from, through, and against pain. That pain is not self-inflicted, it is caused and thus directed to the black. The pained existence of the black is the site from where More's philosophical project is. Azania is the country in pain, it is what is yet to be birthed. To exist in Azania is to exist in tragedy. It is this tragedy that cannot be disavowed. The formations of those who are in pain mean that those who stand for the painful truth of realizing that the declared freedom in the sham of post-1994 liberal democracy is the continuation of the racist colonial encounter that remains undisturbed.

Yes, More may be known as a philosopher, but in the first instance, he is the figure of black. Making his disposition clear, More philosophizes from the reality that he sees it necessary for him to intervene and to interrupt is believed to be the given. What informs More's ontology is tragedy which has nothing to do with the naturality of his blackness, but how he is paradigmatically structured, as Frank Wilderson will say, in antiblackness that became the mark of his existence through and through.[21] What is a given is what More will not take. The restlessness and relentlessness spirit that drives ways of altering the state of things through the necessity of liberation is the motif.

That liberation which has been fought before More, and during his lifetime, is what is necessary. It shall be, as always, that necessity. There is nothing out there to be gained by not painstakingly working through this pain. Such is the effort of the politics of being the black. It is a painful one, the project of formations, folds and forms of formations—the necessity of life itself. For, Azania still lives in tragedy and it has to be birthed, yet again, from this tragedy.

NOTES

1. Mabogo P. More, *Looking through Philosophy in Black: Memoirs* (Lanham: Rowman and Littlefield International, 2019). Liberation is what matters and it is not

its attainment that is the last say, but the very idea of struggling for it. So, liberation is lived by way of putting it into realization. Even in the midst of failure, the continuing struggle of liberation is, in itself, its radical insistence.

2. Frantz Fanon, *Black Skin, White Masks*. Translated by Charles L. Markman (New York: Grove Press, 1967).

3. Mabogo P. More, *Sartre and the Problem of Racism*. Unpublished PhD Thesis (Pretoria: University of South Africa, 2005).

4. Frantz Fanon, *The Wretched of the Earth*. Translated by Constance Farrington (London: Penguin Books, 1969).

5. Lewis R. Gordon, *Existentia Africana: Understanding Africana Existential Thought* (New York and London: Routledge, 2000).

6. Achille Mbembe, *On the Postcolony* (Berkeley: University of California Press, 2001).

7. Archie Mafeje, "Africanity: A Combative Ontology." *CODESRIA Bulletin* 1 (2011): 66–67.

8. Mabogo P. More, "Black Consciousness Movement's Ontology: The Politics of Being," *Philosophia Africana* 14, no. 1 (2012): 23–39. Cited in 24.

9. Ibid., 30.

10. More, *Looking through Philosophy in Black*.

11. Enrique Dussel, *Philosophy of Liberation*. Translated by Aquilina Martinez and Christene Morkovsky (Oregon: Wipf and Stock Publishers, 1985).

12. Nelson Maldonado-Torres, *Against War: Views from the Underside of Modernity* (Durham and London: Duke University Press, 2008).

13. Mabogo P. More, *Biko: Philosophy, Identity, and Liberation* (Cape Town: HSRC Press, 2017).

14. Gordon, *Existentia Africana*.

15. Enrique Dussel, *Ethics of Liberation: In the Age of Globalization and Exclusion*. Translated by Eduardo Mendieta, Camilo P. Bustilo, Yolanda Angulo, and Nelson Maldonado-Torress. Translation edited by Alejandro A. Vallega (Durham and London: Duke University Press, 2013), 414.

16. Maldonado-Torres, *Against War*.

17. Mabogo P. More, "Fanon, Apartheid, and Black Consciousness," in *Shifting the Geography of Reason: Gender, Science, and Religion*, edited by Marina P. Banchetti-Robino and Clevis R. Headley, 241–254 (New Castle: Cambridge Scholars Press, 2006).

18. John E. Drabinsky, *Glissant and the Middle Passage: Philosophy, Beginning, Abyss* (Minneapolis and London: University of Minnesota Press, 2019), 184.

19. Cedric J. Robinson, *Black Marxism: The Making of the Black Radical Tradition* (Chapel Hill: The University of North Carolina Press, 2000).

20. Drabinsky, *Glissant and the Middle Passage*, 23.

21. Frank B. Wilderson, III, *Red, Black, and White: Cinema and the Structure of US Antagonisms* (Durham and London: Duke University Press, 2010).

References

Agamben, Giorgio. *Creation and Anarchy: The Work of Art and the Religion of Capitalism*. Translated by Adam Kotso. Stanford: Stanford University Press, 2019.

_______. *What is an Apparatus? And Other Essays*. Translated by David Kishik and Stefan Pedatella. Stanford: Stanford University Press, 2009.

Althusser, Louis. "Ideology and Ideological State Apparatus (Notes towards an Investigation)." In: *On Ideology*, edited by Louis Althusser, 1–60. London and New York: Verso, 1971.

ANC. "A Time to End the Myth." *Sechaba* 11, no. 3 (1977): 64.

Anidjar, Gil. "Terror Right." *CR: The New Centennial Review* 4, no. 3 (2004): 35–69.

Arendt, Hannah. *The Human Condition*. London and Chicago: The Chicago University Press, 1958.

Badiou, Alain. *Philosophy for Militants*. Translated by Bruno Bosteels. London and New York: Verso, 2015.

_______. *Conditions*. Translated by Stephen Corcoran. New York: Continuum, 2008.

Bass, Alan. "The Signature of the Transcendental Imagination." *The Undecidable Unconscious* 1 (2014): 31–51.

Benjamin, Walter. *The Arcades Project.* Translated by Howard Eiland and Kevin McLaughlin. Cambridge and London: The Belknap Press of Harvard University Press, 2002.

_______. *Illuminations*. Edited and with an Introduction by Hannah Arendt. Translated by Harry Zohn. London: Fontana Press, 1973.

Bhabha, Hommi K. *The Location of Culture*. London: Routledge, 1994.

Biko, Steve. *I Write What I Like*. Oxford and Johannesburg: Heinemann, 1978.

Broeck, Sabine. "Legacies of Enslavism and White Abjectorship." In: *Postcoloniality-Decoloniality-Black Critique: Joints and Fissures*, edited by Sabine Broeck and Carsten Junker, 109–128. Frankfurt and New York: Campus Verlag, 2014.

Buzan, Barry, and H. O. Nazareth. "South Africa Versus Azania: The Implications of Who Rules." *International Affairs* 1 (Winter 1986): 35–40.

Campt, Tina M. "The Loophole of Retreat—An Invitation." *E-Flux Journal* 105 (December 2019): 1–3.

Camus, Albert. *The Rebel*. New York: Penguin, 1971.

Césaire, Aimé. *Notebook of a Return to the Native Land*. Translated and edited by Clayton Eshleman and Annete Smith. Connecticut: Wesleyan University Press, 2001.

_______. *Discourse on Colonialism*. Translated by Joan Pinkham. New York: Monthly Review Press, 1972.

Chandler, Nahum D. *X—The Problem of Negro as the Problem for Thought*. New York: Fordham University Press, 2014.

Ciccariello-Maher, George. "The Commune is the Plan." *The South Atlantic Quarterly* 119, no. 1 (2020): 113–132.

_______. *Decolonizing Dialectics*. Durham and London: Duke University Press, 2017.

Coetzee, John M. *White Writing: On the Culture of Letters in South Africa*. Braamfontein: Pentz Publishers, 2007a.

________. *Diary of a Bad Year*. London: Harvill Secker, 2007b.

da Silva, Denise Ferreira. "1 (Life) ÷ 0 (Blackness) = & - & or &: On Matter beyond the Equation of Value." *E-Flux Journal* 79 (2017): 1–11.

de Certeau, Michel. *Practices of Everyday Life*. Translated by Steven F. Rendall. Berkeley and London: University of California Press, 1984.

Derrida, Jacques. "Countersignature." *Paragraph* 27, no. 2 (2004): 7–42.

________. *The Works of Mourning*. Edited by Pascale-Anne Brault and Michael Naas. Chicago and London: The University of Chicago Press, 2001.

________. *The Gift of Death*. Translated by David Wills. Chicago and London: The University of Chicago Press, 1995.

________. *Margins of Philosophy*. Translated by Alan Bass. Sussex: The Harvester Press, 1986.

________. *Of Grammatology*. Translated by Gayatri C. Spivak. Baltimore: John Hopkins University Press, 1976.

Dorrian, Mark. "Transcoded Indexicality." *Log* 12 (Spring/Summer 2008): 105–115.

Drabinsky, John E. *Glissant and the Middle Passage: Philosophy, Beginning, Abyss*. Minneapolis and London: University of Minnesota Press, 2019.

Du Bois, W. E. B. *The Souls of Black Folk*. New Haven and London: Yale University Press, [1903] 2015.

Dussel, Enrique. *Ethics of Liberation: In the Age of Globalization and Exclusion*. Translated by Eduardo Mendieta, Camilo P. Bustilo, Yolanda Angulo, and Nelson Maldonado-Torres. Translation edited by Alejandro A. Vallega. Durham and London: Duke University Press, 2013.

______. *Philosophy of Liberation*. Translated by Aquilina Martinez and Christene Morkovsky. Oregon: Wipf and Stock Publishers, 1985.

Düttmann, Alexander. "The Feeling of Life." *Oxford Literary Review* 36, no. 1 (2014): 49–61.

Fanon, Frantz. *The Wretched of the Earth*. Translated by Constance Farrington. London: Penguin Books, 1969.

_______. *Black Skin, White Masks*. Translated by Charles L. Markman. New York: Grove Press, 1967.

Farley, Anthony P. "Perfecting Slavery." *Loyola University Chicago Law Journal* 36 (2005): 221–251.

_______. "Behind the Wall of Sleep." *Law and Literature* 15, no. 3 (2003): 421–434.

Farmer, Paul. "An Anthropology of Structural Violence." *Current Anthropology* 43, no. 3 (2004): 305–325.

Fišerová, Michaela. "Pragmatical Paradox of Signature." *Signata* 9 (December 2018): 485–504.

Freire, Paulo. *Pedagogy of the Oppressed*. New York: Continuum, 1994.

Glick, Jeremy M. *The Black Radical Tragic: Performance, Aesthetics, and the Unfinished Haitian Revolution*. New York: New York University Press, 2016.

Gordon, Jane A. *Creolizing Political Theory: Reading Rousseau through Fanon*. New York: Fordham University Press, 2014.

Gordon, Jane A., and Lewis R. Gordon. *Divine Warning: Reading Disaster in the Modern Age*. Boulder and London: Paradigm Publishers, 2009.

Gordon, Lewis R. "Shifting the Geography of Reason in an Age of Disciplinary Decadence." *Transmodernity* 1, no. 2 (2011): 95–103.

_______. *An Introduction to Africana Philosophy*. Cambridge: Cambridge University Press, 2008.

_______. "The Problematic People and Epistemic Decolonization: Toward the Postcolonial in Africana Thought." In: *Postcolonialism and Political Theory*, edited by Nalini Persram, 121–141. Lanham: Lexington Books, 2007.

_______. *Disciplinary Decadence: Living Thought in Trying Times*. Boulder and London: Paradigm Publishers, 2006.

_______. *Existentia Africana: Understanding Africana Existential Thought*. New York and London: Routledge, 2000.

_______. *Her Majesty's Other Children: Sketches of Racism from a Neocolonial Age*. Lanham: Rowman and Littlefield Publishers, 1997.

_______. *Bad Faith and Antiblack Racism*. New York: Humanity Books, 1995a.

_______. *Fanon and the Crisis of European Man: An Essay on Philosophy and the Human Sciences*. London and New York: Routledge, 1995b.

Gretchko, John M. "The Will of Herman Melville." *Leviathan* 20, no. 2 (2018): 95–96.

Grosfoguel, Ramon. "What is Racism?" *Journal of World System Research* 22, no. 1 (2016): 9–15.

_______. "Epistemic Extractivism: A Dialogue with Alberto Acosta, Leanne Betasamosake, and Silvia Rivera Cusicanqui." In: *Knowledges Born in the Struggle: Constructing the Epistemologies of the Global South*, edited by Boaventura de Sousa Santos and Maria Paula Meneses, 203–218. London: Routledge, 2012.

Gwala, Mafika P. "The Thing Black… is Honest… is Human." *SASO Newsletter*, January/February (1972): 13–15.

Hadfield, Leslie A. *Liberation and Development: Black Consciousness Community Programs in South Africa*. East Lansing: Michigan State University Press, 2016.

Harney, Stefano, and Fred Moten. *The Undercommons: Fugitive Planning and Black Study*. Wivenhoe and New York: Minor Compositions, 2013.

Harris, Leonard. "'Believe It or Not' or the Ku Klux Klan and American Philosophy Exposed." *Proceedings and Addresses of the American Philosophical Association* 68, no. 5 (1995): 369–380.

_______. "Introduction." In: *Philosophy Born of Struggle: Anthology of Afro-American Philosophy from 1917*, edited by Leonard Harris, xi–xxv. Dubuque: Kendal/Hunt, 1983.

Hartman, Saidiya V. "The Belly of the World: A Note on Black Women's Labors." *Souls* 18, no. 1 (2016): 166–173.

_______. *Scenes of Subjection: Terror, Slavery, and Self-Making in Nineteenth-Century America*. Oxford: Oxford University Press, 1997.

Heidegger, Martin. *Being and Time*. New York: Harper and Row, 1962.

Henry, Paget. "Africana Political Philosophy and the Crisis of the Postcolony." *Socialism and Democracy* 21, no. 3 (2007): 36–59.

_______. *Caliban's Reason: Introducing Afro-Caribbean Philosophy*. London and New York: Routledge, 2000.

Hilton, John L. "People of Azania." *Scholia* 2 (1993): 3–16.

_______. "Azania—Some Etymological Considerations." *Acta Classica* 35 (1992): 151–159.

Hook, Derek. *(Post)Apartheid Conditions: Psychoanalysis and Social Formations*. Cape Town: HSRC Press, 2014.

JanMohammed, Abdul R. *The Death-Bound-Subject: Richard Wright's Archaeology of Death*. Durham and London: Duke University Press, 2015.

Joja, Athi. "Jafta Masemola's Master Key: Experimental Notes on Azanian Aesthetic Theory." Unpublished Paper, 2019.

Kamuf, Peggy. *Signature Pieces: On the Institution of Authorship*. Ithaca: Cornel University Press, 1988.

Kelley, Robin D. G. *Freedom Dreams: The Black Radical Imagination*. Boston: Beacon Press, 2002.

________. *Race Rebels: Culture, Politics, and the Black Working Class*. New York: Free Press, 1994.

Mafeje, Archie. "Africanity: A Combative Ontology." *CODESRIA Bulletin* 1 (2011): 66–67.

Maldonado-Torres, Nelson. "Thinking through the Decolonial Turn: Post-continental Interventions in Theory, Philosophy and Critique—An Introduction." *Transmodernity* 1, no. 2 (2011): 1–15.

_______. *Against War: Views from the Underside of Modernity*. Durham and London: Duke University Press, 2008a.

_______. "Lewis Gordon: Philosopher of the Human." *CLR James Journal* 14, no. 1 (2008b): 103–137.

Mandela, Nelson. *Long Walk to Freedom*. London: Abacus, 1995.

Manganyi, N. Chabani *Being-Black-in-the-World*. Braamfontein: SPRO-CAS/Ravan Press, 1973.

Marriott, David. "The Ocular Truth: C. L. R. James's England." *Critical Quarterly* 57, no. 3 (2015): 35–50.

Massumi, Brian. *Parables for the Virtual: Movement, Affect, Sensation*. Durham and London: Duke University Press, 2002.

Mbembe, Achille. *Necropolitics*. Durham and London: Duke University Press, 2019.

_______. *Critique of Black Reason*. Johannesburg: Wits University Press, 2017.

_______. *On the Postcolony*. Berkeley: University of California Press, 2001.

Mignolo, Walter D. *The Darker Side of Western Modernity: Global Futures, Decolonial Options*. Durham and London: Duke University Press, 2011.

_______. "Epistemic Disobedience, Independent Thought and De-Colonial Freedom." *Theory, Culture, and Society* 26, nos. 7–8 (2009): 1–23.

Mngxitama, Andile. "Blacks Can't Be Racist." *New Frank Talk* 3, 2009.

Moodley, Strini. "Black Consciousness, the Black Artist and the Emerging Black Culture." *SASO Newsletter*, May/June (1972): 18–20.

More, Mabogo P. "About the Will." Unpublished Notes, 2020.

_______. *Looking through Philosophy in Black: Memoirs*. Lanham: Rowman and Littlefield International, 2019a.

_______. "The Transformative Power of Lewis Gordon's Africana Philosophy in Mandela's House." Unpublished Paper, 2019b.

_______. "Thoughts on Death." Unpublished Paper, 2018.

_______. *Biko: Philosophy, Identity, and Liberation*. Cape Town: HSRC Press, 2017a.

_______. "Isn't Identity Informed by Experience?" *Mail and Guardian*, February 24 to March 2 (2017b): 25.

_______. "Biko and Douglass: Existential Conception of Death and Freedom." *Philosophia Africana* 17, no. 2 (2015/2016):101–118.

_______. "The Intellectual Foundations of Black Consciousness Movement." In: *Intellectual Traditions in South Africa: Ideas, Individuals and Institution*, edited by Peter Vale, Lawrence Hamilton, and Estelle H. Prinsloo, 173–195. Scottsville: UKZN Press, 2014a.

_______. "Locating Frantz Fanon in Post-Apartheid South Africa." *Journal of Asian and African Studies* 49, no. 6 (2014b): 1–15.

_______. "Black Consciousness Movement's Ontology: The Politics of Being." *Philosophia Africana* 14, no. 1 (2012): 23–39.

_______. "Fanon and the Land Question in (Post)Apartheid South Africa." In: *Living Fanon: Global Perspectives*, edited by Nigel C. Gibson, 173–185. New York: Palgrave Macmillan, 2011.

________. "Gordon and Biko: Africana Existential Conversation." *Philosophia Africana* 13, no. 2 (2010/2011): 71–88.

_______. "Black Solidarity: A Philosophical Defense." *Theoria* 56, no. 120 (2009): 20–43.

_______. "Sartre and South African Apartheid." In: *Race after Sartre: Antiracism, Africana Existentialism, Postcolonialism*, edited by Jonathan Judaken, 173–190. Albany: State of University of New York Press, 2008a.

_______. "Gordon on Contingency: A Sartrean Interpetration." *C.L.R. James Journal* 14, no. 1 (2008b): 26–45.

_______. "Aimé Césaire." *Hydrarchy*, 12 May 2008c. http://hyrdracy.blogspot.com/2008/05/aim0csaire.html?=1 [O] accessed 22 February 2015.

_______. "Fanon, Apartheid, and Black Consciousness." In: *Shifting the Geography of Reason: Gender, Science, and Religion*, edited by Marina P. Banchetti-Robino and Clevis R. Headley, 241–254. New Castle: Cambridge Scholars Press, 2006.

_______. *Sartre and the Problem of Racism*. Unpublished PhD Thesis. Pretoria: University of South Africa, 2005.

_______. "Philosophy in South Africa under and after Apartheid." In: *Philosophy and an African Culture*, edited by Kwasi Wiredu, 149–160. Cambridge: Cambridge Scholar, 2004a.

_______. "Biko: Africana Existentialist Philosopher." *Alternation* 11, no. 1 (2004b): 79–108.

_______. "What Difference Does Difference Make?" *Alternation* 6, no. 2 (1999): 332–349.

_______. "Complicity, Neutrality or Advocacy? Philosophy in South Africa. Ronald Aronson's *Stay Out of Politics*." *Theoria* 87 (June 1996): 124–135.

Moten, Fred. *Stolen Life*. Durham and London: Duke University Press, 2018.

_______. *Black and Blur*. Durham and London: Duke University Press, 2017.

_______. *In the Break: The Aesthetics of the Black Radical Tradition*. Minneapolis and London: University of Minnesota Press, 2003.

Moya, Paula M. L. "Who We Are and from Where We Speak." *Transmodernity* 1, no. 2 (2011): 79–94.

Ndlovu-Gatsheni, Sabelo J. *The Decolonial Mandela: Peace, Justice and the Politics of Life*. New York and Oxford: Berghahn, 2016.

Nkrumah, Kwame. *Consciencism: Philosophy and Ideology for Decolonization and Development in Particular Reference to the African Revolution*. London: Heinemann, 1964.

Nuttal, Sarah, and Achille Mbembe. "Mandela's Mortality." In: *The Cambridge Companion to Nelson Mandela*, edited by Rita Barnard, 267–289. Cambridge: Cambridge University Press, 2014.

Outlaw, Lucius. "Africana Philosophy." *The Journal of Ethics* 1 (1997): 265–290.

________. "African, African American, Africana Philosophy." *Philosophical Forum* 23, nos. 2–3 (1992): 63–93.

Patterson, Orlando. *Slavery and Social Death: A Comparative Study* .Cambridge and London: Harvard University Press, 1982.

Pityana, Nyameko. "The Politics of Powerlessness." *SASO Newsletter*, September (1970): 8–9.

Posel, Deborah. "'Madiba Magic': Politics as Enchantment." In: *The Cambridge Companion to Nelson Mandela*, edited by Rita Barnard, 70–91. Cambridge: Cambridge University Press, 2014.

Rabaka, Reiland. *Concepts of Cabralism: Amilcar Cabral and Africana Theory*. Lanham: Lexington Books, 2014.

________. *Forms of Fanonism: Frantz Fanon's Critical Theory and the Dialectics of Decolonization*. Lanham: Lexington Books, 2010.

Ramose, Mogobe B. "On the Contested Meaning of Philosophy." *South African Journal of Philosophy* 24, no. 4 (2015): 551–558.

Rancière, Jacques. *The Future of the Image*. London and New York: Verso, 2007.

Raunig, Gerald. *Factories of Knowledge: Industries of Creativity*. Los Angeles: Semiotext(e), 2013.

Reddy, Thiven. *South Africa, Settler Colonialism and the Failures of Liberal Democracy*. Johannesburg: Wits University Press, 2016.

Robinson, Cedric J. *Black Marxism: The Making of the Black Radical Tradition*. Chapel Hill: The University of North Carolina Press, 2000.

________. *The Terms of Order: Political Science and the Myth of Leadership*. Chapel Hill: The University of North Carolina Press, 1980.

Said, Edward W. *Humanism and Democratic Criticism*. New York: Columbia University Press, 2004.

________. *Culture and Imperialism*. New York: Vintage, 1994.

________. *The Representation of the Intellectual*. New York: Vintage, 1993.

________. *Orientalism*. New York: Vintage, 1978.

Sanders, Chris. "Reflections on Mandela's Role in Ending Apartheid and Promoting South African Democracy." In: *Nelson R Mandela: Decolonial Ethics of Liberation and Servant Leadership*, edited by Busani Ngcaweni and Sabelo J. Ndlovu-Gatsheni, 203–216. Trenton: Africa World Press, 2018.

Sandoval, Chela. *Methodology of the Oppressed*. Minneapolis and London: University of Minnesota Press, 2000.

Sartre, Jean-Paul. *Colonialism and Neocolonialism*. London and New York: Routledge, 2001.

________. *Imagination: A Psychological Critique*. Translated by Forrest Williams. Ann Arbor: The University of Michigan Press, 1962.

________. *Being and Nothingness: An Essay on Phenomenological Ontology*. Translated by Hazel E. Barnes. London: Methuen, 1957.

________. "Paris Alive: The Republic of Silence." *The Atlantic Monthly*, December (1944): 39–40.

Sexton, Jared. "Affirmation in the Dark: Racial Slavery and Philosophical Pessimism." *The Comparist* 43 (October 2019): 90–111.

Sharpe, Christina. *In the Wake: On Blackness and Being*. Durham and London: Duke University Press, 2010.

Sithole, Tendayi. *Steve Biko: Decolonial Meditations of Black Consciousness*. Lanham: Lexington Books, 2016.

Smolensky, Kirsten R. "Rights of the Dead." *Hofstra Law Review* 37 (2009): 763–803.

Sono, Themba. "Solitaire, Solitariness and Solidarity." *SASO Newsletter*, January/February (1972): 5–7.

Sontag, Susan. "For Nelson Mandela." *The Threepenny Review* 28 (Winter 1987): 27.

Spillers, Hortense J. "Mama's Baby, Papa Maybe: An American Grammar Book." *Diacritics* 17, no. 2 (1987): 64–81.

Suárez-Krabbe, Julia. *Race, Rights and Rebels: Alternatives to Human Rights and Development from the Global South*. Lanham: Rowman and Littlefield International, 2016.

Thiam, Cheikh. *Return to the Kingdom of Childhood: Re-envisioning the Legacy and Philosophical Relevance of Negritude*. Columbus: The Ohio State University Press, 2014.

Walker, Corey D. B. "'How Does it Feel to be a Problem?' (Local) Knowledge, Human Interests, and the Ethics of Opacity." *Transmodernity* 1, no. 2 (2011): 104–119.

Walsh, Catherine. "Shifting the Geopolitics of Critical Knowledge: Decolonial Thought and Cultural Studies 'Other' in the Andes." *Cultural Studies* 21, nos. 2–3 (2007): 224–239.

Wauchope, George. "Azania = Land of the Black People." *Frank Talk*, (1984): 7–8.

Wilderson, Frank B., III. *Red, Black, and White: Cinema and the Structure of US Antagonisms*. Durham and London: Duke University Press, 2010.

________. "The Prison Slave as Hegemony's (Silent) Scandal." *Social Justice* 30, no. 2 (2003): 18–27.

Wolfson, Susan J. "Will Plus Words Plus Worth: What's in a Name?" *ELH* 84, no. 3 (2017): 649–688.

Žižek, Slavoj. *The Plague of Fantasies*. London and New York: Verso, 1997.

Index

About the Author

Tendayi Sithole is professor in the Department of Political Sciences, University of South Africa. He is the author of *The Black Register* (2020) and *Steve Biko: Decolonial Meditations of Black Consciousness* (2016).

www.ingramcontent.com/pod-product-compliance
Lightning Source LLC
Chambersburg PA
CBHW021813270326
41932CB00007B/171
* 9 7 8 1 5 3 8 1 6 6 1 3 0 *